HEROES OF THE ALBERT MEDAL

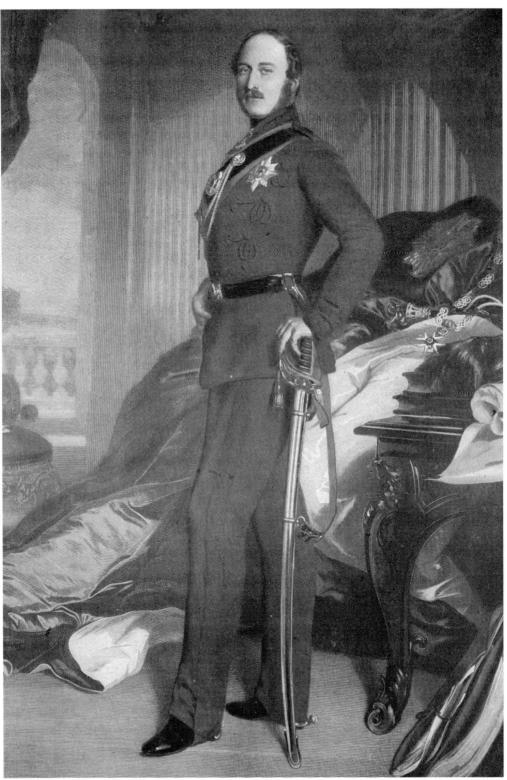

HRH Prince Albert, Prince Consort, in whose memory the medal was named. By E. Woodbury after the painting by Winterhalter in the Royal Collection.

HEROES
OF THE
ALBERT MEDAL

*Service recipients who did not receive
the George Cross*

by

Allan Stanistreet

2002

First published in Great Britain, 2002
by
Token Publishing Ltd.,
Orchard House, Duchy Road, Heathpark, Honiton, Devon EX14 1YD
Telephone: 01404 46972   Fax: 01404 44788
e-mail: info@tokenpublishing.com   Website: http//www.tokenpublishing.com

British Library Cataloguing in Publication data:
A catalogue for this book is available from the British Library
ISBN 1 870 192 53 2

Printed in Great Britain by
Ebenezer Baylis

Contents

To the memory of my friends
Rose Coombs, MBE and Don Henderson, GM
and all those whose names appear in these pages

Acknowledgements

Like so many similar works, this book has been a team effort and I would like to record my grateful thanks to the following, in alphabetical order, for their valuable assistance:

Jonathan Collins, ARRC
Lieutenant-Colonel (Retired) Jim Condon, MBE
    and the Staff of the Army Medal Office
Brett Delahunt (New Zealand)
Sarah Dyson
Chris Fagg (Australia)
Mrs M. Gammie
Mrs A. Herzberg
Mrs Christine Leighton, Archivist, Cheltenham College
Lieutenant-Colonel (Retired) Maxwell Macfarlane
The late Bob Mansell
John D. O'Malley (USA)
Philip O'Shea, LVO, New Zealand Herald of Arms Extraordinary
Alan Polaschek (New Zealand)
Anthony Staunton (Australia)
Paul Street (Australia)
Brigadier (Retired) Bill Strong
Dominic Walsh
Terry Ward
The Registrar, The Royal Archives, Windsor Castle
John Mussell and the Staff at Token Publishing Ltd
Steve Kelly of Concept Graphics, Exeter
HMSO (for *London Gazettes*)

Last, but by no means least, I would like to thank my friend Mrs Margaret Purves, GC, for her kindness in agreeing to write the Foreword to this book. As the last living person to receive the Albert Medal, in 1949, it is fitting that she should do this, having served as an officer in the QARANC, although she was still a schoolgirl when she won her award. A former member of the Albert Medal Association she now lives in quiet retirement in Wiltshire.

Also by Allan Stanistreet

The Malayan Railway—Keretapi Tanah Melayu

'Gainst All Disaster—Gallant Deeds Above and Beyond the Call of Duty

Brave Railwaymen

Portrait of the West Somerset Railway—25 Years of Preservation Progress

Foreword

WHEN Queen Victoria instituted the Albert Medal on March 7, 1866, it was for saving life endangered by shipwrecks and other perils of the sea. In 1877 the Warrant was extended to saving life on the land. It was then that the Albert Medal was regarded by people in general as the "Civilian Victoria Cross"; it remained so until King George VI instituted the George Cross in 1940.

Until the Albert Medal was translated to the George Cross in 1971, little was known of the 560 recipients of this award. Allan Stanistreet has done more to publicise the human stories that go with the award of this decoration than anyone else. I was awarded the Albert Medal in 1949—the last living recipient of the Medal, for it became a posthumous award only in 1950. I applaud his tenacity and efforts in researching these awards, and I believe that he has done a great service to this country in investigating, collating and recording these details, some of which were never held by Government departments. The Home Office, for instance, never held the names of civilian recipients of this award. As late as 1992 an Albert Medallist was discovered living in Canada—knowing nothing of the translation of his medal to the George Cross.

We as a country must not forget our gallant history or how successive governments have toyed with Royal Warrants after the death of the monarch concerned.

Margaret Purves, GC

Introduction

*T*HIS is an attempt to chronicle, in as much detail as possible, those Service recipients of the Albert Medal who did not survive, so far as is known, to exchange their awards for the George Cross in 1971. Those who did so exchange, or were eligible to do so, are described in *'Gainst all Disaster* (see Bibliography).

Those Service recipients who did survive, as at October, 21, 1971, numbered some 47 and there is one exception to the criterion above. He is included here because he was not discovered until 1992 and therefore does not appear in *'Gainst All Disaster.* His name is Ernest Alfred Wooding and he appears here after all other entries. He also, when finally discovered, elected to retain his original award. The 250 people featured in the following pages number rather under half the total of 571 awards of the Albert Medal.

It has been a difficult task over many years trying to assemble biographical details and photographs of those mentioned in these pages and the list is still far from complete. Much disparity will be noted in the information available between the individuals. One continues to rely, as ever, largely on the almost invariable kindness and help of the next-of-kin and descendants of those concerned and one of the objects of this book is hopefully to elicit more information on those of whom we still, sadly, know so little.

The Albert Medal in Gold, which was only awarded to 70 men, is probably our rarest gallantry award, while the Albert Medal (in Bronze) was almost as hard earned, so it is extraordinary that more is not known of the recipients, even allowing for the large number awarded during the First World War and the security considerations at that time. Communications during the first half-century of the decoration's existence were not what they are today and this may have contributed to the lack of awareness on the part of the general public. Even during its currency, it was so sparingly given that few had heard of it and even fewer had actually seen one.

Like the Victoria Cross, of which it was the "civilian" equivalent, the Albert Medal was classless and included recipients from every station in life. In the Forces, too, all ranks from General to Private, Admiral to Boy, featured among those who received it. At least two members of the House of Lords earned it and among the civilian recipients were several teenagers, one boy of eight and two boys of ten. A man of 67 received it posthumously.

Any further information on those featured within these pages will be welcomed by the author and the publisher. As usual, all responsibility for errors and omissions may be laid firmly at the door of the author!

The box in which the Albert Medal was presented to William John Nutman.

Colour illustrations generously supplied by John D. O'Malley

The box in which the Albert Medal was presented to William Thomas.

Albert Medal First Class (Gold)
for Sea Service.

Albert Medal Second Class (Bronze)
for Sea Service.

Albert Medal First Class (Gold)
for Land Service.

Albert Medal Second Class (Bronze)
for Land Service.

Obverse and reverse of the
Albert Medal in Gold for Sea Service
illustrating the naming.

Obverse and reverse of the
Albert Medal for Sea Service
with original ribbon.

Awards to William Nutman, including the Albert Medal in Gold for Sea Service.
Although Nutman was not a serviceman and therefore does not appear in this book, his group illustrates
the esteem in which many Albert Medallists are held.

*DSC and Albert Medal group
with the Russian Order of
St Anne and St Stanislas.*

DSO group including Albert Medal with original ribbon.

A brief history

IN December 1864, the then Home Secretary, Mr Milner Gibson, put forward a proposal to the Queen for a decoration to be awarded to persons who risked their lives in gallant efforts to save the lives of others found drowning in the sea. Just over a year later, on March 7, 1866, the Albert Medal was instituted by Royal Warrant.

It appears to have been completely overlooked by those concerned that there had been just such a reward for rescues at sea since the institution of the Board of Trade Medal for Saving Life at Sea (also known as the Sea Gallantry Medal) by the passing of the Merchant Shipping Act of 1854. Indeed, it seems likely that at least 200 SGMs had been awarded prior to the appearance of the AM, although at that time the SGM was not designed to be worn by the recipients.

Nevertheless, the Albert Medal was now up and running. Only one award was made under the original Warrant, a Gold medal to Samuel Popplestone and after some further thoughts on the matter, another Royal Warrant, dated April 12, 1867, appeared, which created two different types of Albert Medal: First Class (in Gold) and Second Class (in Bronze). Both medals were "For Gallantry in Saving Life at Sea". The ribbon for the First Class was dark blue, an inch and three-eighths wide, with four white longitudinal stripes. The ribbon for the Second Class was darke blue, five-eighths of an inch wide, with two white longitudinal stripes. It was intended to be awarded to those who endangered their own lives in saving or attempting to save others from the perils of the sea or shipwreck and bars might be awarded for further such acts, although no bars were ever awarded and it is possible that none was ever designed. Presumably, it would have been possible to wear both classes of medal, if appropriate, though this situation never arose during the medal's existence.

Principally, it is thought, due to the heroic behaviour of rescuers in a colliery disaster at Tynewydd, South Wales, in 1877, the Albert Medal was extended, by a Royal Warrant dated April 30, 1877, to acts of "Gallantry in Saving Life on Land" and this Warrant also created a medal in two classes but there were design differences in the medals, as can be seen from the illustrations and the ribbons were crimson and white, to the same dimensions as before.

It should be noted that the Albert Medal, of whatever type, was for saving life, although, particularly during the First World War, this was broadly interpreted in awards to service personnel. 154 AMs went to service personnel between 1915 and 1918, as against over 600 VCs for the same period. Certainly during the early years of its existence, the AM was known as "the civilian VC" and the standards required for either class were on a par with those required for the VC. During the First World War, its bestowal was considered by the VC Committee.

The AM underwent relatively few changes during its life of just over a century. In

1904, the ribbon of both Second Class medals was altered to one and three-eighths inches wide and in 1917, the titles of the awards were altered to "Albert Medal in Gold" and "Albert Medal". Around the end of the First World War, recipients were authorised to use the post-nominal initials AM.

Its order of wear has varied but was generally after decorations and before other medals for gallantry. Strangely, it is often referred to as a decoration in the *London Gazette*.

Between 1922 and 1940, the Albert Medal ran in parallel with the Medal of the Order of The British Empire for Gallantry, otherwise known as the Empire Gallantry Medal (EGM). This was a considerably lesser award in terms of the degree of gallantry displayed but embraced a far wider spectrum of situations. As far as Service recipients are concerned, during the period mentioned above, 21 AMs were awarded (including seven for the Quetta earthquake in 1935), while there were 64 EGMs (nine for Quetta).

Upon the institution of the George Cross in September 1940, it was decreed that all surviving recipients of the EGM, less the four honorary awards to foreign subjects but including any posthumous awards made subsequent to the outbreak of war on September 3, 1939, were to return their medals to the Central Chancery of the Orders of Knighthood and receive the GC in exchange. Thus, those who had originally received the lesser award were to be elevated above those who had received the greater. There were several occasions when both AMs and EGMs had been awarded, e.g. Quetta, and this was eventually to cause considerable upset amongst Albert Medallists.

At least five people were refused the AM and awarded the EGM instead, of whom two survived to exchange their awards for the GC in 1940! Two of these were posthumous and one died prior to 1940 but the last of these died only in 1992.

In 1949, an administrative decision was taken to discontinue the award of both types of Albert Medal in Gold and to confine the award of the Albert Medal to posthumous cases only. This was probably because for some incomprehensible reason, when the George Medal was instituted (at the same time as the GC), no provision was made for its posthumous award. Thus, the AM became, quite improperly, a posthumous GM. No Royal Warrant ever legitimised this decision.

In 1965, the late Instructor-Commander David Evans AM RN (Retired), who had won his AM in an explosion on board HMS *Glatton* in 1918, decided to try to organise a reunion of surviving Albert Medallists to coincide with the centenary of the decoration, on somewhat similar lines to that held for Victoria Cross holders in 1956. He advertised widely for recipients to contact him and this led, in due course, to the formation of The Albert Medal Association. Before its ultimate demise in 1972, it was to enrol 73 members, as well as a number of Associate Members, normally widows or next-of-kin of previous holders of the AM.

It was only after the formation of the AM Association that it dawned upon its members that their prestigious decoration was no longer being awarded to living recipients and that its status appeared considerably diminished subsequent to the institution of the GC. There followed a further five years of lobbying, undertaken reluctantly on their part, as they had no wish for the matter to become political, before the ultimate compromise was reached.

This compromise also included holders of the Edward Medal, for bravery in mines and industry generally but not, for whatever reason, the King's and Queen's Police (and Fire Service) Medals for Gallantry. So in October 1971, by Royal Warrant, everyone received the same prize and no fewer than three (five, if one counts the two different grades of each award) medals were exchanged for the George Cross - no matter that some deeds had originally been deemed more worthy than others!

The whole business was, it has to be said, a bureaucratic shambles. Deceased holders of the Albert and Edward Medals were not eligible to be considered GCs and presumably their status remained below those who had exchanged. 64 AMs were still alive in October, 1971, of whom 15 elected to retain their original insignia, although they would be considered as GCs and use these post-nominal initials. The exchange was not widely publicised and the writer long suspected that some remained undetected, particularly among Commonwealth recipients. His suspicions were confirmed when, twenty-one years after the exchange, in 1992, a previously unknown recipient turned up in Canada.

It will be noted that after 1935, the Army does not figure in awards of the Albert Medal at all, right up to the end of medal's existence - a span of 36 years. All the Service awards during this time went to the Royal Navy, its Reserves and the Commonwealth equivalents. No reason is known for this, although it may be purely fortuitous, since one or two refusals in the other two services are recorded. Hence, both the first and last Service awards of the Albert Medal went to members of the Royal Navy.

THE GRAVE OF H. FITSIMMONS, AM (Q.V.), IN GAUHATI WAR CEMETARY

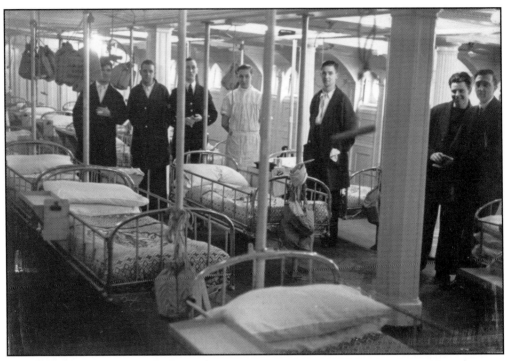

SBA THORPE (Q.V.) (CENTRE IN WHITE) WITH SICK BERTH COLLEAGUES AN PATIENTS ON BOARD HMS BROKE

HMS BROKE

Apparent anomalies in the award of the Albert Medal

*T*WO matters arise under the above heading. They are taken in no particular order. The first relates to the decision as to whether the Land or Sea award should be made in what might be described as grey areas. Even acts of life-saving at sea attracted both Land and Sea awards: in general, however, it may be said that the saving of life from shipwreck attracted the Sea medal, while rescues, launched from the shore, of drowning bathers and others, were rewarded with the Land medal.

This did not apply to gallant deeds performed in docks and there were occasions when Servicemen involved gained the Land award and civilians, even Merchant Navy personnel, were given the Sea medal. It seems that the official channel used to make any recommendation was instrumental in deciding which type of medal should be given.

All the Polar AM awards were in the Land category, despite the fact that the deeds were performed at sea, albeit over very thick ice. Kevin Walton, GC DSC, tells the story of how he went to Buckingham Palace to receive his Albert Medal from the King and the King made a comment about his wearing the wrong AM ribbon; His Majesty thought it should have been the Sea ribbon. Lieutenant Walton told the King that that was the ribbon he had been ordered to wear and happily is still wearing, for he declined to exchange his original award for the GC and is now the only person still wearing the Albert Medal for Gallantry in Saving Life on Land.

Two Sea awards were made in Canada, one for gallantry at Orillia, Ontario for a motor launch fire (see WOODING) and posthumously for gallantry on Lake Ontario, both a thousand miles from the sea!

Out of 150 awards of the AM during WWI, nearly half were given for what might be described as grenade incidents. Twelve of these were in Gold (including seven posthumous) and 37 in Bronze (including four posthumous). Several recipients of both types of award had exhibited great gallantry in similar situations on more than one occasion, although only one of these (2Lt HANKEY) was to receive the AM in Gold.

The circumstances of each individual incident is, understandably, so similar to all the others that it is difficult to imagine what must have influenced the minds of those considering the matter to make the Judgment of Paris required in each case. Of those who survived, many were dreadfully injured and their lives afterwards must surely have been radically transformed.

It is invidious to make comparisons in such cases but those of two men bear comparison. They have a certain amount in common.

Both were officers, both held the MC in addition to the AM and both performed gallantly in three separate grenade incidents, yet one (HANKEY) was to receive the AM in Gold while the other, NEVITT, was awarded the Bronze version. Both, serendipitously, appear to have emerged unscathed by their experiences and both survived the war.

At this distance from events, we may only speculate as to why one man was thought more worthy than another but it does rather beg the question as to how the standards were applied in each case.

Service recipients of the Albert Medal - 1866-1971 - who did not survive to become holders of the George Cross

Note: Abbreviations have been used in the entries to save space. A glossary is to be found at the end of this book. The citations are as they appear in the London Gazettes, although some have been shortened as necessary (indicated by …).

AIMANSING PUN

No. 3790.
Rank: Rfn.
Unit/Force: 1/6 GR.
Other decorations: Nil.
Date of deed: May 16, 1926.
Date of Gazette: October 5, 1926.
Place/Date of Birth: Not known.
Place/Date of Death: Not known but probably prior to 1971.
Place of memorial: Nil.
Town/County connections: Nepal.
Remarks: Presented with AM at Abbotabad, NWFP, January 17, 1927.

Citation

His Majesty The KING has been pleased to award the Albert Medal to Rifleman Aimansing Pun, 1/6th Gurkha Rifles, in recognition of his gallantry in endeavouring to save life at Attock, India, in May last.

On May 16th, 1926, a party of men were washing their clothes on the banks of a wide river, which by reason of the strong converging currents was extremely dangerous to swimmers.

Contrary to orders, one of the party Kishanbahadur Thapa, entered the stream, swam out some fifty yards from the bank, was caught by the current and rendered helpless.

Although well acquainted with the danger involved, Rifleman Aimansing Pun without hesitation went to the rescue of his comrade and succeeded in getting hold of the drowning man. He commenced to swim with him to the further bank, but his efforts proved ineffectual owing to the violent struggles of Kishanbahadur Thapa, who dragged his rescuer under water. On coming to the surface Pun, whose hold on the drowning man had been broken, could see no trace of his comrade. He reached land only with great difficulty, in a most exhausted condition.

7

ALDERSON, George

No. 12231.
Rank: LCPL.
Unit/Force: 10 Bn DLI.
Other decorations: Nil.
Date of deed: October 14, 1915.
Date of Gazette: May 19, 1916.
Place/Date of birth: Easington, Co Durham, April 10, 1884.
Place/Date of death: October 14, 1915.
Place of memorial: Lijssenhoek Mil Cemy, plot 1, row B, grave 14A.
Town/County connections: Dunston-on-Tyne.
Remarks: Went to France, May 21, 1915. Also awarded 1914-15 Star, British War and Victory Medals. The AM was presented to his widow, Mrs Ethel Alderson, 10 Stephenson Street, Dunston-on-Tyne, who received it from FM Sir John French at The Haymarket, Newcastle-upon-Tyne.

Citation

The KING has been graciously pleased to award the Decoration of the Albert Medal to the undermentioned ... of His Majesty's Forces serving in France in recognition of (his) gallantry in saving life:-

Albert Medal of the First Class.

Lance Corporal George Alderson, 10th Battalion, Durham Light Infantry.

On the evening of the 14th October, 1915, Alderson, with two other non-commissioned officers, was moving some bombs into a room in a farmhouse where they were to be stored. While the bombs were being stacked, one of them fell to the floor and the percussion cap was fired. Alderson, knowing that the bomb would explode in four seconds, and that to throw it out of the window would endanger the men who were outside, picked it up and tried to reach the door. Before he could get out of the door the bomb exploded, blowing off his hand and inflicting other serious wounds, from which he shortly died.

By his prompt action in picking up and carrying the bomb he probably saved the lives of the three men who were in the room with him, and by his presence of mind in not throwing it out of the window he certainly saved the lives of those standing outside.

This act was the more meritorious as Alderson was fully aware of the deadly nature of the bomb and the danger to himself that his act involved.

ALLAN, Arthur Duff Hadden

No. 308058.
Rank: PTE.
Unit/Force: RAMC(T). 3 Malta Coy RAMC.
Other decorations: Nil.
Date of deed: February 5, 1917.
Date of Gazette: November 9, 1917 & February 8, 1918.

Place/Date of birth: Not known.
Place/Date of death: Not known.
Place of memorial: Not known.
Town/County connections: Aberdeen.
Remarks: Also served in Labour Corps as PTE 723448. Awarded British War Medal only. Presented with AM by His Majesty the King at Buckingham Palace on April 3, 1919. Address c/o Mrs Ogg, 195 George Street, Aberdeen.

Citation

The KING has been graciously pleased to confer the Decoration of the Albert Medal upon Acting Quartermaster-Serjeant James William Brown, Royal Army Medical Corps, Serjeant William Seymour, Northumberland Fusiliers, and Privates Arthur Duff Hadden Allan and James Cuthbertson, of the Royal Army Medical Corps(T.).

The following is an account of the services in respect of which the Decoration has been conferred:

On the morning of the 5th February, 1917, a serious explosion, followed by a fire, occurred on the French troopship "St Laurent" at Malta.

After some time it was observed that three men in the forepart of the ship, where the flames were fiercest, were cut off from the rest.

None of the boats near would approach the ship owing to the heat and danger of a further explosion, until Acting Quartermaster-Serjeant Brown persuaded a labourer to row him out; but when within thirty yards of the ship the labourer refused to go further.

Brown returned, and was then joined by Seymour, Allan and Cuthbertson. They rowed directly to the forepart of the ship, the sides of which were by this time red hot, while the plates were falling into the sea.

ANDERSON, *Alexander*

No. M2076596.
Rank: Mech SSGT.
Unit/Force: ASC. GHQ Tps Sup Col Wksp ASC.
Other decorations: Nil.
Date of deed: May 2, 1916.
Date of Gazette: August 29, 1916.
Place/Date of birth: Not known.
Place/Date of death: Not known.
Place of memorial: Not known.
Town/County connections: Not known.
Remarks: To France May 2, 1915. Awarded 1914-15 Star, British War and Victory Medals. To Class Z Res July 2, 1919. Presented with AM by His Majesty the King at Buckingham Palace on January 24, 1917.

Citation

The KING has been graciously pleased to award the Decoration of the Albert Medal of the Second Class to Lieutenant Sidney Albert Rowlandson, Mechanic Staff Serjeant Thomas Michael Walton, Private Alexander Anderson, and Private Joseph Thomas Lawrence, of the

Army Service Corps, serving in France, in recognition of their gallantry in saving life.

On 2nd May last, whilst a German 21-centimetre shell, in which several holes had been bored, was being "steamed" in a laboratory for the purpose of investigation, the box of shavings in which it was packed caught fire. The officer in charge of the laboratory at once sent for help to the nearest Army Service Corps fire station, ordered all persons to leave the building, and warned the inhabitants of the neighbouring houses that a serious explosion was imminent.

On receipt of the request for help, Lieutenant Rowlandson, with Walton, Anderson and Lawrence, at once collected fire extinguishers and proceeded by motor to the laboratory. They entered the building, played on the fire (which had spread considerably), and after about two minutes were able to reach the burning shell, which they dragged into the yard and extinguished there.

At any moment after the fire broke out the shell might have exploded with disastrous results.

ANDERSON, Charles Alexander

Rank: Col (A / Maj-Gen).
Unit/Force: RA: Comd Peshawar Inf Bde.
Other decorations: KCB (1915) KCIE (1919).
Date of deed: August 31, 1906.
Date of Gazette: September 26, 1911.
Place/Date of birth: ?India, February 10, 1857.
Place/Date of death: Ivybridge, Devon, February 20, 1940.
Place of memorial: Not known.
Town/County connections: Ivybridge, Devon; Kilworth, Co Cork.
Remarks: Also awarded IGS 54 (Jowaki 1877-78, Burma 1885-87) Afghanistan Medal 1878-80 (Ali Musjid, Kabul), IGS 95 (Punjab Frontier 1897-98), IGS 08 (NWF 08), 1914 Star, British War and Victory Medals (MID), 1935 Jubilee and 1937 Coronation Medals. Retired 1920 as Lt-Gen. MID 9 times - 1880, 1897, 1898 (twice), 1908 (twice), 1915 (twice), 1916. Col Comdt RA 1919-1920. M. Ellen Katherine Russell 1893. Two sons were both army officers; one RAMC, the other in the Leicesters and the YLI. Both served WWI. He was appointed a Grand Commander of the Order of the Sacred Treasure of Japan for his services in WWI. His AM and some other medals (but not, apparently, the 1914 Star, 1935 Jubilee, 1937 Coronation or any of his orders) are in a private collection.

Citation

The KING has been pleased to approve of the Albert Medals of the First and Second Class being conferred upon the undermentioned Officers and others of the Indian Ordnance Department in recognition of their gallantry in saving life on the occasion of fires caused by explosions of cordite at ... Ferozepore in the year 1906:-

FEROZEPORE EXPLOSION
Albert Medal of the First Class
Captain Charles Creaghe Donovan
Albert Medal of the Second Class
Major-General Charles Alexander Anderson, C.B.
Major (now Lieutenant-Colonel) Malcolm Sydenham Clarke Campbell, C.I.E.

C. A. ANDERSON
Source: RA Institution

Captain Hugh Clarke
Assistant Commissary and Honorary Lieutenant Frederick Handley
Conductor Henry Pargiter
Sergeant (now Sub-Conductor) Arthur James Robinson
Sergeant George Smith, and
Robert Dunn Dow

On the 30th August, 1906, a fire broke out in one of the Magazines of the Ferozepore Arsenal comprising 5 cells, in which were stored cordite, small arms' ammunition and gunpowder. At an early stage the ends of one of the outer cells (No. 10) were blown out by an explosion of cordite, while from cell No. 9, where small arms' ammunition was stored, smoke was seen to be issuing.

Major-General Anderson, who directed the subsequent operations from a roof at the edge of the Magazine Compound, at a distance of some 20 yards, having ordered all persons to be cleared out of the fort, and placed a cordon round it at 1,000 yards distance, a steam fire engine was got to work, and the fire party which had been organised commenced their highly dangerous task of clearing cell No. 8 in which was stored some 19,000 lbs. of gunpowder; they eventually succeeded in so doing, thereby cutting off the fire by the intervention of an empty cell. Had the powder in this cell exploded, the explosion must have been communicated to cells in an adjoining magazine, where 300,000 lbs. of gunpowder were stored.

Captain Donovan volunteered to clear cell No. 8, and led the fire party, and all concerned acted with the greatest coolness in circumstances calling for a high degree of courage. The door of the cell was opened and the fire hose turned on. Major Campbell joined the party by the cell, and returned in a short while and reported to General Anderson that though the cell was full of smoke, and the barrels hot, there was no actual fire in the cell. As, however, the explosions in the ruined cell No. 10 were becoming more violent, General Anderson, fearing that the barrels of powder which were being removed from cell No. 8 would be ignited, ordered the discontinuance of efforts to clear the cell; the pumping engine was, however, kept at work by Mr Dow and some native assistants.

A series of heavy explosions of cordite now took place, and on the occurrence of a lull Captain Clarke went to reconnoitre, and reported that cell No. 9 was still apparently intact. Major Campbell and Mr. Pargiter subsequently went into the enclosure to investigate, and on their report being received a party including 50 lascars was organized, and the removal of the powder barrels in cell No. 8 was recommenced under cover of the fire hose. During their removal the last important explosion of cordite took place some 12 yards away. Eventually all the barrels were removed without accident.

ANDERSON, Charles Henry

No. 2326.
Rank: LCPL.
Unit/Force: 1/14 London Regt (TF).
Other decorations: Nil.
Date of deed: November 28, 1916.
Date of Gazette: June 29, 1917.
Place/Date of birth: c1890.
Place/Date of death: November 28, 1916.

Place of Memorial: St Venant Communal Cemy, France, Plot 2, Row K, Grave 3.
Town/County connections: Wallingford, Berks.
Remarks: Regt was part of 188 Inf Bde, 56 Div. Also awarded British War and Victory Medals. AM presented to mother, Mrs Charles Anderson, by GOC Southern Comd at Bradfield College on July 20, 1917. His mother lived at The Nest, North Stoke, Wallingford, Berks.

Citation

The KING has been graciously pleased to award the Decoration of the Albert Medal of the First Class in recognition of the gallantry of Lance-Corporal Charles Henry Anderson, late of the 1/14th Battalion of the London Regiment, who lost his life in France in November last in saving the lives of others.

On the 28th November, 1916, Lance-Corporal Anderson was in a hut in France with eleven other men when, accidentally, the safety pin was withdrawn from a bomb. In the semi-darkness he shouted a warning to the men, rushed to the door, and endeavoured to open it so as to throw the bomb into a field. Failing to do this, when he judged that the five seconds during which the fuse was timed to burn had elapsed, he held the bomb as close to his body as possible with both hands in order to screen the other men in the hut. Anderson himself and one other man were mortally wounded by the explosion, and five men were injured. The remaining five escaped unhurt.

Anderson sacrificed his life to save his comrades.

C. H. ANDERSON
Source: Regimental magazine

ANNIS, Percy Fairborn

No. 57778.
Rank: CPL.
Unit/Force: 20 Canadian Bn, 4 Canadian Inf Bde.
Other decorations: Nil.
Date of deed: February 11, 1916 & December 23, 1915.
Date of Gazette: January 4, 1918.
Place/date of birth: Orillia,Ontario, August 20, 1894.
Place/date of death: November 3, 1943.
Place of memorial: Not known.
Town/County connections: Orillia, Ontario, Canada.

Remarks: Also awarded 1914-15 Trio. Enlisted November 9, 1914, Toronto. Served Canada, GB and France. Discharged as SGT July 22, 1918. Presented with AM by Governor-General of Canada.

Citation

The KING has been graciously pleased to award the Decoration of the Albert Medal to the undermentioned ... Non-Commissioned Officer of His Majesty's Forces serving in France or elsewhere in recognition of (his) gallantry in saving life:-

Corporal Percy Fairborn Annis, Canadian Infantry.

On the 23rd December, 1915, Annis was instructing a class in the use of the trench catapult, when a lighted bomb fell from the catapult into the trench. Annis at once picked up the bomb and threw it away. On the 11th February, 1916, on a similar occasion, the catapult failed to act properly, with the result that the bomb was thrown only a short distance, and fell close to another party under instruction. Annis at once ran out to pick up the bomb. The bomb exploded just as he reached it and wounded him.

ATKINSON, Edward Leicester

Rank: Surg LT-CDR.
Unit/Force: RN. HMS *Glatton*.
Other decorations: DSO (LG June 21, 1916).
Date of deed: September 16, 1918.
Date of Gazette: May 20, 1919.
Place/date of birth: November 23, 1882, St Vincent, W Indies.
Place/date of death: At sea, February 20, 1929.
Place of memorial: Forest School, London: Scott Polar Research Institute, Cambridge
Town/County connections:
Remarks: Trained as surgeon 1900-1905 at St Thomas' Hosp. Joined RN 1908. With Scott on *Terra Nova* 1910. Polar Medal (Antarctic 1910-13). Discovered bodies of Scott and companions and wrote words on Oates' memorial. To China early 1914 but returned on outbreak of WWI. Served Gallipoli and Western Front. Wounded in France and thrice MID. Lost left eye. To Archangel May 1919 and UK October 1919. Specialised in ophthalmics. To Royal Naval College, Greenwich 1920. With British Naval Mission to Greece aboard HMS *Ramillies* 1920. To Chatham 1926. Wife, Jessie, died July 1928 at Chatham. Retired List as medically unfit November 1928. Promoted Surgeon-Captain, youngest in RN at 46. Sailed for India aboard SS *City of Sparta* as Ship's Surgeon, November 1928. Married second wife, Mary Flint Hunter at Glasgow, November 15, 1928. She died at Glasgow, January 12, 1954. No children of either marriage. Also awarded 1914-15 Trio.

Citation

The KING has been graciously pleased to approve of the award of the Albert Medal for gallantry in saving life at sea to-
Surgeon Lieutenant-Commander Edward Leicester Atkinson, D.S.O., R.N.
   The account of the services, in respect of which this decoration has been conferred, is as follows:-

On the 16th September, 1918, a serious explosion occurred amidships on board H.M.S. "Glatton" whilst lying in Dover Harbour. This was followed immediately by an outbreak of fire, the oil fuel burning furiously and spreading fore and aft. Efforts were made to extinguish the fire by means of salvage tugs. The foremost magazines were flooded, but it was found impossible to get to the after magazine flooding positions. The explosion and fire cut off the after part of the ship, killing or seriously injuring all the Officers who were on board with one exception. The ship might have blown up at any moment.

At the time of the explosion Surgeon Lieut.-Commander Atkinson was at work in his cabin. The first explosion rendered him unconscious. Recovering shortly, he found the flat outside his cabin filled with dense smoke and fumes. He made his way to the quarter deck by means of the ladder in the Warrant Officers flat, the only one still intact. During this time he brought two unconscious men on to the upper deck, he himself being uninjured.

He returned to the flat, and was bringing a third man up, when a smaller explosion occurred whilst he was on the ladder. This explosion blinded him, and, at the same time, a piece of metal was driven into his left leg in such a manner that he was unable to move until he had extracted it. Placing the third man on the upper deck, he proceeded forward through the shelter deck. By feel, being totally unable to see, he here found two more unconscious men, both of whom he brought out.

He was found later on the upper deck in an almost unconscious condition, so wounded and burnt that his life was despaired of for some time.

BADENOCH, Ian Forbes Clark.

Rank: Lt.
Unit/Force: 20 Bn RF.
Other decorations: Nil.
Date of deed: March 19, 1917.
Date of Gazette: March 1, 1918.
Place/date of birth: Not known.
Place/date of death: France, March 19, 1917.
Place of memorial: La Neuville Communal Cemetery, Corbie, France.
Town/County connections: Banff, Aberdeenshire, Scotland.
Remarks: Also awarded British War and Victory Medals. Served as CPL (S/13259) in A&SH prior to commissioning in RF on February 26, 1917. AM presented to father, John Alexander of 27 High St, Banff by His Majesty the King at Buckingham Palace, March 16, 1918.

Citation
The KING has been pleased to award the Decoration of the Albert Medal in recognition of the gallantry of Second Lieutenant Ian Forbes Clark Badenoch, 20th Battalion, Royal Fusiliers, in saving life in France, at the cost of his own life, in March of last year. The circumstances are as follows:-

On the 19th March, 1917, during bombing practice, a live bomb thrown by one of the party failed to clear the parapet and fell back into the bombing pit. Lieutenant Badenoch at once rushed to pick up the bomb and throw it out of the pit. He collided with the man who had thrown it, but persisted in his attempt, and was in the act of throwing the bomb when it exploded, and he was mortally wounded.

Lieutenant Badenoch's prompt and courageous action undoubtedly saved the man who threw the bomb from death or severe injury.

BAILEY, Albert Victor.

No. O.N.K.6117 (Dev.)
Rank: SPO.
Unit/Force: RN. HMS *Tiger*.
Other decorations: Nil.
Date of deed: August 27, 1919.
Date of Gazette: April 27, 1920.
Place/date of birth: Not known
Place/date of death: Not known.
Place of memorial: Not known.
Town/County connections: Not known.
Remarks: Also held 1914-15 Trio and RN LS&GC (named to him as SPO HMS *Vivid*.

Citation
The KING has been graciously pleased to approve the award of the Albert Medal to
Mate Henry Buckle, R.N.
Stoker Petty Officer Albert Victor Bailey, O.N.K.6117 (Dev.)
for gallantry in endeavouring to save life at sea.

The following is the account of the services in respect of which the decorations have been conferred:-

While H.M.S. "Tiger" was undergoing repairs at Invergordon, on the 27th August, 1919, two dockyard fitters and an able seaman were overcome by noxious gas in the hold of the ship, and Stoker Petty Officer Bailey, accompanied by a sick berth attendant, made an unsuccessful attempt at rescue. Both he and his companion had put on respirators, but found them useless. Mr. Buckle, the officer of the watch, then arrived on the scene, and in spite of the grave risk to life, which it was now evident would be incurred by further attempts at rescue, immediately went down and succeeded in passing a rope round one of the men. This man was got out, but Mr. Buckle was considerably affected by the gas, and could do nothing further.

Stoker Petty Officer Bailey, though suffering from the effects of his previous attempts, repeated the operation, and succeeded in getting the other two men out, but all efforts to restore them were futile.

Note: Mr Buckle, later Commander, OBE, became a GC in 1971.

BAIN, John Philip.

No. D/K 61978.
Rank: SPO.
Unit/Force: RN. HMS *Foresight*.
Other decorations: Nil.
Date of deed: May 2, 1942.

J. P. BAIN
Source: Family per D.Rose

Date of Gazette: November 10, 1942.
Place/date of birth: c1905.
Place/date of death: May 2, 1942.
Place of memorial: Plymouth Naval Memorial, Panel 69, Column 1.
Town/County connections: Seacombe, Merseyside.
Remarks: Son of Mr and Mrs J. C. Bain of 53 Demesne St, Seacombe, Wirral. Married, one son.

Citation
For great bravery and devotion in saving life at sea: The Albert Medal (Posthumous)
Stoker Petty Officer John Philip Bain, D/K.61978, who was in charge of a boiler room when it was hit by a 5.1-in. shell, which damaged two main steam pipes and filled the compartment with steam. Stoker Petty Officer Bain ordered his shipmate out of the boiler room; but to save his ship and her company from disaster he stayed there to shut off the main and auxiliary feed check valves, and so prevent the water for the ship's boilers from escaping as steam through the damaged pipes. Had this happened it would have been impossible to get the ship under way, and she would certainly have fallen victim to enemy aircraft or submarine attack. Stoker Petty Officer Bain thus saved his ship, but this selfless devotion cost him his life, for he died of his injuries.

BARBER, John.

Rank: AB.
Unit/Force: RN. HMS *Lily*.
Other decorations: Nil.
Date of deed: September 16, 1889.
Date of Gazette: December 20, 1889.
Place/date of birth: Not known.
Place/date of death: Not known.
Place of memorial: Not known.
Town/County connections: Not known.

Citation
HER Majesty the Queen has been graciously pleased to confer the Decoration of the Albert Medal of the Second Class on JOHN BARBER, A.B., of Her Majesty's ship "Lily".
The following is an account of the services in respect of which the Decoration has been conferred:-
Her Majesty's ship "Lily" was wrecked off Amour Point, Forteau Bay, Coast of Labrador, on the 16th September, 1889, and seven of her crew were drowned. After her boats had capsized, and although it was known that two of the crew had been drowned near the same spot in attempting to effect communication with the shore, JOHN BARBER, A.B., volunteered to swim with a line through the surf, which he successfully accomplished, enabling a 4-inch hawser to be hauled ashore, whereby communication was established and the rest of the crew saved.
The service was one of great risk and gallantry, the bottom being rocky, and there being at the time a dense fog with an ebb tide and considerable swell.

BARTLETT, *Charles Edward Cox.*

Rank: Lt.
Unit/Force: 4 Bn S Staffs Regt.
Other decorations: MC (LG Feb 18, 1915). No citation.
Date of deed: February 22, 1916.
Date of Gazette: May 19, 1916.
Place/date of birth: January 30, 1893.
Place/date of death: February 6, 1960.
Place of memorial: Not known.
Town/County connections: Not known.
Remarks: Comsd South Staffs Regt February 5, 1913. Served WWI and MID. Awarded Croix de Guerre (France). CO 1 South Staffs 1938-40 and served throughout WWII, retiring as Col January 29, 1946. Between the wars, served in Singapore, Burma, India and Sudan. Married. In addition to his MC, AM and Croix de Guerre, he held 1914 Star with bar, British War, Victory, and GSM (bar 'Palestine'), 1939-45 and Africa Stars, Defence, War (MID) and KGVI Coronation 1937 Medals. All his decorations and medals are now in the Staffs Regt Museum at Lichfield.

Citation

The KING has been graciously pleased to award the Decoration of the Albert Medal of the Second Class to Lieutenant Charles Edward Cox Bartlett, South Staffordshire Regiment, in recognition of his gallantry in saving life at St. Peter's Barracks, Jersey, in Feb-ruary last:-

On the 22nd February, 1916, at St Peter's Barracks, Jersey, one of the men under instruction at a bombing class, of which Lieutenant Bartlett was in charge, was practising with a catapult bomb thrower, and had removed the safety pin from a bomb, holding back the lever with his finger. In placing the bomb in the sling he dropped it, and, in a fright, ran backwards, colliding with Lieutenant Bartlett, who had started to pick up the bomb. Lieutenant Bartlett, however, succeeded in reaching the bomb in time to throw it over the parapet into the air, where it exploded harmlessly. The bomb was timed to explode five seconds after the lever was released.

This officer has already been awarded the Military Cross.

C. E. C. BARTLETT
Source: Regt Mus Lichfield

BATTYE, Basil Condon.

Rank: Lt.
Unit/Force: RE.
Other decorations: DSO (LG June 24, 1916 & July 27, 1916).
Date of deed: August 30, 1906.
Date of Gazette: August 26, 1913.
Place/date of birth: September 24, 1882.
Place/date of death: May 16, 1932.
Place of memorial: Not known.
Town/County connections: Not known.
Remarks: Educated South Eastern College, Ramsgate and RMA Woolwich. Entered RE 1899 or 1900 (sources differ). Lt August 18, 1903. Somaliland 1903-04. India, 1904. Simla Hydro-Electric Scheme 1910-14. Served WWI. Wounded and MID five times. General Staff 1915-18. AInstCE, MAm Soc CE, MAMInstEE. Also held AGS Medal with bar Somaliland 1902-04, 1914 Star and bar, British War and Victory Medals. Married in 1903 Edith Lilian Cole of Bristol.

Citation

The KING has been pleased to approve of Albert Medals being conferred upon the undermentioned officers and non-commissioned officer in recognition of their gallantry in saving life on the occasion of a fire caused by explosions of cordite at Ferozepore in the year 1906.
Albert Medal of the First Class.
Captain (then Lieutenant) Eglintoune Frederick Ross.
Albert Medal of the Second Class.
Major (then Captain) David Coley Young,
Captain (then Lieutenant) Basil Condon Battye, R.E., and
Staff-Serjeant (then Corporal) Patrick John Fitzpatrick.

A full description of the explosion and of the gallantry of various officers and others to whom Albert Medals were awarded in 1911 will be found in the London Gazette of September 26th, 1911.

Captain Ross discovered the fire, and with a detachment of his regiment entered the magazine compound with a small hand engine fed from tanks in the magazine, and attempted to put out the fire. He also worked at getting the steam engine into position.

Major Young, as General Anderson's Brigade-Major, was constantly with the General in positions of great danger. In particular he joined General Anderson at a critical moment by the door of No. 8 cell, from which the gunpowder was being removed, and remained with the General throughout the rest of the period of danger.

Captain Battye assisted in the removal of the gunpowder from No. 8 cell. He also, with Staff Serjeant Fitzpatrick, directed the operations for piercing two holes through the masonry of the roof of Cell No. 9, where the small arms ammunition was burning, and succeeded in getting the hose through these holes so as to play on the burning ammunition. By this means a check on the fire in No. 9 was effected. Both men were conspicuous throughout the day in the magazine enclosure.

BEARD, Ernest Edmund.

No. VR1731.
Rank: SPO.
Unit/Force: RCNVR.
Other decorations: Nil.
Date of deed: December 6, 1917.
Date of Gazette: February 18, 1919.
Place/date of birth: Hammersmith, London, July 24, 1887.
Place/date of death: Halifax, Nova Scotia, December 6, 1917.
Place of memorial: Not known.
Town/County connections: London.
Remarks: Also held 1914-15 Star, British War and Victory Medals. Enlisted August 11, 1914 at Halifax, NS.

Citation
The KING has been graciously pleased to approve of the posthumous award of the Albert Medal for gallantry in saving life at sea to:-
Mr Albert Charles Mattison, late Acting Boatswain, Royal Canadian Navy, and Stoker Petty Officer Edward S. (sic) Beard, late Royal Canadian Naval Volunteer Reserve.
The following is the account of the services in respect of which these decorations have been conferred:-
On the 6th December, 1917, the French Steamer "Mont Blanc", with a cargo of high explosives, and the Norwegian Steamer "Imo" were in collision in Halifax Harbour. Fire broke out on the "Mont Blanc" immediately after the collision, and the flames very quickly rose to a height of over 100 feet. The crew abandoned their ship and pulled towards the shore. The commanding officer of H.M.C.S. "Niobe", which was lying in the harbour, on perceiving what had happened, sent away a steam boat to see what could be done. Mr. Mattison and six men of the Royal Naval Canadian Volunteer Reserve volunteered to form the crew of this boat, but just as the boat got alongside the "Mont Blanc" the ship blew up, and Mr Mattison and the whole boat's crew lost their lives. The boat's crew were fully aware of the desperate nature of the work they were engaged on, and by their gallantry and devotion to duty they sacrificed their lives in the endeavour to save the lives of others.

BEARD, Walter Richard.

No. 4015.
Rank: LCPL.
Unit/Force: 1 Res Bn RE.
Other decorations: Nil.
Date of deed: August 16, 1918.
Date of Gazette: December 10, 1918.
Place/date of birth: Not known.
Place/date of death: Not known.

Town/County connections: Not known.
Remarks: Went to France March 21, 1915. Also held 1914-15 Trio. Presented with AM at Buckingham Palace by King George V, February 22, 1919.

Citation

The KING has been pleased to award the Albert Medal to Lance-Corporal (acting Second Corporal) Walter Richard Beard, 1st Reserve Battalion, Royal Engineers, in recognition of his gallantry in saving life at bombing practice in August last.

On the 16th August, 1918, Lance-Corporal Beard was instructing recruits in throwing live bombs, when one of the men under instruction, as he was about to throw a bomb, dropped it in the trench. Beard at once ran out from cover, picked up the bomb, and threw it over the parapet, thereby undoubtedly saving the recruit from death or serious injury. The bomb exploded in the air before reaching the ground.

In almost exactly similar circumstances Beard repeated this gallant action on the 23rd August, thereby again saving the life of a man who had dropped a bomb in the trench.

BEARNE, Lewis Collingwood.

Rank: Maj.
Unit/Force: ASC. Serbian (British) MT Coy, ASC.
Other decorations: DSO (LG February 18, 1915).
Date of deed: October 22, 1916.
Date of Gazette: January 1, 1917.
Place/Date of birth: April 5, 1878.
Place/date of death: November 10, 1940.
Place of memorial: Not known.
Town/County connections: Lympne, Kent.
Remarks: Educated at Newton College. Served South African War, first Lumsden's Horse, then DCLI. Comsd DCLI July 27, 1901. Transferred to ASC October 1, 1902. Lt Col IA 1927. Retd 1929. Married 1905. Also held QSA (3 bars), KSA (2 bars), 1914 Star, British War and Victory Medals, Order of White Eagle of Serbia with Swords (4th Class). MID three times.

Citation

Major Lewis Collingwood Bearne, D.S.O., and Private Albert Edward Usher, both of the Army Service Corps.

On the 22nd October, 1916, a French motor lorry, loaded with 3,000lbs. of aeroplane bombs, caught fire in the middle of a camp of the Serbian Army. Efforts to beat out the flames with earth proved ineffectual, and, after the fire had been burning for seven or eight minutes, and the bomb cases were already involved, Major Bearne and Private Usher ran up with extinguishers. Both immediately crawled underneath the lorry, and eventually succeeded in extinguishing the flames, thus averting a serious disaster at the risk of their own lives. Major Bearne was severely burnt about the hands and arms.

Note: Curiously, there is no preamble to this citation, which is part of a series of citations for the Albert Medal.

BECKER, William.

No. J5841.
Rank: AB.
Unit/Force: RN. HMS *Highflyer*.
Other decorations: Nil.
Date of deed: December 6, 1917.
Date of Gazette: March 26, 1918.
Place/date of birth: November 17, 1891.
Place/date of death: Bridlington, Yorkshire, February 17, 1970.
Place of memorial: Not known.
Town/county connections: Bridlington, Yorkshire.
Remarks: Member of the AM Association, 1966-70.

Citation
The KING has been graciously pleased to approve of the posthumous award of the Albert Medal in gold for gallantry in saving life at sea to
Lieutenant-Commander (acting Commander) Tom Kenneth Triggs, R.N., and of the Albert Medal for gallantry in saving life at sea to
Able Seaman William Becker, O.N.J.5841.
The account of the services, in respect of which these medals have been conferred is as follows:-

On the 6th December, 1917, the French steamer "Mont Blanc", with a cargo of high explosives, and the Norwegian steamer "Imo", were in collision in Halifax Harbour. Fire broke out on the "Mont Blanc" immediately after the collision, and the flames very quickly rose to a height of over 100 feet. The crew abandoned their ship and pulled towards the shore.

The Captain of H.M.S. "Highflyer", which was about a mile away, at once sent off a boat to see if anything could be done to prevent loss of life, and Commander Triggs, volunteering for this duty, immediately got into the ship's whaler and pulled to the scene. A tug and the steamboat of H.M.C.S. "Niobe" were seen going there at the same time.

Commander Triggs boarded the tug, and finding it was impossible to do anything for the "Mont Blanc", decided to endeavour to get the "Imo" away, giving directions accordingly to the tug. He returned to the whaler, and was pulling towards the bows of the "Imo", which was about 300 yards from the "Mont Blanc", to pass a line from her to the tug, when a tremendous explosion occurred.

Of the seven people in the whaler, one, Able Seaman Becker, was rescued alive on the Dartmouth shore, whither he had swum; the remainder perished.

It is clear that after communication with the tug, Commander Triggs and the rest of the boat's crew were fully aware of the desperate nature of the work they were engaged in, and that by their devotion to duty they sacrificed their lives in the endeavour to save the lives of others.

BEECHING, George William.

No. C/MX65180.
Rank: SBA.
Unit/Force: RN. HMS *Ibis*.

G. W. BEECHING
Source: Family

Other decorations: Nil.
Date of deed: November 16, 1942.
Date of Gazette: April 20, 1943.
Place/date of birth: 1919.
Place/date of death: November 16, 1942.
Place of memorial: Chatham Naval Memorial, Panel 64, Column 1.
Town/county connections: Wallasey, Cheshire.
Remarks: Aged 23 at death. From Wallasey, Cheshire. Member of Birkenhead Div St John's Amb Bde, then Wallasey Div. Son of George and Rebecca Beeching of Wallasey. Single. His AM was stolen from the Museum of St John, Clerkenwell, in 1992 and not recovered at the time of writing.

Citation

The KING has been graciously pleased to approve the following Rewards and Awards:-

For distinguished services in the operations which led to the landing of the Allied Forces in North Africa:

For gallantry in saving life at sea:

The Albert Medal in Gold (Posthumous).

Sick Berth Attendant George William Beeching, C/MX.65180.

Sick Berth Attendant Beeching was between decks when H.M.S. Ibis was hit. The explosion caused serious damage and the ship took a list to starboard of about 15 degrees. The Emergency Lighting partly failed and the Mess Decks were deep in oil fuel. Sick Berth Attendant Beeching showed great courage and presence of mind. He helped those who came forward with wounds, among them one man very badly burned about the face and hands. Sick Berth Attendant Beeching took him to the Sick Bay and gave him morphia. When the ship began to heel over, and it was apparent that she would capsize, he helped the man to the deck, gave him a life belt, and got him into the water before abandoning ship himself. Sick Berth Attendant Beeching was not seen again.

BELBEN, George Devereux.

Rank: Lt.

Unit/Force: RN. HMS *Trident*.

Other decorations: DSO (LG 4 April, 1944), DSC (LG July 23, 1918) for Zeebrugge (HMS *Thetis*).

Date of deed: September 14, 1918.

Date of Gazette: January 31, 1919.

Place/date of birth: May 14 or 27, 1897.

Place/date of death: Anzio, February 8, 1944.

Place of memorial: Naples War Cemetery, II.O.9.

Town/County connections: Verwood, Dorset.

Remarks: MID (LG August 1, 1944 (posthumous). Capt RN when killed and commanding HMS *Penelope*, aged 46. Son of George and Lucy Belben and husband of Joyce Belben of Verwood.

Citation

The KING has been graciously pleased to approve of the award of the Albert Medal for gallantry in saving life at sea to:-

Lieutenant George Devereux Belben, D.S.C.,R.N.,

Sub-Lieutenant David Hywel Evans, R.N.V.R.

P.O. Albert Ernest Stoker, O.N.227692, and

Able Seaman Edward Nunn, O.N.J.15703.

The account of the services, in respect of which these decorations have been conferred, is as follows:-

On the 16th September, 1918, a serious explosion occurred amidships on board H.M.S. "Glatton" whilst lying in Dover Harbour. This was followed by an outbreak of fire, the oil fuel burning furiously and spreading fore and aft. Efforts were made to extinguish the fire by means of salvage tugs. The foremost magazines were flooded, but it was found impossible to get to the after magazine flooding positions. The explosion and fire cut off the after part of the ship, killing or seriously injuring all the officers who were on board with one exception. The ship might have blown up at any moment.

Lieutenant Belben, Sub-Lieutenant Evans, Petty Officer Stoker, and Able Seaman Nunn were in boats which were rescuing men who had been blown, or who had jumped, overboard. They proceeeded on board H.M.S. "Glatton" on their own initiative, and entered the super-structure, which was full of dense smoke, and proceeded down to the deck below.

Behaving with the greatest gallantry and contempt of danger, they succeeded in rescuing seven or eight badly injured men from the mess deck, in addition to fifteen whom they found and brought out from inside the super-structure.

This work was carried out before the arrival of any gas masks, and, though at one time they were driven out by the fire, they proceeded down again after the hoses had been played on the flames. They continued until all chance of rescuing others had passed, and the ship was ordered to be abandoned, when she was sunk by torpedo, as the fire was spreading, and it was impossible to flood the after magazines.

Note: Sub-Lt Evans became a GC in 1971.

BENNETT, George.

No. 114
Rank: PTE.
Unit/Force: 12 L.
Other decorations: Nil.
Date of deed: February 25, 1918.
Date of Gazette: September 13, 1918.
Place/date of birth: Not known.
Place/date of death: Not known.
Place of memorial: Not known.
Town/county connections: Not known.
Remarks: Went to France August 15, 1914. Also held 1914 Star and bar, British War and Victory Medals and Silver War Badge.

Citation

The KING has been pleased to award the Albert Medal to Private George Bennett, of the 12th Lancers in recognition of his gallantry in saving life in France in February last. The circumstances are as follows:-

G. W. BENNETT
Source: J. D. O'Malley USA

On the 25th February, 1918, at a railway station in France a woman who was crossing the line in front of a troop train, to reach a passenger train, was caught by the buffer of the engine.

Private Bennett, hearing the woman's screams and seeing her position, rushed to help her and pulled her into the six-foot way between the two trains. Infortunately a basket which the woman was carrying was struck by the troop train and knocked Bennett against the passenger train, with the result that he was badly injured and has suffered the amputation of both his legs. Had it not been for his presence of mind and courage the woman would probably have been killed.

BEVAN, George Parker.

Rank: Capt.
Unit/Force: RN. HMS *Iphigenia.*
Other decorations: CMG (1918), DSO (LG March 14, 1916).
Date of deed: November 8, 1916.
Date of Gazette: July 9, 1918.
Place/date of birth: June 23, 1878.
Place/date of death: Aden, January 14, 1920.
Place of memorial: Ma'ala Cemetery, Yemen, G.18.
Town/County connections: Stanwell Moor, Middlesex.
Remarks: Promoted Capt June, 1916. February, 1918, appointed Naval Asst Dir of Tpt and Shipping. December 1918 to Germany with Allied Naval Commission. 1920, commanded HMS *Triad*. Selected as Senior Naval Officer, Persian Gulf. Died en route to take up appt. Married to Lilian of Torquay at death. No children. Also held 1914-15 Star trio (MID twice), Officier de la Légion d'Honneur, Order of St Anne of Russia 2nd Class.

Citation
The KING has been graciously pleased to approve of the award of the Albert Medal to Captain George Parker Bevan, C.M.G., D.S.O., R.N., for gallantry in saving life at sea.

The following is the account of the services in respect of which the decoration has been conferred:-

On the 8th November, 1916, a series of explosions and fires occurred at Bakarista, Port of Archangel, on merchant ships and on the wharves. The S.S. "Baron Driesen" had blown up at 1 p.m. and part of the S.S. "Earl of Forfar" forty minutes later, and fresh explosions were expected every instant. It was thought that all their crews had either escaped or been killed or rescued, but after dark cries of distress were heard from the "Earl of Forfar". The ship was a mass of flame at the time, and burning embers from the fire which was raging on shore were continually showered over her. She had a cargo of explosives on board and was abreast of the main conflagration. The flames were blown towards her by the wind, and the remaining portion of the ship was expected to be blown up at any moment. Captain Bevan, however, on hearing the cries proceeded on board, accompanied by Lieutenant-Commander MacMahon, and, hearing moans from under the smouldering debris of the forecastle, cleared away the wreckage and extricated the mate, who had an arm and a leg and his collarbone broken, and passed him into a tug.

Captain Bevan displayed the utmost gallantry and disregard of his personal safety.

BIGLAND, John Edward.

No. 229006.
Rank: LCPL.
Unit/Force: 12 Lt Rly Tpt Crew Coy RE.
Other decorations: Nil.
Date of deed: April 30, 1918.
Date of Gazette: August 30, 1918.

Place/date of birth: Not known.
Place/date of death: Not known.
Place of memorial: Not known.
Town/County connections: Not known.
Remarks: Served in Manchester Regt as No. 19830, TR Bn as No. 28694 and RE under No. WR/20622. Also held British War and Victory Medals, with Silver War Badge.

Citation

The KING has been pleased to award the Albert Medal in each of the following cases in recognition of gallantry displayed in saving or endeavouring to save life:-
Lance-Corporal John Edward Bigland
Sapper Thomas Henry Woodman, of the Royal Engineers; and
Sapper (acting Company Sergeant-Major) Alfred Henry Furlonger, D.C.M.,
Sapper Joseph Collington Farren,
Sapper George Edward Johnston, late of the Royal Engineers.

In Flanders, on 30th April, 1918, a train of ammunition had been placed at an ammunition refilling point, and after the engine had been detached, and was being run off the train, the second truck suddenly burst into flames. Furlonger immediately ordered Bigland, the driver, to move the engine back on to the train for the purpose of pulling away the two trucks nearest the engine. Bigland did so without hesitation, and the engine was coupled up by Furlonger, assisted by Farren, while the burning truck was uncoupled from the remainder of the train by Woodman. The two trucks were then drawn away clear of the ammunition dump, it being the intention to uncouple the burning wagon from the engine and the first wagon, and so isolate it, with the object of localising the fire as far as possible. The uncoupling was about to be done when the ammunition exploded, completely wrecking the engine and both trucks, killing Furlonger, Farren and Johnston (a member of the train crew), and seriously wounding Bigland. Had it not been for the prompt and courageous action of these men, whereby three of them lost their lives and one was seriously injured, there is not the slightest doubt that the whole dump would have been destroyed and many lives lost.

BLAND, George Hubert.

Rank: Capt.
Unit/Force: 105 Mahratta LI, IA.
Other decorations: MC (LG August 25, 1917). No citation.
Date of deed: August 31, 1921.
Date of Gazette: June 30, 1922.
Place/date of birth: September 1, 1897.
Place/date of death: Not known.
Place of memorial: Not known.
Town/county connections: Not known.
Remarks. Comsd January 30, 1916. Retd January 11, 1923. Recalled for WWII and served in the RAOC attaining rank of Lt Col. Also held British War and Victory Medals, and Africa Stars, Defence and War Medals.

Citation

The KING has been pleased to award the Albert Medal to Captain George Hubert Bland, M.C., 105th Mahratta Light Infantry, in recognition of his gallantry in saving life at Moghal Kot in August of last year.

On the 31st August, 1921, at Moghal Kot, a Stokes Mortar shell fused prematurely, and Captain Bland, with great presence of mind and disregard for his own safety - for a few seconds only would elapse before the shell exploded - at once rushed forward and threw the shell over the parapet. But for his courageous action there would in all probability have been loss of life, and it is unlikely that casualties would have been confined to the Trench Mortar Section, for many Officers and men were in the near vicinity.

BODDY, John Gouldthorpe.

Rank: Lt (E).
Unit/Force: RN. HMS *Trinidad*.
Other decorations: Nil.
Date of deed: May 14, 1942.
Date of Gazette: October 20, 1942.
Place/date of birth: Not known.
Place/date of death: Off North Cape, Norway, May 14, 1942.
Place of memorial: Plymouth Naval Memorial.
Town/County connections: Not known.

Citation

The KING has been graciously pleased to ... approve the following Award(s):-

For great bravery and devotion in trying to save life at sea:

The Albert Medal (Posthumous) Lieutenant (E) John Gouldthorpe Boddy, Royal Navy, whose ship was heavily attacked by enemy aircraft. Lieutenant Boddy was within a few feet of one bomb when it fell: he was badly shaken by the explosion. About ten minutes later he was seen to raise himself on his hands and knees. There were fires now burning round him, and the way was blocked by debris. Cries were heard from the Stokers' mess-deck below, and Lieutenant Boddy asked a rating to help him rescue the men below. He was last seen crawling towards the hatch to try to save them. This devotion cost him his life.

J. G. BODDY
Source: RN College of Engineering, Manadon

BODSWORTH, Samuel Arnold.

No. 70270.
Rank: PTE.
Unit/Force: RAMC. HMHS *Salta*.
Date of deed: April 10, 1917.
Date of Gazette: January 11, 1918.
Place/date of birth: Not known.
Place/date of death: Not known.
Place of memorial: Not known.
Town/county connections: Not known.
Remarks: Also held British War and Victory Medals.

Citation

The KING has been graciously pleased to confer the Decoration of the Albert Medal upon Private Samuel Arnold Bodsworth, Royal Army Medical Corps.

The following is an account of the services in respect of which the Decoration has been conferred:-
On the 10th April, 1917, His Majesty's Hospital Ship "Salta" was sunk in Havre Roads.

His Majesty's Ship "Druid" proceeded to render assistance and got alongside a swamped boat of the "Salta". All the occupants of the boat were rescued except a Hospital Sister and Private Bodsworth. The former was so exhausted that she was unable to hold the ropes thrown to her, and eventually became unconscious.

Although he might have been rescued, Private Bodsworth persisted in remaining in the boat with the Sister, and, after she had fallen overboard and been hauled back again, he finally succeeded in placing a line round her body, by means of which she was hauled on board the "Druid".

Very considerable risk was incurred by Private Bodsworth in rendering the service on account of the rough sea which prevailed at the time.

BRIDGES, William J.

Rank: QM.
Unit/Force: RN. HMS *Thunderer*.
Other decorations: Nil.
Date of deed: January 2, 1879.
Date of Gazette: June 10, 1879.
Place/date of birth: Not known.
Place/date of death: Not known.
Place of memorial: Not known.
Town/county connections: Not known.

Citation

THE Queen has been graciously pleased to confer the Albert Medal of the Second Class on -
WILLIAM J. BRIDGES, Quartermaster of Her Majesty's Ship "Thunderer".

The following is an account of the services in respect of which the decoration has been conferred:-

On the occasion of the recent explosion which took place on board the "Thunderer", BRIDGES was at his station in the shell room. When the explosion occurred, the shell room was immediately filled with smoke and many burning fragments of clothing, &c., were blown down into it. The magazine was also filled with smoke and reported to be on fire. All lights were put out, and the cries of the wounded were distracting. The prevailing impression appears to have been that one of the filled common shells had exploded, and the men stationed in the room made their escape as speedily as possible, with the exception of BRIDGES, who, taking off his woollen comforter, wrapped it round the burning fragments, and brought them up on the flats.

BRIDGES afterwards went down again to make further search for any smouldering material that might have found its way amongst the projectiles.

BROADHURST, George.

G. BROADHURST
Source: S. Wales Weekly Argus

No. 20111.
Rank: LCPL.
Unit/Force: 10 Bn SWB.
Other decorations: Nil.
Date of deed: February 10, 1916.
Date of Gazette: June 30, 1916.
Place/date of birth: Not Known.
Place/date of death: Not known.
Place of memorial: Not known.
Town/county connections:
Sudbrook, Monmouthshire; Swansea. Glamorgan.
Remarks: To France December 3, 1915. Discharged due to wounds incurred when winning his AM September 15, 1916. Also held 1914-15 Star, British War and Victory Medals and Silver War Badge.

Citation
The KING has been graciously pleased to award the Decoration of the Albert Medal of the First Class to Lance-Corporal George Broadhurst, of the 10th Battalion, South Wales Borderers, who is serving in France, in recognition of his gallantry in saving life:-

On the 10th February, 1916, a member of a class which was being instructed in bombing dropped a live bomb, picked it up again and threw it to a corner of the room. Broadhurst immediately placed his foot on the bomb with a view to minimising the effect of the explosion. He was severely wounded in both feet. By his brave action he undoubtedly safeguarded his comrades.

BROOKS, Victor.

No. 522653.
Rank: SGT.
Unit/Force: Canadian Cav Fd Amb, CAMC.
Other decorations: Nil.

Date of deed: June 30, 1918.
Date of Gazette: November 8, 1918.
Place/date of birth: Gorton, Manchester, November 28, 1887.
Place/date of death: Not known.
Place of memorial: Not known.
Town/county connections: Manchester.
Remarks: Discharged Buxton, Derbyshire, May 9, 1919

Citation

The KING has been pleased to award the Albert Medal to Lieutenant-Colonel (Temporary Brigadier-General) Alfred Burt, D.S.O., and Sergeant Victor Brooks, Canadian Cavalry Field Ambulance; and (posthumous awards) to Private Arthur Johnson and Driver Alfred Horn, late of the Army Service Corps, in recognition of their gallantry in saving life or endeavouring to save life in France in June last. The circumstances are as follows:-

On the 30th June, 1918, a Corporal of the Royal Air Force, who had been lowered by rope into a crater caused by a bomb which had been dropped by a hostile aeroplane, was overcome by carbon monoxide gas, which had accumulated in large quantities in the crater. Endeavours were made to haul him out, but his head became caught, and Private Johnson volunteered to descend and re-adjust the rope, which he did successfully, and the Corporal was rescued, but Johnson was himself overcome. Driver Horn at once put on his respirator and lowered himself to the rescue, but was likewise overcome. Sergeant Brooks then volunteered to attempt to rescue both men but was also overcome by the gas; fortunately he was hauled out.

At this stage Brigadier-General Burt refused to permit anyone else to descend, but did so himself, and succeeded in dragging one of the unconscious men some way towards the rope; he, however, became unconscious and had to be pulled out.

There can be no doubt that all knew the risk that they were running, and willingly incurred it in the hope of saving life.

BROWN, James William.

No. 59214.
Rank: WOII (A/QMS).
Unit/Force: 30 Coy RAMC.
Other decorations: Nil.
Date of deed: February 5, 1917.
Date of Gazette: November 9, 1917.
Place/date of birth: Not known.
Place/date of death: Not known.
Place of memorial: Not known.
Town/county connections: Not known.
Remarks: Also held British War Medal.

Citation
As for ALLAN, A. D. H.

J. E. BROWN
Source: Globe & Laurel

BROWN, *John Edwin.*

No. PO/13676.
Rank: PTE.
Unit/Force: RMLI.
Other decorations: Nil.
Date of deed: January 31, 1917.
Date of Gazette: September 7, 1917.
Place/date of birth: London, c1887.
Place/date of death: Off Isle of Man, February 26, 1918.
Place of memorial: Portsmouth Naval Memorial, Column 30.

Remarks: Also held RHS medal in Bronze. Son of John and Emily Brown of Bethnal Green and husband of Lilian Sarah Brown of Tottenham, London. AM was probably lost at sea.

Citation

The KING has been graciously pleased to confer the Decoration of the Albert Medal upon John David Bulmer, boatswain of the steamship "Rhydwen", of Cardiff, and Private John Edward Brown, R.M.L.I.

The following is an account of the services in respect of which the Decoration has been conferred:-

On the 31st January, 1917, while the steamship "Rhydwen" of Cardiff, was lying at Genoa, a fire broke out in the ship's magazine.

A fire signal was immediately hoisted, but before assistance arrived Bulmer and Brown went below, unlocked the door of the magazine and got the hose at the seat of the fire.

Water was then played on the magazine and the ammunition was taken out on deck, and, owing to the prompt action of the ship's crew, the fire was extinguished.

Considerable risk was incurred by Bulmer and Brown in rendering the service.

BUGG, *Rupert Walter.*

No. SD5042 (SD5046 according to CWGC)
Rank: Ldg Deckhand.
Unit/Force: RNR. ML 285.
Other decorations: Nil.
Date of deed: December 29, 1917.
Date of Gazette: May 21, 1918.
Place/date of birth: c1886.
Place/date of death: March 22, 1919.
Place of memorial: Holbrook Churchyard, Suffolk. 129.
Town/county connections: Stoke, Ipswich, Suffolk.
Remarks: Aged 32 at death. Probably died of influenza. Husband of Hettie J. Bugg, 21 Ashley St, Stoke, Ipswich.

Citation

The KING has been pleased to award the Decoration of the Albert Medal to John George Stanners, Deckhand, R.N.R., O.N. 17562 D.A., and to Rupert Walter Bugg, Leading Deckhand, R.N.R.,

O.N. 5046 S.D., in recognition of their gallantry in the following circumstances:-

On the 29th December, 1917, some cotton waste, which had been stored in a wooden cupboard in the Magazine of H.M. Motor Launch No. 289, caught fire from an unknown cause. On the fire being discovered by the smell of burning and by the issue of smoke from the Magazine hatch, when opened, Deckhand Stanners, without hesitation, went down into the Magazine and brought up a quantity of burning waste.

Leading Deckhand Bugg, who was in Motor Launch No. 285, alongside No. 289, smelt something burning, and on observing Deckhand Stanners coming up from the Magazine with burning material, immediately went down and extinguished the remainder of the cotton waste.

The promptitude of action and the high courage shown by these men in the face of very grave danger averted a serious fire, and in all probability saved both Motor Launches and the lives of those on board.

Note: Stanners became a GC in 1971.

A. BURT

Source: Regiment

BURT, Alfred.

Rank: Lt-Col (T/Brig-Gen).
Unit/Force: 3 DG. Comd 7 Cav Bde.
Other decorations:
CB, CMG, DSO* (LG June 18, 1917 & July 26, 1918).
Date of deed: June 30, 1918.
Date of Gazette: November 8, 1918.
Place/date of birth: London, April 18, 1875.
Place/date of death: Chertsey, Surrey, February 26, 1949.
Place of memorial: Not known.
Town/county connections: London, Chertsey, Stoke Poges.
Remarks: Son of F. J. Burt of Stoke Poges, Bucks. Educated Oundle, Heidelberg. Joined Artists Vols 1894; 3 Bn R Warks Regt 1895-6; 2Lt 3 DG June 6, 1896. Ret as Brig-Gen 19 March 16, 1920. Chief of Mil Mission to Latvia and Lithuania June 1919 - February 1920. Served South African War and awarded QSA (5 clasps) and KSA (2 clasps). Awarded 1914-15 Star, British War and Victory Medals. MID for SA War and WWI. Awarded Légion d'Honneur.

Citation
As for BROOKS, V.

BUSH, George Robert.

No. P/KX96548.
Rank: Sto Cl 1.
Unit/Force: RN. HMS *Bagshot.*
Other decorations: Nil.
Date of deed: February 18, 1942.
Date of Gazette: August 11, 1942.

Place/date of birth: c1918.
Place/date of death: February 19, 1942.
Place of memorial: Alexandria War Memorial Cemetery (Hadra), Egypt. Plot 1, Row C, Grave 7.
Town/county connections: Not known.

Citation

The KING has been graciously pleased to approve the following award:
    For great gallantry in saving life at sea:
                    The Albert Medal (Posthumous)
Stoker First Class George Robert Bush, P/KX.96548.

When a pipe in one of H.M. Ships burst, filling the boiler-room with steam, Stoker Bush and three others took refuge in a bunker. They tried to make those on the upper deck hear them but could not. As the bunker was filling with steam, Stoker Bush made a dash up the ladder. He reached the top, gasped out "Three men, port bunker," and fainted. The bunker plate on the upper deck was at once removed and the three men saved. Stoker Bush died next morning from the shock of his many burns.

BUSWELL, Richard Walker.

Rank: Lt.
Unit/Force: Ches Yeo, att 7 Gp RAF.
Other decorations: Nil.
Date of deed: May 31, 1918.
Date of Gazette: August 30, 1918.
Place/date of birth: Not known.
Place/date of death: Not known.
Place of memorial: Not known.
Town/county connections: Not known.
Remarks: T/Capt RAF. Went to France September 9, 1914. He also served in the Oxford Yeomanry. Presented with AM by His Majesty the King at Buckingham Palace September 18, 1918. Also held 1914 Star, British War and Victory Medals and the Territorial Efficiency Medal (AO 107/12).

Citation

The KING has been pleased to award the Albert Medal ... in recognition of gallantry displayed in ... endeavouring to save life:-
Lieutenant Richard Walker Buswell, Cheshire Yeomanry (temporary Captain, Royal Air Force).

On the 31st May, 1918, Captain Buswell was flying at Yatesbury, when he saw another machine sideslip to the ground and burst into flames. He flew to the spot and landed; and seeing that the pilot, who was enveloped in flames, was still living, he dashed into the fire and endeavoured to rescue him. Several attempts had already been made to reach the pilot, but owing to the very intense heat they were unsuccessful. Captain Buswell, however, managed to get hold of the pilot's clothes, which, being in flames, came away in his hand,. He then procured a belt and succeeded in extricating the pilot, but was too late to save his life.

CALTHROP, Walter Henry Calthrop.

Rank: Cdr.
Unit/Force: RN.. Director Naval Transport Operations.
Other decorations: Nil.
Date of deed: April 14/15, 1918.
Date of Gazette: October 1, 1918.
Place/date of birth: Not known.
Place/date of death: Not known.
Place of memorial: Not known.
Town/county connections: Not known.

Citation

The KING has been graciously pleased to approve of the award of the Albert Medal for gallantry in saving life at sea to Commander Walter Henry Calthrop Calthrop, R.N.

The account of the services in respect of which this decoration has been conferred is as follows:-

On the night of 14th/15th April, 1918, a fire broke out on board the S.S. "Proton", an ammunition ship, at Port Said. Commander Calthrop, on being informed on the telephone that the ship was on fire, immediately proceeded to the scene. The ship had already been abandoned by her crew, and was ablaze in Nos 1 and 2 holds. The forecastle was also alight, and it was impossible to get down to the fore well deck owing to the heat of the flames. Knowing that the "Proton" had 240 tons of ammunition on board, Commander Calthrop decided to endeavour to flood the ship, and for this purpose obtained assistance and went down into the engine-room and opened the sea inlet. He also tried to break the main sea valve cover, but was not successful in this. He accordingly sent for a gun-cotton charge for the purpose of sinking the ship, and warned all ships in the vicinity to get under weigh. He then returned to the "Proton", which was now blazing fiercely forward, the sides being red hot as far aft as the bridge, and the bridge screen all alight, He again boarded her with the first and second engineers and went below, trying to break the doors of the condenser with sledge hammers. After about five minutes this was found to be impossible, and they returned on deck. By this time a picket boat had arrived with the gun-cotton charge, and it was decided that the ship ought to be sunk as soon as possible. This operation was accordingly carried out.

Commander Calthrop displayed the utmost gallantry and disregard of his own personal safety in making protracted efforts, first to flood and then to sink the ship, whilst exposed to continual risk of an explosion of the ammunition on board. His efforts undoubtedly prevented serious loss of life.

CALVERLEY, Frank Herbert.

Rank: 2 Lt.
Unit/Force: RE. 1 Spec Coy RE.
Other decorations: Nil.
Date of deed: July 19/20, 1918.
Date of Gazette: October 29, 1918.
Place/date of birth: Not known.

Place/date of death: Not known.
Place of memorial: Not known.
Town/county connections: Batley, Yorks.
Remarks: To France April 15, 1915. Also served in ranks of RE as No. 91644 and Pte 445 West Riding Fd Amb RAMC. Att to 2 Australian Div. Presented with AM by His Majesty the King at Buckingham Palace May 17, 1918. Also held 1914 Star, British War and Victory Medals. Came from 27 Pulwell Hall Road, Batley, Yorks.

Citation

The KING has been pleased to award the Albert Medal to Second Lieutenant Frank Herbert Calverley, Royal Engineers, in recognition of his gallantry in saving life in July last. The circumstances are as follows:-

In France, on the night of the 19th July, 1918, Lieutenant Calverley was in charge of a party of men unloading 4-inch Stokes gas bombs from limbers, when he noticed that the safety lever on one of the bombs had been broken and that the fuze was burning. Regardless of personal danger, he at once rushed forward and picked up the bomb, fully realising the disaster that would inevitably occur should it explode among the men and horses. He carried it to leeward of the dump, where it burst, wounding him in several places. But for his prompt and gallant action there would have been numerous gas casualties and, in all probability, loss of life.

CAMPBELL, *John Dudley Pitts.*

Rank: 2 Lt.
Unit/Force: RFA. 112 Bty 24 Bde RFA.
Other decorations: MC LG February 1, 1919.
Date of deed: March 9, 1917.
Date of Gazette: August 21, 1917.
Place/date of birth: Melbourne, Australia, c1885.
Place/date of death: Melbourne, Australia, November 5, 1957.
Place of memorial: Cremated, Spring Vale Crematorium, Melbourne.
Town/county connections: Melbourne, Victoria, Aust.
Remarks: Also held British War and Victory Medals. To France January 12, 1916. Joined RFA as 2Lt August 13, 1915. Major October 30, 1917. Returned to Aust and demobilised September 4, 1919. His exploit was featured in the "Victor" comic on May 31, 1986.

Citation.

The KING has been pleased to award the Albert Medal of the Second Class to Second Lieutenant John Pitts Campbell, Royal Field Artillery, in recognition of his gallantry in saving life in France in March last.

On the 9th March, 1917, in the Rutoire Plain, near Loos, a British aeroplane fell to the ground and turned completely over, throwing out the pilot and bursting into flames. The machine-gun ammunition caught fire, with the result that bullets were flying in all directions. Lieutenant Campbell ran up and at great personal risk dragged the pilot, who was wounded, out of danger. He then placed him in a neighbouring dug-out, sent for medical assistance and organised a party of stretcher-bearers to carry him to a dressing-station.

CAMPBELL, Malcolm Sydenham Clarke.

Rank: Maj.
Unit/Force: RA. IOD.
Other decorations: CB (1919), CIE (1907).
Date of deed: August 30, 1906.
Date of Gazette: September 26, 1911.
Place/date of birth: November 2, 1863.
Place/date of death: Wallingford, Berks, July 22, 1949.
Place of memorial: Cremated. Ashes interred at Ivybridge.
Town/county connections: Ivybridge, Devon; Crowthorne, Berks
Remarks: Son of Maj-Gen A. H. E. Campbell, late Madras Cavalry. Educ. Cheltenham Coll and RMA Woolwich. Comsd February 14, 1883. Third Burma War 1886-7. Att IOD June 10, 1888. Third China War 1900. Ordnance Consulting Officer for India in London 1911-19. Col December 15, 1914. Rctd December 4, 1919. Deacon 1919, Priest 1920. Vicar of Ivybridge, Devon, 1922-46. Retd from Holy Orders 1946. Went to reside at Hamtun, Crowthorne, Berks. Married 1889 to Jessie (died 1933). Also held IGS 1854 bar Burma 1885-7 and China Medal 1900 with bar. He was MID for China.

Citation
See citation for ANDERSON, C. A.

CARLIN, Gertrude Walters.

Rank: Sister.
Unit/Force: TFNS. 36 CCS RAMC.
Other decorations: ARRC (LG June 13, 1918).
Date of deed: October 1, 1918.
Date of Gazette: January 31, 1919.
Place/date of birth: Not known.
Place/date of death: Gore, New Zealand, April 9, 1969.
Place of memorial: Not known.
Town/county connections: Gore, New Zealand.
Remarks: Member of 3 North Gen Hosp. Called up September 2, 1914. Staff Nurse. To France February 6, 1915. Prom Sister July 5, 1916. Returned to UK December 24, 1918. Resigned May 29, 1920 on marriage. Became Mrs Dickison. Described as above average; an excellent worker. Also held 1914-15 Star, British War and Victory Medals. No citation for ARRC.

Citation
The KING has been pleased to award the Albert Medal to
Sister Gertrude Walters Carlin
Staff Nurse Harriet Elizabeth Fraser,

both of the Territorial Force Nursing Service; and to
Sister Gladys White,
of the British Red Cross Society, in recognition of their gallantry in saving life at a Casualty Clearing Station in Belgium in October last.

Early on the morning of the 1st October, 1918, a serious fire occurred in No. 36 Casualty Clearing Station at Rousbrugge, in Belgium. At the time some of the patients were undergoing serious operations in the abdominal and general operating theatres, the walls of which were composed of wood. The first intimation of danger in the theatres was the extinction of the electric light accompanied by volumes of smoke, and almost immediately the wooden walls burst into flames. The two sisters and the staff nurse assisted in carrying the unconscious patients to safety, and returned to the burning wards to assist in carrying out other patients. During this time ether bottles and nitrous oxide cylinders were continually exploding, filling the air with fumes and flying fragments of steel.
Note: Staff Nurse Fraser (later Mrs Barry) exchanged her AM for the GC in 1971.

CARPENTER, Alfred.

Rank: Lt.
Unit/Force: RN. HMS *Challenger*.
Other decorations: DSO (LG January 13, 1887).
Date of deed: January 31, 1876.
Date of Gazette: June 23, 1876.
Place/date of birth: Brighton, Sussex, August 2, 1847.
Place/date of death: 1926.
Place of memorial: Not known.
Town/county connections: Not known.
Remarks: Son of Cdr Charles Carpenter RN (JP for Sussex) and Sophie Wilson, daughter of Thomas Wilson of Walthamstow. Educated Brighton College. Entered RN 1861. In charge of Marine Survey of India 1885. Author of "Nature Notes for Ocean Voyagers". Married twice (1) Henriette Shadwell (one son, one daughter) and (2) Aetheldreda Cox. Also held IGS 1854 (one bar), Egypt Medal (one bar) and Khedive's Star. Father of Capt (later Vice Adm) A. F. B. Carpenter VC of HMS *Vindictive* at Zeebrugge.

Citation
THE Queen has been graciously pleased to confer the Albert Medal of the Second Class on:-
LIEUTENANT ALFRED CARPENTER, R.N., of Her Majesty's Ship "Challenger".

The following is an account of the services in respect of which the decoration has been conferred:-

At 10.30 P.M. on the 31st January 1876, while the "Challenger" was at anchor in Stanley Harbour, Falkland Islands, in five fathoms of water, distant a quarter of a mile from the shore, Thomas Bush, an Able Seaman, fell overboard from the steam pinnace, which was coming alongside, and sank without uttering a cry. The night was dark, the weather very boisterous and raining, there was a short chopping sea (which rendered swimming extremely difficult), and an outsetting current.

LIEUTENANT CARPENTER, without a moment's hesitation, jumped from the gangway, and swam towards the spot where the man disappeared, which was some twenty feet from the ship, and touched him with his feet under water. He then dived, seized hold of Bush, and brought him to the surface, and supported him from three to five minutes; but Bush being a very heavy man, and encumbered with thick waterproof clothing, and, moreover, being quite insensible, LIEUTENANT CARPENTER, as he got exhausted with his exertions, was obliged to let him slip down. He supported him with his legs for a few moments, and then they were both taken on board the "Challenger".

When picked up, they were between forty and fifty yards from the ship's stern, which distance they were drifted by the current and wind. Every effort was at once made by the medical officers to restore Bush, but without success. There were several patches of floating kelp round the ship, amongst which the strongest swimmer would be helpless, which materially increased the risk incurred.

From the unusual and strange fact that the man was not seen from the time of his falling overboard until brought to the surface by LIEUTENANT CARPENTER, no boat, but for his prompt action, could have attempted to save the man with any chance of success.

CHESHIRE, William Donald.

Rank: Capt.
Unit/Force: 17 Bn LF.
Other decorations: Nil.
Date of deed: May 1, 1916.
Date of Gazette: August 21, 1917.
Place/date of birth: Not known.
Place/date of death: Not known.
Place of memorial: Not known.
Town/county connections: Not known.
Remarks: To France June 1916. Later served as Maj in 1 London Rifle Brigade. MID LG May 22, 1917. Also awarded British War and Victory Medals. Presented with AM by His Majesty the King at Buckingham Palace July 17, 1917.

Citation
The KING has been pleased to award the Albert Medal of the Second Class to Captain William Donald Cheshire, Lancashire Fusiliers, in recognition of (his) gallantry in saving life in France.

At Neuve Chapelle, on the 1st May, 1916, while practice with live grenades was being carried out, one of the class, in attempting to throw a grenade from which the safety pin had been withdrawn, struck his hand against the parados, so that the grenade was knocked out of his hand and fell into the trench, in which about twenty men were collected.

Captain (then Lieutenant) Cheshire rushed forward, but was hampered and delayed by the men, who were trying to get clear. Nevertheless, he seized the grenade and threw it over the parapet. It exploded immediately after leaving his hand.

CLARKE, Hugh.

Rank: Capt.
Unit/Force: RA. IOD.
Other decorations: Nil.
Date of deed: August 30, 1906.
Date of Gazette: September 26, 1911.
Place/date of birth: Sydney, NSW, Australia, January 13, 1877.
Place/date of death: June 22, 1940.
Place of memorial: Not known.
Town/county connections: Southsea, Hants.
Remarks: Enlisted 5 (Militia) Inniskilling Fusiliers, 1898. 2LT RA June 24, 1898. Att IOD September 1902. Served in France and Flanders in WWI. Col March 14, 1927. Transferred to Indian Army August 25, 1927. DDOS Southern Comd (India) 1927-31. Retired August 25, 1931. Married February 6, 1903, to Kathleen Johnston at St Thomas' Cathedral, Bombay. Two sons. Also held 1914-15 Trio and Delhi Durbar Medal 1911.

Citation
As for ANDERSON C. A.

H. CLARKE (SEATED RIGHT)

CLOW, Malcolm Joseph.

Rank: T/Surg-Lt.
Unit/Force: RNVR. HMS *Ibis*.
Other decorations: Nil.
Date of deed: November 10, 1942.
Date of Gazette: April 20, 1943.
Place/date of birth: Hale, Cheshire, November 9, 1914.
Place/date of death: Sydney, NSW, Aust, February 11, 1945.
Place of memorial: Sydney War Cemetery, Rookwood, Plot 5, Row C, Grave 8.
Town/county connections: Hale, Cheshire.
Remarks: Comsd October 23, 1940. Unmarried. BA, MB, ChB. Son of J. P. Clow, a Manchester accountant. Worked at Crumpsall Hosp, Manchester, before joining RNVR. Qualified 1938. Home address: Melbrook, Cambridge Road, Hale, Cheshire. He took his own life at Warwick Farm Naval Base, Liverpool, NSW. One of the last two awards of the Albert Medal in Gold for Gallantry in Saving Life at Sea (the other was BEECHING, q.v.).

Citation
The KING has been graciously pleased to approve the following ...
  For gallantry in saving life at sea:
           The Albert Medal in Gold
Temporary Surgeon Lieutenant Malcolm Joseph Clow, M.B., B.Ch., R.N.V.R.
  Surgeon Lieutenant Clow was between decks when H.M.S. Ibis was hit and badly damaged. Wounded men were brought to him in the Sick Bay, among them an Engine Room Artificer badly burnt about the arm. Surgeon Lieutenant Clow gave him an injection of morphia, and, as the ship was now sinking, helped the man up the ladder and out on to the upper deck. As the man had no life belt, he put his own on him. Then he got him into the water and made sure he was free of the ship before he himself abandoned it. In doing this Surgeon Lieutenant Clow became entangled in the rigging and was taken down some way before he got clear. He then swam for three hours without a life belt before he was picked up.

COLLINS, James.

J. COLLINS

No. 49809.
Rank: PTE (A/LCPL).
Unit/Force: RAMC. 14 Fd Amb RAMC.
Date of deed: November 11, 1917.
Date of Gazette: January 1, 1918.
Place/date of birth: Not known.
Place/date of death: Not known.
Place of memorial: Not known.
Town/county connections: Not known.
Remarks: To France May 27, 1915. Also awarded 1914-15 Trio. Presented with AM by His Majesty the King at Buckingham Palace April 6, 1918.

Citation

The KING has been graciously pleased to award the Decoration of the Albert Medal in Gold to Private (acting Lance-Corporal) James Collins, of the 14th Field Ambulance, Royal Army Medical Corps, in recognition of his gallant action in saving life in France in the following circumstances:-

On the 11th November, 1917, near an advanced dressing station in France, a lunatic soldier escaped from his escort and ran away along a trench. Collins ran after him, and when he got near him the man threatened to throw a bomb at him. Collins closed with the man, who then withdrew the pin from the bomb and let it fall in the trench. In an endeavour to save the patient and two other soldiers who were near, Collins put his foot upon the bomb, which exploded, killing the lunatic and injuring Collins severely; fortunately the two soldiers were not hurt.

Collins, who could easily have got out of the way, ran the gravest risk of losing his life in order to save others.

W. J. CONDON
Source: Sydney Morning Herald

CONDON, William Joseph.

No. R.47279.
Rank: EM (E) 1.
Unit/Force: RAN. HMAS *Voyager.*
Date of deed: February 10, 1964.
Date of Gazette: March 19, 1965.
Place/date of birth: Not known.
Place/date of death: Off NSW, Aust, February 10, 1964.
Place of memorial: Not known.
Town/county connections: Not known.
Remarks: One GC, two AMs, one GM, five BEMs and three Queen's Commendations for Brave Conduct were awarded for the sinking of HMAS *Voyager.* The GC and AMs were all posthumous.

Citation
Except for the GC mentioned above, there are no citations for any of the other awards, save "for courage and devotion to duty at the time of the sinking of H.M.A.S. Voyager *on 10th February 1964."*

CONNOR, Douglas Mortimer.

Rank: T/Lt.
Unit/Force: RNVR. ML 387.
Date of deed: March 5, 1944.
Date of Gazette: December 19, 1944.

Place/date of birth: c1911.
Place/date of death: Off Beirut, Lebanon, March 5, 1944.
Place of memorial: Beirut War Cemetery, Lebanon. Plot 7, Row C, Grave 1.
Town/county connections: Trowbridge, Wilts.
Remarks: Son of H. B. and M. Connor of Trowbridge, Wilts and husband of Norah Marion Connor of Trowbridge. Also awarded 1939-45, Atlantic and Pacific Stars and War Medal, all of which carry impressed naming.

Citation

The KING has been graciously pleased ... to approve the following awards:
    For saving life at sea:

Albert Medal (Posthumous).

Temporary Lieutenant Douglas Mortimer Connor, R.N.V.R.

On 5th March, 1944, fire broke out in the starboard corner of the engine room of one of H.M. Motor Launches at Beirut. An explosion occurred immediately afterwards and the fire spread rapidly throughout the ship. Lieutenant Connor straightaway organised all the fire-fighting gear on board and sent a runner to inform Coastal Forces base and Naval Base so that the civilian and Naval fire-fighting organisation might be got into action as soon as possible. The heat from the burning ship was intense and it was well known that with the burning high octane petrol the ship was likely to blow up at any moment.

The burning ship was a grave menace to other shipping berthed alongside and Lieutenant Connor made valiant efforts to make fast a tow line so that she could be towed out of the port. So great was the heat, however, that the tow line parted. At about 19.15 a third and more violent explosion occurred in which Lieutenant Connor lost his life.

Lieutenant Connor well knew the risks involved, but sacrificed his life in an endeavour to prevent the spread of the fire which might well have become a major conflagration involving the loss of many lives.

CORSCADDEN, Arthur Latimer.

Rank: Sub-Lt.
Unit/Force: Royal Canadian Sea Cadets.
Date of deed: June 6, 1954.
Date of Gazette: August 7, 1956.
Place/date of birth: Toronto, Canada, December 6, 1930.
Place/date of death: Lake Ontario, Canada, June 6, 1954.
Place of memorial: Not known.
Town/county connections: Toronto.
Remarks: Son of Harold and Emilie Corscadden. Flt Cadet 33580 RCAF October 23, 1950 to March 22, 1951. Honorably discharged. Midshipman Royal Canadian Sea Cadets June 15, 1949. Married May, 1952, to Audrey May Monkley. No children. Graduate of Jarvis Collegiate Institute, Toronto. Chartered accountant. Employed by Toronto brokerage firm at the time of his death.

Citation

The QUEEN has been graciously pleased to approve the posthumous award of the Albert Medal

for gallantry in attempting to save life at sea to:-
Sub-Lieutenant Arthur Latimer CORSCADDEN, Royal Canadian Sea Cadets.

On 6th June, 1954, Sub-Lieutenant Corscadden took nine Sea Cadets of the training establishment Royal Canadian Sea Cadet Corps ARK ROYAL in a whaler on a training exercise on Lake Ontario. During the exercise a sudden gust of wind struck the sail of the whaler and capsized it. Sub-Lieutenant Corscadden ordered the cadets to stay by the boat but one of them drifted away. The boy could not swim in the cold water and Sub-Lieutenant Corscadden at once swam after him. He put a life jacket on the cadet and lashed him to himself in an effort to keep him afloat, but the water was so cold that they both sank before help arrived. The gallant action of this junior officer is in keeping with the highest traditions of the Royal Canadian Navy.

COTTON, *Arthur Steadman.*

Rank: Lt-Col (Brev Col).
Unit/Force: RA. Artillery Adviser BMMS Russia.
Other decorations: CB (1930), CMG (1919), CBE (LG March 15,1920), DSO (LG June 23, 1915).
Date of deed: October 14, 1919.
Date of Gazette: July 16, 1920.
Place/date of birth: London, August 18, 1873.
Place/date of death: Bournemouth, Hants, September 13, 1952.
Place of memorial: Not known.
Town/County connections: London, Bournemouth.
Remarks: Son of Maj J. W. M. Cotton JP of 2 Chester Terrace, Regent's Park, London (late 21H and 9 Foot). Educated Merchant Taylors School and RMA Woolwich. Joined RA May 30, 1893. Served China and WWI (wounded three times). BGRA 41 Div. CRA 28 Div (Chanak, Turkey) 1922-23. Comd 28 Div 1923, CRA 56 (Lond) Div TA 1924-25. CRA Southern Comd (India) 1926-27. BRA Northern Comd (India) 1927-30. Retd as Brig-Gen 1930. Married Rose Bousfield 1903. One daughter. Also held China Medal 1900, 1914 Star and bar Trio, Defence Medal, Officer Order of St Maurice and St Lazarus (Italy), Order of St Vladimir 3rd Class (Russia), Croix de Guerre avec Palmes (France), Croix de Guerre (Belgium). MID nine times. There is no citation for the D.S.O.

Citation
The KING has been pleased to award the Albert Medal to Lt.-Col. (Bt. Col.) Arthur Stedman Cotton, C.M.G., D.S.O., Royal Artillery, in recognition of his gallantry in saving life in the following circumstances:-

On the 14th October, 1919, at Novorossisk, South Russia, an ammunition dump exploded, setting fire to the ss. "War Pike", which was carrying a cargo of munitions, including shells. Colonel Cotton, as explosions were taking place both on the quay and on board the ship, cleared the bystanders from the neighbourhood, and assisted in casting off the hawsers from the vessel. He then organised a small party to follow the steamer in a tug, when it was towed out to sea, in order to render all possible assistance, and, although the vessel was burning fiercely, the hold and bunkers being well alight, he boarded her and endeavoured to get the fire under control. It was not until the fore part of the ship began to settle down that he and his party left the vessel.

Colonel Cotton's prompt action, which was attended by great personal risk, in all probability saved many lives.

COYNE, David Emmitt.

No. 3347.
Rank: SGT.
Unit/Force: 31 Aust Inf Bn, AIF.
Date of deed: May 15, 1918.
Date of Gazette: October 18, 1918.
Place/date of birth: Ballinrush, Qld, Aust, March 14, 1896.
Place/date of death: Voire-sur-Corbie, Amiens, France, May 15, 1918.
Place of memorial: Vignacourt British Cemetery, France, Plot 2, Row D, Grave 6.
Town/county connections: Ballinrush, Mackay, Qld, Aust.
Remarks: Son of David and Anne Coyne. Educated at Marian State School and then worked on the land with father. Horse breaker. To France May 1916. Promoted Sgt June 1917. Also awarded British War and Victory Medals. The only Australian serviceman to win the AM in Gold.

Citation

The KING has been pleased to award the Albert Medal in Gold in recognition of the gallantry of Sergeant David Emmitt Coyne, of the 31st Battalion, Australian Imperial Force, in saving life in France at the cost of his own life.

D.E. COYNE

On the night of the 15th May, 1918, in order to test some Mills grenades, Sergeant Coyne threw one of them, but it failed to clear the parapet and fell into the trench in which there were a number of other men. Sergeant Coyne shouted to them to run for their lives, and endeavoured to find the bomb in order to throw it away, but owing to the darkness he was unable to lay his hand on it in time and, the men not being clear of the trench, he deliberately threw himself on to the top of it and let it explode under him, receiving fatal injuries, but saving the lives of his comrades.

T. CREAN
Source: "An Unknown Few"

CREAN, Thomas.

Rank: PO 1.
Unit/Force: RN. Scott Expedition.
Other decorations: Nil.
Date of deed: February 9 - 19, 1912.
Date of Gazette: July 29, 1913.
Place/date of birth: Co Kerry, Ireland, July 20, 1877.
Place/date of death: Anascaul, Co Kerry, Ireland, July 27,
Place of memorial: Anascaul, Co Kerry, Ireland. Mt
Crean and Crean Glacier, Antarctica.
Town/county connections: Anascaul, Co Kerry, Ireland.
Remarks: Served WWI, receiving British War and
Victory Medals. Also awarded RN LS&GC and Polar Medal (bars Antarctic 1902-04,
Antarctic 1910-13 and Antarctic 1914-16). Received Scott Medal 1904 and Scott
Memorial Medal 1913. Promoted CPO December 27, 1916 and returned to RN 1917.
The exploit which won him the AM was featured in "The Hornet" comic, December
25, 1971. He was one of those who rowed in the epic voyage from Elephant island
on Shackleton's expedition of 1914. Retd from RN as WO (Bos'un) 1920.

Citation

*The KING was pleased, on Saturday, the 26th instant, at Buckingham Palace, to present to Chief
Stoker William Lashley, R.N., and Petty Officer (First Class) Thomas Crean, R.N., Albert
Medals of the Second Class, which had been conferred upon them by His Majesty in recognition
of their gallantry in saving life as detailed below:-*

*At the end of a journey of 1,500 miles on foot the final supporting party of the late Captain
Scott's expedition towards the South Pole, consisting of Lieutenant Edward Ratcliffe Garth
Russell Evans, R.N. (now Commander Evans, C.B.), Chief Stoker William Lashley, R.N., and
Petty Officer (First Class) Thomas Crean, R.N., were 238 miles from the base when Lieutenant
Evans was found to be suffering from scurvy. His condition rapidly became worse. When 151
miles from the base he was unable to stand without support on his ski sticks, and after struggling
onward on skis in great pain for four days, during which Lashley and Crean dragged their sledge
fifty-three miles, he collapsed, and was unable to proceed further.*

*At this point Lieutenant Evans requested his two companions to leave him, urging that
eighty-three miles lay between the party and the nearest refuge hut, and that unless they left him
three lives would be lost instead of one. This, however, they refused to do, and insisted on
carrying him forward on the sledge.*

*Favoured by a southerly wind, Lashley and Crean dragged Lieutenant Evans on the sledge
for four days, pulling for thirteen hours a day, until, on the evening of February 17, 1912, a
point was reached thirty-four miles from a refuge hut, where it was thought possible that
assistance might be obtained. During the following twelve hours, however, snow fell incessantly,
and in the morning it was found impossible to proceed further with the sledge.*

*As the party now had only sufficient food for three more meals, and both Lashley and Crean
were becoming weaker daily, it was decided that they should separate, and that Crean should
endeavour to walk to the refuge hut, while Lashley stayed to nurse Lieutenant Evans.*

T. CREAN
Source: "An Unsung Hero"

After a march of eighteen hours in soft snow Crean made his way to the hut, arriving completely exhausted. Fortunately Surgeon Edward L. Atkinson, R.N. was at the hut with two dog teams and the dog attendant. His party, on February 20, effected the rescue of Lieutenant Evans and Lashley.

But for the gallant conduct throughout of his two companions Lieutenant Evans would have undoubtedly lost his life.

Note: Lieutenant Evans (later known as Evans "of the Broke") was to become Admiral Lord Mountevans and never forgot his rescuers, keeping in touch with them for the rest of their lives.

CUTHBERTSON, James.

No. 324094.
Rank: PTE.
Unit/Force: RAMC. 3 Malta Coy RAMC.
Other decorations: Nil.
Date of deed: February 5, 1917.
Date of Gazette: November 9, 1917 and February 8, 1918.
Place/date of birth: Not known.
Place/date of death: Not known.
Place of memorial: Not known.
Town/county connections: Edinburgh.
Remarks: Presented with AM by His Majesty the King at Aldershot.

Citation
See Citation for ALLAN, A. D. H.

D.W. DALE
Source: "An Unknown Few"

DALE, Donald William.

No. N/Z.4861.
Rank: Sto 1.
Unit/Force: RNZN. HMNZS *Achilles*.
Date of deed: June 22, 1943.
Date of Gazette: November 23, 1943.
Place/date of birth: Timaru, NZ, September 13, 1922.
Place/date of death: Waimate, NZ, October 28, 1969.
Place of memorial: Not known.
Town/county connections: Timaru and Waimate, NZ.
Remarks: Educated Fairview School then worked as labourer and farmhand. Served NZ Army 1940-41. Joined RNZN May 20, 1942. Discharged May 3, 1946. Married Lois Chamberlain, March 28, 1947. One son, three daughters. Only member of RNZN ever to win AM. Attended 1953 Coronation. Also held 1939-45, Atlantic, Pacific Stars (bar Burma), War Medal, NZ War Service Medal 1939-45 and Coronation Medal 1953.

Citation

The KING has been graciously pleased ... to approve the following awards:-
   For bravery in saving life at sea:
                    The Albert Medal
Stoker First Class Donald William Dale, N/Z.4861, (Timaru, New Zealand).
   When there was a bad explosion in his ship in dock, Dale, as all anti-smoke apparatus was already in use, tied a handkerchief round his mouth, and went down into a smoke-filled compartment, from which he helped rescue four workmen.

He then came up for a spell, after which he went down in another part of the ship to the compartment in which the explosion had taken place. With help from one other man, he here rescued two dockyard workmen, getting them up through a manhole with ropes. To reach the scene of destruction Dale, who was still without apparatus, had to grope his way through smoke and debris. The last twisted vertical ladder down which he went fell short of the deck below. Hearing the cries of those trapped, he trusted to chance and jumped. Luckily the deck proved firm.

Although unaware of the full damage which had been caused to the ship Dale well knew that he was facing the gravest danger.

C. C. DARLEY

DARLEY, Charles Curtis.

Rank: Sqn Ldr.
Unit/Force: RAF. 274 Sqn RAF.
Other decorations: CBE (1931).
Date of deed: September 28, 1919.
Date of Gazette: July 25, 1922.
Place/date of birth: Caynham Manor, Salop, July 31, 1890.
Place/date of death: June 10, 1962.
Place of memorial: Not known.
Town/county connections: Ludlow, Salop; Birmingham; London.
Remarks: Son of Capt Charles Edward and Emily Louisa Darley. Married 1925, Hilda, daughter of H. P. Stephenson of London. No children. Educated Dulwich College and RMA Woolwich. 2Lt RFA 1910. Served WWI, seconded to RFC 1914. POW 1916-17. Invalided out of RAF as Air Cdre in 1939. Civilian in WWII. Airfields Control Board till 1959. MID (LG January 1, 1916). Also awarded 1914 Star and bar, British War, Victory, IGS '08 (bar NWF 1930-31), IGS 1936 (Bar NWF 1937-39), Defence, Durbar 1911, Jubilee 1935, Coronation 1937 and Coronation 1953 Medals, plus the Silver Medal of the Society for the Protection of Life from Fire.

Citation
The KING has been pleased to award the Albert Medal to Squadron Leader Charles Curtis Darley, of the Royal Air Force, in recog-nition of his gallantry in endeavouring to save life.

On the night of the 27th September, 1919, a Vickers-Vimy Aeroplane, piloted by Captain Cecil Hill Darley, brother of Squadron Leader (then Flight Lieutenant) Darley, who was acting as Navigation Officer, made a forced landing by Lake Bracciano, some twenty miles north of Rome, when on a flight from England to Egypt.

On the following morning, in taking off, the aeroplane failed to clear a telegraph pole, and crashed, immediately bursting into flames. Squadron Leader Darley was thrown clear, but at once rushed to the blazing wreckage and displayed very conspicuous bravery and devotion in persistent, but unavailing, attempts to rescue his brother, who was pinned in the pilot's seat. His efforts to release his brother were only brought to an end by his collapse. He sustained such severe burns that he was a patient in hospital for over eighteen months.

DAVIS, David.

No. 2349.
Rank: TPR.
Unit/Force: 16 (Queen's) L.
Other decorations: Nil.
Date of deed: May 17, 1890.
Date of Gazette: June 27, 1890.
Place/date of birth: St Pancras, London, ?April, 1865.
Place/date of death: Not known.
Place of memorial: Not known.
Town/county connections: London.
Remarks: Enlisted February 20, 1885 in London, giving age as 19 years and 10 months. His trade was Carman. Described as 5' 8³/₄" in height, weighing 135 lbs. Eyes were hazel and hair brown. Fresh complexion. His father was John Joseph Davis of 16 Bryer Road, Kilburn, London. Spent the whole of his service (5 years 330 days) in Aldershot and Dublin, being medically discharged on June 15, 1891. He appears to have had no other medals.

Citation
The QUEEN has been graciously pleased to confer the "Albert Medal of the Second Class" upon David Davis, of the 16th (Queen's) Lancers, in recognition of the gallantry displayed by him in attempting to save life at Aldershot on the 17th May, 1890.
Note: According to "Heroic Endeavour" (see Bibliography), Davis saved several children in Aldershot, Hampshire, by stopping two runaway horses with a wagon, in doing which he incurred severe injuries.

DAVIS, David Thomas.

No. 7716.
Rank: PNR.
Unit/Force: 2 Bn CG.
Other decorations: Nil.
Date of deed: November 12, 1890.
Date of Gazette: December 23, 1890.
Place/date of birth: Moreton-in-Marsh, Glos, 1869.
Place/date of death: Fulham, London, June 1926.

Place of memorial: Sheen Cemetery, London, Plot EC21.

Town/county connections: Moreton-in Marsh, Glos; Fulham, London.

Remarks: Son of George and Mary Davis of Moreton-in-Marsh. Married June 17, 1893 to Carrie Charlotte Venison. Three daughters. Master builder in later life. Served 4 Bn Gloucestershire Regt 1887-89, then Coldstream Guards from May 30, 1889 to May 15, 1902. Awarded QSA Medal with one bar Cape Colony. He was a slater on enlistment.

Citation

THE Queen has been graciously pleased to confer the "Albert Medal of the Second Class" upon Pioneer David Thomas Davis, 2nd Battalion, Coldstream Guards, and upon Color-Sergeants Henry Pickersgill and William Wilson, 1st Battalion Scots Guards, in recognition of gallantry displayed by them on the occasion of a fire which took place at the Wellington Barracks, London, on the 12th November last.

Note: The fire was in the soldiers' married quarters and he and the others saved a number of children from the roof.

D.T. DAVIS AM
Source: Grandson: W. Vaughan

DAVIS, *Edward Peverall Meggs.*

Rank: Lt.

Unit/Force: RNAS. Seaplane School, Calshot, RNAS.

Other decorations: AFC (LG November 1, 1918). No citation.

Date of deed: October 3, 1917.

Date of Gazette: December 18, 1917.

Place/date of birth: October 20, 1898.

Place/date of death: Detling, Kent, August 13, 1940 (KIA).

Place of memorial: Runnymede Memorial.

Town/county connections: Not known.

Remarks: Entered RNAS April 3, 1916. Probationary Flt Sub Lt April 3, 1916. Flt Lt October 1, 1917. Comsd Capt RAF April 1, 1918. F/O August 1, 1919. May 15, 1925 PA to AOC Middle East. April 1, 1935 PA to Chief of Air Staff as Sqn Ldr. Wg Cdr July 1, 1938. Gp Capt Stn Comd RAF Detling when KIA at 1600 hours on August 13, 1940. Medal entitlement unknown, though he appears only to be entitled to 1939-45 Star and War Medal for WWII and none for WWI.

Citation

The KING has been graciously pleased to confer the Albert Medal on:-
Flight Lieutenant Edward Peverall Meggs Davis, R.N.A.S.

    The following is the account of the services in respect of which the decoration has been conferred:-

    On the 3rd October, 1917, whilst carrying out a practice flight, a seaplane, piloted by Flight Sub-Lieutenant James Douglas Grant, fell into the sea. The seaplane turned over and the pilot was enclosed in the boat under water.

    Flight Lieutenant Edward Peverall Meggs Davis immediately flew a seaplane to the position of the accident, made fast to the wreck, and dived under the wreck in his uniform and endeavoured to extricate Flight Sub-Lieutenant Grant.

    To do this it was necessary for him to dive amongst and struggle through the mass of wires and broken parts of the wreck. Notwithstanding the imminent danger of being caught up amongst them, Lieutenant Davis continued his efforts to get Flight Sub-Lieutenant Grant out, until the emergency boat arrived on the scene.

    No other help was at hand until the arrival of this motor boat, which at the time of the accident was about a mile and a half away.

    Flight Lieutenant Davis risked his life in endeavouring to save that of his brother officer, as there was every chance of his becoming caught under water in the wires of the wreck.

DAWES, Nicholas Bernard Edwin.

Rank: Capt.
Unit/Force: RE.
Other decorations: Nil.
Date of deed: July 30, 1909.
Date of Gazette: October 14, 1910.
Place/date of birth: Not known.
Place/date of death: Krishnarajkatte, Mysore, India, July 30, 1909.
Place of memorial: Not known.
Town/county connections: Not known.
Remarks: Son of Cdr (Retd) H. M. Dawes, HM Bombay Marine. Married to Lilian Nathalie Dawes. Two sons.

Citation

The KING was pleased, on Wednesday last, the 12th October, at Marlborough House, to present to Mrs Lilian Nathalie Dawes the Albert Medal of the Second Class which, but for his untimely death, would have been awarded to her late husband, Captain Nicholas Bernard Edwin Dawes, R.E., Officiating Chief Engineer and Secretary to the Government of Mysore, in recognition of his gallantry in endeavouring to save life as detailed below:-

    On the afternoon of Friday, the 30th July, 1909, Captain Dawes was engaged upon the difficult and dangerous work of reconstructing a large dam across the Canvery River at Krishnarajkatte, Mysore State, while the river was in full flood.

    Captain Dawes and a workman were on a raft towed by a boat consisting of two dugouts lashed together. Weighted barrels had been lowered to the river bottom from the raft, which was then pulled towards the boat and allowed to drift towards a hawser for the purpose of being drawn to an island in the river. While the party were being hauled to land the strong current caused the dugouts to heel over, and the coolies becoming frightened matters were made worse, the occupants of the last boat and raft having to jump into the river.

Captain Dawes swam to within about 10 feet of the island, and then turned round and seemed to be counting the men to see that all were safe. He noticed one man being carried down midstream towards the breach, and swam out to help him. He was swept through the breach, and must have been dashed against a rock, as there was no shout for help or other signal of distress. His body was not recovered until three days later. The Indian was washed ashore some 500 or 600 yards down stream in a badly bruised condition.

DICKSON, Thomas Johnstone.

Rank: Lieutenant.
Unit/Force: 4 Res Bn Yorkshire Regt.
Other decorations: Nil.
Date of deed: June 26, 1917.
Date of Gazette: January 4, 1918.
Place/date of birth: c1893.
Place/date of death: West Bridgeford, Notts, August 6, 1945.
Place of memorial: Radcliffe-on-Trent Cemetery, Notts. Sec B, Grave 197L.
Town/county connections: West Bridgeford, Notts.
Remarks: To France 1916. Son of T. J. and Catherine Dickson and husband of C. A. Dickson, West Bridgeford, Notts. Served WWII in RAPC. Also awarded British War, Victory, Defence and War Medals.

Citation
The KING has been graciously pleased to award the Decoration of the Albert Medal to the undermentioned ... in recognition of (his) gallantry in saving life:-
Lieutenant Thomas Johnstone Dickson, Yorkshire Regiment.

On the 26th June, 1917, Lieutenant (then Second Lieutenant) Dickson was instructing a man in throwing live bombs. One of the bombs failed to clear the parapet and fell back into the breast-work. Lieutenant Dickson told the man to run to safety, and himself did so. On reaching shelter he found that the man had not followed. He at once ran back into the breastwork, and saw the man crouching in a corner on the far side of the bomb. He ran past the bomb, seized the man, and dragged him back past the bomb into safety just before the bomb exploded. Had not Lieutenant Dickson deliberately returned into the danger zone, the man would almost certainly have been killed.

DONOVAN, Charles Creaghe.

Rank: Capt.
Unit/Force: RA. IOD.
Other decorations: Nil.
Date of deed: August 30, 1906.

Date of Gazette: September 26, 1911.
Place/date of birth: June 30, 1870.
Place/date of death: Dover, Kent, January 4, 1923.
Place of memorial: Charlton Cemetery, Kent.
Town/county connections: Not known.
Remarks: Educated RMA Woolwich. 2Lt RA February 14, 1890. Lt Col May 1, 1917. DDOS Northern Comd (India) 1918-19. Retd June 5, 1920. Married Mabel Jennings December 3, 1896 (no children) and 1921 Alice Edith Keeble (no children). Also awarded British War Medal, IGS 1908 with bar Afghanistan NWF 1919 and Delhi Durbar Medal 1911.

Citation
See citation for ANDERSON, C. A.

PRIVATE J. DUNN
Source: Family

DUNN, James.

No. 9389.
Rank: PTE.
Unit/Force: 2 Bn CG.
Other decorations: Nil.
Date of deed: June 12, 1918.
Date of Gazette: August 30, 1918.
Place/date of birth: Clitheroe, Lancs, June 12, 1889.
Place/date of death: London, February 16, 1943.
Place of memorial: Guards Plot, Brompton Cemetery, London.
Town/county connections: Clitheroe, Lancs; London.
Remarks: Son of Joseph W. Dunn and Catherine Dunn. Enlisted 2 CG London January 4, 1912. France, Belgium and Germany from August 12, 1914 to March 6, 1919. Orderly to Maj Gen Comd Lond Dist 1919-22. Discharged March 13, 1927. Special Constable during General Strike, 1926. Employed in hotel trade as waiter and attendant, also warehouse keeper. Married, three daughters. Also served under No. 2646522. Awarded 1914 Star with bar, British War and Victory Medals. Medals now in CG Museum, Wellington Barracks, London.

Citation
The KING has been pleased to award the Albert Medal ... in recognition of gallantry displayed in saving ... life:-
Private James Dunn, Coldstream Guards.
*   At a railhead in France, on the evening of the 12th June, 1918, several trucks loaded with heavy ammunition caught fire, causing an explosion. Several men were wounded, and some lay*

underneath the burning trucks. Dunn at once rushed forward, regardless of his own safety, and carried two of the wounded men to a shelter trench close by, where he rendered them first aid. He then returned to the assistance of the other wounded men, when a second explosion took place. Notwithstanding this, and also the very grave danger of further explosions, he continued to assist the wounded and to help to rescue those who were lying helpless under the burning trucks. His bravery, coolness and prompt action undoubtedly saved several men from being burned to death.

ELLAYA.

Rank: Sub-Maj.
Unit/Force: 1/88 Carnatic Inf Bn.
Other decorations: Nil.
Date of deed: June 18, 1920.
Date of Gazette: July 15, 1921.
Place/date of birth: Not known.
Place/date of death: Not known.
Place of memorial: Not known.
Town/county connections: Not known.
Remarks: Enlisted April 22, 1893. Comsd Jemadar September 1, 1913. Subedar-Major July 16, 1919. Hon Lt July 1, 1920. Retd 1921.

Citation

The KING has been pleased to award the Albert Medal to Lieutenant Ian William Galbraith, M.C., 19th Lancers (Fane's Horse), and to Subadar-Major Ellaya, 1/88th Carnatic Infantry, in recognition of their gallantry in saving life at St. Thomas' Mount Arsenal, Madras, in June of last year.

On the night of June 18th, 1920, a dangerous fire broke out at the Arsenal at St Thomas' Mount, and the flames, 20 ft. high, had reached a spot within 5 yards of which a large quantity of aerial bombs were stacked. Lieutenant Galbraith superintended the removal of the bombs for nearly three-quarters of an hour, remaining until the last bomb had been removed, and he set a splendid example to the Troops by his gallantry and perseverance. Four thousand of these bombs were stored in the Arsenal, and an explosion would have resulted in heavy loss of life.

Subadar-Major Ellaya, with 43 men of "C" Company, took a prominent part in the work of removing the bombs which were lying close to the flames. He was the first member of his Regiment to arrive on the scene, and he too set a fine example to the men under him by carrying away the bombs and continuing to do so until ordered to another duty by his Commanding Officer. The work he performed in removing the bombs exposed him to very great danger.

FANCONI, Arturo.

No. C/MX554517.
Rank: SBA.
Unit/Force: RN.
Other decorations: Nil.

SBA A. FANCONI
Source: Family per Mrs R. David

Date of deed: June 28, 1944.
Date of Gazette: May 15, 1945.
Place/date of birth: c1906.
Place/date of death: Quineville, France, June 28, 1944.
Place of memorial: Bayeux War Cemetery, France, Plot 2, Row G, Grave 16.
Town/county connections: Ilminster, Somerset.
Remarks: Single. Son of Giulio and Anna Fanconi of Ilminster, Somerset. His action was the subject of a Swiss TV documentary entitled "Arturo Fanconi's Longest Day".

Citation
The KING has been graciously pleased to ... approve the following award:-
For gallantry in saving life:
The Albert Medal in Gold (Posthumous).

Sick Berth Attendant Arturo FANCONI, C/MX.554517.

On 28th June, 1944, Fanconi was summoned to help men wounded by mines at Quineville in Normandy. He at once ran almost half a mile and went through what later proved to be a field of anti-personnel mines to reach them.

He applied tourniquets and bandages; then, with help, carried two patients out of the drive which was the scene of the incident. This was a tiring and difficult task as it entailed hugging a wall all the way. Fanconi was on the more dangerous side throughout. While the rescue party were considering how best to help a third man who lay some distance within the minefield, another mine burst beneath the rubble on which they stood. This killed one helper and wounded Fanconi and another.

Despite this, Fanconi tried to collect his scattered medical kit and to help his comrade. He had to crawl to do so, and was in great pain.

In his attempt, he exploded a further mine which blew off one of his feet. The explosion hurled him into the air, and when he fell he set off a third mine which severed his other foot. A Corporal made every effort to help him, but the kit was now of little use and Fanconi could not be saved.

All who had witnesses his selfless courage, his speed and skill in giving aid to others, all the while exposing himself to immediate danger, were inspired by his great example.
Note: This was the last award of the Albert Medal in Gold.

FARABANI.

Rank: Seedie Tindal of Stokers.
Unit/Force: RN. HMS *Wild Swan*.
Other decorations: Nil.
Date of deed: August 8, 1880.
Date of Gazette: November 23, 1880.
Place/date of birth: Not known.

Place/date of death: Not known.
Place of memorial: Not known.
Town/county connections: Not known.
Remarks: Like the majority of native Indian recipients of the Albert Medal, we know little or nothing about him.

Citation

THE Queen has been graciously pleased to confer the "Albert Medal of the First Class" on - FARABANI, Seedie Tindal, serving in Her Majesty's ship "Wild Swan".

The following is an account of the services in respect of which the decoration has been conferred:-

On the 8th August last, while the "Wild Swan" was off the coast of Mozambique, a fugitive slave boy, named Farejallah, having jumped overboard from a stage alongside the ship, was immediately seized by an enormous shark, which bit off his leg at the knee, dragging him under the water. When he rose to the surface, the shark again attacked him, tearing off his remaining leg and part of the thigh. On Farejallah beginning to rise to the surface again, closely followed by the shark, FARABANI jumped from the netting into the water, and brought the unfortunate boy to the surface, nor did he leave the water till he had placed him in a position of safety.

The Captain of the "Wild Swan" adds, that what makes this, if possible, a more gallant deed, is the fact that FARABANI saw the whole of the horrible catastrophe from the first seizure of the boy, and that, when he jumped into the water, not only the attacking shark, but three others were seen close to the ship, attracted no doubt by the blood.

Note: See "Heroic Endeavour" page 7 under "Maintaining Standards". There seems to have been considerable official resistance to the grant of this well-deserved award, mainly on the ground that the recipient was a native Indian and might not appreciate its significance as much as a British recipient!

J.C. FARREN
Source: Family

FARREN, Joseph Collinton.

No. 267361.
Rank: SPR.
Unit/Force: RE. 12 Lt Rly Op Coy RE.
Other decorations: Nil.
Date of deed: April 30, 1918.
Date of Gazette: August 30, 1918.
Place/date of birth:
Carlton, Leics, February 16, 1893.
Place/date of death: Crombeke, Belgium, April 30, 1918.
Place of memorial: Haringhe Military Cemetery, Belgium. Stained Glass Window, Carlton Parish Church.
Town/county connections:
Carlton, Leicestershire.
Remarks: Son of Charles and Mary Farren. Educated at village school and then believed

J.C. FARREN
Source: Courtesy Mrs. A. M. Hunt

to have worked for local farmer. Thought to have joined the L&NW Railway Co between 1908 and 1910. Served on L&NWR till 1916, by which time he had become a Porter/Goods Guard. Joined RE as Sapper 267361 but also had No. WR/273247. Bachelor. Awarded British War and Victory Medals.

Citation
See citation for BIGLAND, J. E.

FELDWICK, Arthur Edward.

No. 370031.
Rank: CPL.
Unit/Force: 8 Bn London Regt (TF).
Other decorations: Nil.
Date of deed: May 6, 1916.
Date of Gazette: August 7, 1917.
Place/date of birth: Not known.
Place/date of death: Not known.
Place of memorial: Not known.
Town/county connections: Not known.
Remarks: To France March 18, 1915. Also served with No. 349. Awarded 1914-15 Trio.

Citation
The KING was pleased, on Friday the 3rd instant, at Buckingham Palace, to present to Captain (then Second Lieutenant) William Leslie Coutts Rathbone, 15th Battalion, London Regiment, the Albert Medal of the Second Class, which had been conferred upon him by His Majesty for gallantry in saving life, as detailed below:-

On the night of the 6th May, 1916, as a working party under Lieutenant Rathbone was proceeding down a communication trench, they were fired upon from close quarters. On enquiry Lieutenant Rathbone ascertained that the shots came from a soldier who had run amok, and had posted himself with loaded rifle and fixed bayonet further down the trench. Lieutenant Rathbone borrowed a rifle and accompanied by Corporal Feldwick, advanced along the trench until in view of the mentally deranged man. They then advanced with rifles at the ready; the officer calling upon the man to surrender. Receiving no reply they then dropped their rifles and rushed him, and after disarming him took him to the nearest dressing station.

Corporal Feldwick, who is a prisoner of war, has also been awarded the Albert Medal of the Second Class.

FIROZE KHAN

No. 4351.
Rank: L-Nk.
Unit/Force: 5 Bn 8 Punjab Regt.
Other decorations: Nil.

Date of deed: May 31, 1935.
Date of Gazette: November 19, 1935.
Place/date of birth: Not known.
Place/date of death: Not known.
Place of memorial: Not known.
Town/county connections: Not known.
Remarks: His AM was presented at Fort Salop on June 3, 1936.

Citation
His Majesty The KING has been graciously pleased to award the Albert Medal ... for services rendered in connection with the recent earthquake in Baluchistan:-
Lance-Naik Firoze Khan, 5th Battalion, 8th Punjab (Burma) Regiment.

   On the morning of May 31st Lance-Naik Firoze Khan was in charge of a party engaged in rescue work and fire fighting in the city. Hearing cries for help from beneath the ruins in the close vicinity of a fire, Lance-Naik Firoze Khan and his party commenced to dig and cut their way down into the building. After nearly two hours' work, the Lance-Naik was able to enter the building from above and discovered two people pinned down by beams and rubble. The fire had by this time spread to the building in question, which was full of smoke and fumes. In spite of this the Lance-Naik with pick and saw spent over half an hour beneath the ruins and finally released the injured people. He did this at great risk to his own life as throughout there was grave danger of the ruins subsiding from the effect of the fire and further earthquake shocks.

FISKE, Charles William.

Rank: T/Capt.
Unit/Force: 7 E Kent Regt ("The Buffs").
Other decorations: MC (LG October 4, 1919).
Date of deed: December 14, 1917.
Date of Gazette: March 22, 1918.
Place/date of birth: August 4, 1877.
Place/date of death: Tavistock, Devon, April 14, 1970.
Place of memorial: Not known.
Town/county connections: Tavistock, Devon.
Remarks: Also awarded British War and Victory Medals.

Citation
The KING has been pleased to award the Decoration of the Albert Medal to Lieutenant (temporary Captain) Charles William Fiske, 5th Battalion, East Kent Regiment ... in recognition of (his) gallantry in saving life. The circumstances are as follows:-
   On the 14th December, 1917, while bombing practice was being carried out at Margate under the supervision of Captain Fiske, a man threw a live bomb which failed to clear the parapet and fell back into the pit. Captain Fiske at once placed himself under cover expecting that the man would do likewise. On finding, however, that the man had lost his head and was unable to move, Captain Fiske ran back into the pit, seized the man, forced him into a

corner and covered him with his own body. In the subsequent explosion Captain Fiske was wounded in both thighs.

Captain Fiske by his gallant action undoubtedly saved the man from death or severe injury.

FITZHERBERT, The Honourable Thomas Charles.

T. C. FITZHERBERT
Source: Family

Rank: Capt.
Unit/Force: Lancs Hrs Yeo.
Other decorations: Nil.
Date of deed: July 10, 1916.
Date of Gazette: January 1, 1918.
Place/date of birth: August 30, 1869.
Place/date of death: September 20, 1937.
Place of memorial: Not known.
Town/county connections: Stafford.
Remarks: 4th son of Basil Fitzherbert of Swynnerton Hall, Stafford. Educated Oscott College, Birmingham. Private Secretary to Governors in West Indies and Newfoundland. Served South African War as Trooper in Staffordshire Yeomanry. Awarded QSA Medal. Married April 30, 1925, Beryl, second daughter of John Michael Waters of Farnham, Surrey and widow of Major Henry Brougham RA. Two sons. Grandfather of present Baron Stafford.

Citation

The KING has been graciously pleased to award the Decoration of the Albert Medal to the undermentioned Officer ...in recognition of (his) gallantry in saving life:-
Captain the Hon. Thomas Charles Fitzherbert, Lancashire Hussars.

On the 10th July, 1916, an instructional party was throwing live bombs from separate pits. A volley was ordered. All the bombs were thrown successfully except one, which hit the parapet and stuck in the mud. For three or four seconds the accident was unnoticed, as everyone was watching the bombs in the air, and the man who threw the bomb was too frightened to call out or to move. Suddenly, Captain Fitzherbert noticed smoke issuing from the parapet and saw the bomb. He might have placed himself in safety by throwing himself on the bottom of the pit; but seeing that the man would be exposed to the full force of the explosion, he picked the bomb out of the mud and threw it clear just as it exploded. By his courage and presence of mind he undoubtedly saved the man's life, while risking his own.

FITZPATRICK, Patrick John.

Rank: CPL.
Unit/Force: RE. MWS (India)
Other decorations: DCM (LG January 14, 1916 & March 11, 1916.
Date of deed: August 30, 1906.

Date of Gazette: August 26, 1913.
Place/date of birth: April 10, 1880.
Place/date of death: India, May 13, 1928.
Place of memorial: Not known.
Town/county connections: Not known.
Remarks: Also held 1914 Star, British War, Victory and IGS 1908 (bars Afghanistan NWF 1919 and Waziristan 1921-24). Comsd RE August 25, 1918. Capt November 10, 1922.

Citation
See citation for BATTYE, B. C. (No 14).

FITZSIMMONS, Harry.

No. 4532418.
Rank: PTE.
Unit/Force: 1 Bn W Yorks Regt. (PWO).
Other decorations: Nil.
Date of deed: May 31, 1935.
Date of Gazette: November 19, 1935.
Place/date of birth: Armley, Leeds, February 17, 1911.
Place/date of death: Burma, April 8, 1944.
Place of memorial: Gauhali Military Cemetery, Plot 1, Row H, Grave 28.
Town/county connections: Leeds, Yorks.
Remarks: Joined army at 15. In Palestine before WWII. Transferred to Glos Regt (No. 4352418) and became Sgt, in which rank he was KIA. Awarded GSM 1918 (bar Palestine), 1939-45 and Burma Stars, Defence and War Medals.

HARRY FITZSIMMONS (EXTREME RIGHT, BACK ROW)
Source: Family

Citation

His Majesty The KING has been graciously pleased to award the Albert Medal ... for services rendered in connection with the recent earthquake in Baluchistan:-

Private Harry Fitzsimmons, 1st Battalion, The West Yorkshire Regiment (The Prince of Wales's Own).

On the 31st May and 1st and 2nd June, 1935, Fitzsimmons was on rescue duty in the area of Quetta City to the east of Sandeman Hall. He worked with conspicuous energy and devotion to duty throughout the period of rescue work, and in conjunction with others was responsible for saving several lives. On 1st June, in order to rescue an Indian whom he knew to be buried alive, Fitzsimmons, at great risk to his own life, made a passage under the debris of a house into which he was able to crawl. On reaching the man he discovered a woman lying dead on top of him, who was pinned down by a stout beam across her leg. In order to release the man, whom he eventually saved, he had to saw off the woman's leg with a carpenter's saw. The remains of the building, and the passage he made, were in imminent danger of collapse during the whole period he was working. Fitzsimmons' action was a very gallant one and worthy of special recognition.

FLETCHER, Walter Edmund.

Rank: Lt-Cdr.
Unit/Force: RN. HMS *Haslemere*.
Other decorations: Nil.
Date of deed: May 16, 1941.
Date of Gazette: May 16, 1941.
Place/date of birth: Buckinghamshire, 1906.
Place/date of death: Thames Estuary, January 5, 1941.
Place of memorial: Gillingham (Woodlands) Cemetery, Grave 1379.
Town/county connections: Monks Risborough, Bucks.
Remarks: Son of Rev Canon E. S. B. Fletcher MA and Bertha May Fletcher of Monks Risborough, Bucks. Joined TS Conway 1919. Prom Lt April 1, 1929. Served on *Winchelsea, Nelson* and *Vivid*. Was on 1934 Wordie Canadian Arctic Expedition and later served on *Whitehead and Pembroke*. Prom Lt Cdr April 1, 1937 and served on *Londonderry and Fiji*. Joined trawler *Haslemere* November 7, 1940.

Citation

The KING has been graciously pleased to approve the posthumous Award of the Albert Medal, for gallantry in trying to save life at sea, to:

Lieutenant-Commander Walter Edmund Fletcher, Royal Navy, H.M.S. Haslemere.

On 5th January, 1941, Lieutenant-Commander Fletcher took his ship to the rescue of Miss Amy Johnson, who was piloting an aircraft which had fallen into the sea. Snow was falling and it was bitterly cold. The seas were heavy and a strong tide was running, but he dived in fully clothed. This brave and selfless action, which cost him his life, was typical of the fine spirit which Lieutenant-Commander Fletcher showed at sea and under fire while serving with the Channel Mobile Balloon Barrage.

FOLEY, Richard.

No. 27620.
Rank: DVR.
Unit/Force: RFA. 41 Bde RA.
Other decorations: MM (LG July 18, 1917).
Date of deed: January 2, 1916.
Date of Gazette: May 19, 1916.
Place/date of birth: Not known.
Place/date of death: Not known.
Place of memorial: Not known.
Town/county connections: Sunderland.
Remarks: To France May 11, 1915. Also awarded 1914-15 Trio. All his medals, which are offical replacements, are in the RA Museum, Woolwich. They were replaced in 1941. Presented with AM by His Majesty the King at Buckingham Palace September 12, 1917.

Citation

The KING has been graciously pleased to award the Decoration of the Albert Medal to the undermentioned ... in recognition of their gallantry in saving life:-
Albert Medal of the Second Class
Corporal James Webb, Royal Army Medical Corps.
Driver Richard Foley, Royal Field Artillery.
On 2nd January, 1916, during a heavy bombardment, Webb and Foley, acting entirely on their own initiative, left a place where they were safe and ran out to bring two wounded French civilians into a dug-out. They got both men into a cellar. During this operation heavy shells were falling all around them, and a motor-cyclist, who was assisting to bring in the second man, was killed.

FORBES, William Balfour.

Rank: Lt.
Unit/Force: RN. HMS *Rapid*.
Other decorations: Nil.
Date of deed: September 17, 1870.
Date of Gazette: March 10, 1871.
Place/date of birth: 1845.
Place/date of death: May 9, 1928.
Place of memorial: Not known.
Town/county connections: Not known.
Remarks:

Citation

THE Queen has been graciously pleased to confer the decoration of the "Albert Medal of the Second Class" on:-
LIEUTENANT WILLIAM BALFOUR FORBES, R.N., of Her Majesty's ship "Rapid".

The following is an account of the services in respect of which the decoration has been conferred:-

On the night of the 17th of September last, whilst Her Majesty's ship "Rapid" was proceeding from Tarrogona to Gibraltar a boy fell from the main yard-arm, and in his fall struck his head against the gunwale of one of the boats, and was thereby rendered insensible. SUB-LIEUTENANT WILLIAM BALFOUR FORBES (now LIEUTENANT), at once, and in the dark, jumped overboard, and seized him and persisted in keeping him up at imminent risk to his own life, for when the ship's boat, which was lowered to pick them up, reached them, SUB-LIEUTENANT FORBES was quite exhausted, and with the boy was under water.

Had the boat arrived a minute later both would have been drowned.

PTE W. H. FOSTER
Source: Regimental magazine.

FOSTER, William Henry.

No. 4854105.
Rank: PTE.
Unit/Force: 1 Bn Leics Regt.
Date of deed: June 11, 1931.
Date of Gazette:
November 27, 1931.
Place/date of birth:
Willenhall, Staffs, October 12, 1906.
Place/date of death: Not known.
Place of memorial: Not known.
Town/county connections:
Willenhall and Wednesbury, Staffs.
Remarks: Son of Job and Frances S. Foster of 37 Wood St, Wednesbury. Occupation: Moulder. Enlisted in Leics Regt May 21, 1926. Dischgd December 29, 1933. Attested September 4, 1939 and dischgd as unfit April 30, 1940. Married Florence (née Griffiths) April 24, 1935 at Wednesbury. One son. Also awarded 1939-45 Star and War Medal.

Citation

His Majesty The KING has been graciously pleased to award the Albert Medal to Private William Henry Foster, 1st Battalion, The Leicestershire Regiment, in recognition of his gallantry in the following circumstances:-

Shortly before 9 p.m. on the evening of 11th of June, 1931, a forest fire broke out in the neighbourhood of Sabathu, Simla Hills, on a hillside which was covered with highly inflammable pine needles. A Company of the Leicestershire Regiment on Fire Picquet immediately proceeded to the scene and attempted to beat out the fire. The wind, however, fanned the flames which became so fierce that the Company was withdrawn, but on the roll being called, it was found that two men, Private A.L. Smith and Private Foster, were missing. Private Smith had been cut off by the fire and in endeavouring to escape he slipped on the hillside where he lay with his clothing alight surrounded by flames and unable to move. Private Foster, who had been detached from his Company, was informed by an Indian that one of his comrades was lying ablaze on the hill. He at once rushed down through 200 yards of flaring undergrowth and found Smith lying helpless in the fire. Foster picked Smith up and carried him some 300 yards to a place of safety, whence both men were taken to hospital in a state of shock, Smith being so badly burned that he never rallied and died the same night.

Foster's action in endeavouring to save his comrade was an extremely brave one. He went into the fire at grave peril to his own life, and had he fallen on the slippery hillside no one would have been there to go to his assistance.

FOY, Clifford.

Rank: Lt.
Unit/Force: 10 Bn Manchester Regt.
Other decorations: Nil.
Date of deed: September 7, 1917.
Date of Gazette: March 22, 1918.
Place/date of birth: Not known.
Place/date of death: Not known.
Place of memorial: Not known.
Town/county connections: Not known.
Remarks: To France August, 1916. Also served as 2Lt in Buckinghamshire Hussars Yeomanry. Awarded British War and Victory Medals.

Citation
The KING has been graciously pleased to award the Decoration of the Albert Medal to ... Lieutenant Clifford Foy, 10th Battalion, The Manchester Regiment, in recognition of (his) gallantry in saving life. The circumstances are as follows:-

On the 7th September, 1917, while bombing practice was being carried out under the supervision of Lieutenant Foy, one of the party withdrew the pin from a live bomb and, when in the act of throwing it, dropped the bomb and fainted, falling upon the bomb. Lieutenant Foy at once lifted the man off the bomb and carried him to a place of safety.

A short time afterwards another man threw a bomb which hit the parapet and fell back into the pit. He made no endeavour to run out of the pit, whereupon Lieutenant Foy entered the pit and dragged him out.

On the same occasion a third man threw a live bomb which hit the parapet and rolled to the side. He was running out to throw the bomb farther away when Lieutenant Foy stopped him by tripping him up and dragged him into safety.

By these repeated acts of gallantry Lieutenant Foy undoubtedly saved the men concerned from serious injury or death.

H. C. *CUMMINGS*
Source: British Medical Journal

FRENCH, Herbert Cummings.

Rank: Capt.
Unit/Force: RAMC.
Other decorations: Nil.
Date of deed: November 17, 1902.
Date of Gazette: March 10, 1903.
Place/date of birth: Quebec, Canada, November 22, 1869.
Place/date of death: October 13, 1913.
Place of memorial: Not known.
Town/county connections: Quebec, Canada.
Remarks: Son of Maj-Gen Sir George A. French KCMG, late RA, first Commissioner of the Royal Canadian Mounted Police. Surgeon Lt July 29, 1903. Surgeon Maj April 29, 1905. Served South African War. QSA (Bars: Transvaal, Orange Free State). Awarded RHS Silver Medal for his act. Expert on syphilis and published several papers on the subject.

Citation

The KING has been graciously pleased to confer the decoration of the Albert Medal of the Second Class upon Captain Herbert C. French, Royal Army Medical Corps.

The following is an account of the services in respect of which the decoration has been conferred:-

While His Majesty's transport "Wakool" was steaming, at the rate of about 12 knots an hour, through the Straits of Malacca, on the 17th November, 1902, a native fireman jumped overboard. Captain French, who was a passenger on board, immediately dived off the promenade deck, a height of about 36 feet from the water, and swam to the place where he had observed the man. Before he reached the spot the man had disappeared, and Captain French was obliged to make for a lifebuoy, as he was exhausted with the weight of his clothing. Subsequently both were rescued by the ship's lifeboat.

Captain French incurred considerable risk, as a strong current was running at the time, and he might have been drawn under the propellers of the ship. He was also in danger of sharks and water snakes, which are known to frequent the Straits of Malacca.

FURLONGER, Alfred Henry.

No. 109599.
Rank: PTE (A/CSM).
Unit/Force: RE. 26 Lt Rly Op Coy RE.
Other decorations: DCM (LG February 6, 1918).
Date of deed: April 30, 1918.
Date opf Gazette: August 30, 1918.
Place/date of birth: 1887.
Place/date of death: Crombeke, Belgium, April 30, 1918.
Place of memorial: Haringhe Military Cemetery, Belgium.

A. H. *FURLONGER*
Source: RE Museum

Town/county connections: Wimbledon, London.
Remarks: Also served with No. WR/355209. Awarded British War and Victory Medals.

Citation
See citation for BIGLAND, J. E.

GALBRAITH, William.

Rank: Lt.
Unit/Force: 19 Lancers (Fane's Horse), IA.
Other decorations: MC (LG August 16, 1917).
Date of deed: June 18, 1920.
Date of Gazette: July 15, 1921.
Place/date of birth: Not known.
Place/date of death: Not known.
Place of memorial: Not known.
Town/county connections: Not known.
Remarks: Also awarded British War and Victory Medals. Prom Capt January 31, 1921. To Indian Police Service October 24, 1922.

Citation
See citation for ELLAYA.

GEAKE, William Henry Gregory.

Rank: Lt.
Unit/Force: AIF.
Other decorations: MBE (New Year's Honours, 1918).
Date of deed: September 18, 1917.
Date of Gazette: November 27, 1918.
Place/date of birth: Earley, Berks, February 23, 1880.
Place/date of death: RAAF Hospital, Richmond, NSW, March 14, 1944.
Place of memorial: Australian War Memorial.
Town/county connections: Earley, Berks; Sydney, NSW; Melbourne, Victoria.
Remarks: Educated Sydney Grammar School, NSW. Consulting Engineer. OC AIF Research Section, Esher, Surrey, during WWI. Inventor. Wounded 1917. Served RAAF WWII. Sqn Ldr. Died of cancer during service. Medals now in the Australian War Memorial, Canberra, ACT.

Citation
The KING has been pleased to award the Albert Medal to Lieutenant William Henry Gregory Geake, of the Australian Imperial Force, in recognition of his gallantry in saving life in September of last year. The circumstances are as follows:-

W. H. G. GEAKE (CENTRE FRONT)
Source: Sabretache, April 1978

On the 26th September 1917, at about 8 p.m., an explosion occurred in the pressing room of a munitions inventions experimental station. The room contained 25 lbs. of thermit and 300 lbs. of gunpowder, pressed into rocket heads. Lieut. Geake, whose services had been placed at the disposal of the Ministry of Munitions, and who was standing outside at the time, at once ran into the building, where explosions were still taking place, and helped one man out. He then ran back into the building, passed through the place where the thermit and powder were exploding, and carried out an injured man whom he found under a burning bench. Notwithstanding the fact that he was himself badly burned, Lieut. Geake entered the building a third time, under the mistaken impression that another man was still inside, but was eventually driven out by the fire and explosions.

Lieut. Geake then worked for two hours to alleviate the injuries of the rescued men, one of whom was dying.

Unfortunately, at a demonstration on the following morning, which he attended, although unfit for duty, Lieut. Geake suffered further injuries owing to a premature explosion, three fingers being blown off his right hand, and his right leg being broken and almost severed.

GERRIGHTY, Anthony.

Rank: PTE.
Unit/Force: RM. HMT *Baron Colonsay.*
Other decorations: Nil.
Date of deed: July 28, 1878.
Date of Gazette: November 29, 1878.
Place/date of birth: Liverpool, August 31, 1851.
Place/date of death: Not known.
Place of memorial: Not known.

Town/county connections: Liverpool, Lancs.
Remarks: Also awarded RHS Bronze Medal for this act. He had no other medals. Trade on enlistment August 28, 1869, was saltmaker. Dischgd July 6, 1883. Married.

Citation

THE Queen has been graciously pleased to confer the Albert Medal of the Second Class on - ANTHONY GERRIGHTY, Private, Royal Marines.

The following is an account of the services in respect of which this decoration has been conferred:-

On the night of the 27th July last, at 10 P.M., a lunatic named Field, on is passage home in the transport ship "Baron Colonsay", of Greenock, broke away from the sentry in the sick berth and climbed to the fore topgallant-yard. Men were sent aloft to try and prevent his falling, but on their approach he struck one of them on the head. After remaining aloft all night calling "murder", &c., he came down about 5 A.M. on the 28th. The sentries that were placed to watch him then tried to secure him but he jumped overboard. GERRIGHTY instantly jumped after him and though struck at with a knife which Field had in his hand, succeeded in rescuing him.

This occurrence took place in latitude 36 deg 26 min N., longitude 2 deg 52 min W., the ship going eight knots and a fresh breeze blowing.

GIBSON, Alexander.

No. 112204.
Rank: SGT.
Unit/Force: RE. RE Depot, South Bde RE.
Other decorations: Nil.
Date of deed: January 17, 1919.
Date of Gazette: July 8, 1919.
Place/date of birth: Not known.
Place/date of death: Not known.
Place of memorial: Not known.
Town/county connections: Not known.
Remarks: Presented with AM by His Majesty the King at Buckingham Palace July 31, 1919.

Citation

The KING has been pleased to award the Albert Medal to Lieutenant (acting Major) William Revell Smith, M.C., R.F.A., Sergeant Alexander Gibson, Royal Engineers, and Corporal James Smith, Military Mounted Police, in recognition of their gallantry in endeavouring to save life at Wizernes in January last.

On the 17th January, 1919, a fire occurred at the brewery at Wizernes. In the engine room a Frenchman, whose cries for help could be heard, had been entombed by a fall of masonry, which completely blocked the entrance. The upper part of the building was blazing fiercely, and the only entrance to the engine room was by a small hole in the wall which carried the machinery belting. Major Smith, Sergeant Gibson, and Corporal Smith succeeded in making their way through this hole into the room, and worked for three-quarters of an hour before they exposed the head and shoulders of the entombed man, who was found to be dead.

They undoubtedly risked their lives in endeavouring to save life, for a further collapse of masonry (which appeared imminent) would have completely cut off their exit.

GILES, Edward.

Rank: Capt.
Unit/Force: Indian Navy. Master Attendant, Karachi.
Other decorations: Nil.
Date of deed: June 20, 1868.
Date of Gazette: December 2, 1870.
Place/date of birth: Not known.
Place/date of death: Not known.
Place of memorial: Not known.
Town/county connections: Not known.
Remarks:

Citation

THE Queen has been graciously pleased to confer the decoration of the "Albert Medal of the Second Class" on:-

CAPTAIN EDWARD GILES, Indian Navy, Master Attendant at Kurrachee.

The following is an account of the services in respect of which the decoration has been conferred:-

The barque "Alicia" of Greenock, was driven upon the bar of Kurrachee Harbour, at 4.20 P.M. of the 20th June, 1868, in very heavy weather, and at the height of a south-west monsoon, when the bar is covered with a continuous line of heavy breakers at all times of tide. The sea at once made a complete breach over the vessel, washing boats and everything else from her decks, and obliging the crew to take to the mizen rigging.

CAPTAIN GILES, the Master Attendant, and Mr. Robert Henry Mason, Senior Pilot at Kurrachee, made attempts to reach the stranded vessel in two boats twenty-five feet long, fitted as life boats, and manned by natives.

CAPTAIN GILES' boat on entering the breakers was swept back half filled, but was carried into comparatively smooth water.

By great exertion however, he brought her within 50 feet of the vessel, the confused mass of surging wreck threatening instant destruction if he had approached nearer.

The shipwrecked crew were at first too frightened to attempt to leave their vessel, but eventually, upon a light line being successfully flung on board of her, two seamen and the pilot hauled themselves by means of it through the water, and were got into the boat. The boat up to this time had been kept clear by bailing, but now, being half filled by a heavy sea which struck her, was compelled at once to return, and the three men were transferred to another boat waiting in smooth water.

A little before sunset, CAPTAIN GILES was again by the wreck, passing through the midst of broken spars and all kinds of wreckage. Having rescued six more men, he was taking them ashore when a wave rolled over the boat and filled her, breaking her rudder and six oars, and sweeping three of her crew overboard. The following roller fortunately carried these men into smooth water, where they were picked up by the waiting boats.

Both of the station life boats were now disabled; but as some of the crew still remained on board the "Alicia", CAPTAIN GILES determined upon a further attempt in the boat of the tug "Dagmar". This boat was fitted with cork floats, but was heavy. After great exertion the wreck was reached, and the remaining men, with the exception of the master, were got into the boat, when she was carried away half filled.

The master of the "Alicia", who had jumped overboard with a plank, was carried in the direction of the waiting boats, and ultimately picked up.

The Commissioner of Scinde, in bringing the case to the notice of the Governor of Bombay, bears testimony to the "conspicuous bravery" of CAPTAIN GILES, in thus rescuing fourteen persons during a strong gale of wind and very high sea, a service which occupied three hours, at any moment of which the boats in the surf ran risk of being swamped.

GIMBLE, Edward.

No. G/861.
Rank: PTE.
Unit/Force: 1 Bn Middx Regt.
Other decorations: Nil.
Date of deed: October 26, 1915.
Date of Gazette: April 18, 1916 and May 11, 1916.
Place/date of birth: Not known.
Place/date of death: Not known.
Place of memorial: Not known.
Town/county connections: Not known.
Remarks: To France December 3, 1914. Awarded 1914-15 Trio. Presented with AM by His Majesty the King at Buckingham Palace May 16, 1916.

Citation
The KING was pleased, on Wednesday, the 10th instant, at Buckingham Palace, to present to Private Edward Gimble, 1st Battalion, Middlesex Regiment, who was home on leave from France, the Albert Medal of the Second Class which was conferred upon him for gallantry in saving life on the occasion of an outbreak of fire on the Ammunition Ship "Maine" at Boulogne, on 26th October, 1915. Full particulars are set forth in the notice appearing in the London Gazette of the 18th April last.

On the morning of the 26th October, 1915, the Orderly Officer on duty at the Bassin Loubet, Boulogne, was informed that a fire had broken out in the after hold of the S.S. "Maine" Ammunition Ship, in which a quantity of high explosives was stowed, and he at once reported the fact to Lieutenant-Commander Warden at the Office of the Naval Transport Officer.

In the meantime the ship was abandoned by her officers and crew, and steps were taken by the local fire brigade to rig the shore fire hoses.

Lieutenant-Commander Warden immediately proceeded on board, and on arrival at the after hold found smoke issuing from between the high explosive cases in the centre of the hatch. He went down into the hold, lifted up one of the cases, and called for the fire hose, which was passed to him by Private Edward Gimble, 1st Battalion, Middlesex Regiment, who had followed him on board.

Warden played the hose on them and extinguished the fire. Subsequent investigation showed that the fire was in all probability due to the ignition by friction or spontaneous combustion of amorphous phosphorous, which had leaked from boxes containing that substance stowed above the cases containing the high explosives.

There is little doubt that the prompt and gallant action of Lieutenant-Commander Warden prevented an explosion which would have had serious and possibly disastrous results with almost certain loss of life.

GOODHART, Francis Herbert Heaveningham.

Rank: Cdr.
Unit/Force: RN. HMS/MK. 13.
Other decorations: DSO (LG May 31, 1916).
Date of deed: January 29, 1917.
Date of Gazette: April 23, 1918.
Place/date of birth: Sheffield, Yorks, July 10, 1884.
Place/date of death: Gareloch, January 31, 1917.
Place of memorial: Faslane Cemetery.
Town/county connections: Sheffield, Yorks; Chigwell, Essex.
Remarks: Son of Vicar of St Barnabas, Sheffield. Educated Chigwell Grammar School and HMS *Britannia*. Midshipman May 15, 1900. Sub Lt July 15, 1903. Lt January 15, 1904. Cdr December 31, 1915. Served HMS *Ramillies* 1900-03, *Magnificent* and *Agamemnon* 1910-11. HMS *Maidstone* August 1914 for command of submarine E8. Despatches for reconnaissance of Heligoland Bight. Joined submarines January 10, 1905. Married 1912 Isabella Turner. Two daughters. He was also awarded the Order of St Vladimir 4th Class (Russia), the Order of St George 4th Class (Russia) and was a Chevalier de la Légion d'Honneur. He was entitled to a 1914-15 Star Trio but they do not appear to have been claimed on his behalf. His DSO, AM and two Russian orders are in the Imperial War Museum, London.

Citation

The KING has been graciously pleased to approve of the posthumous award of the Albert Medal in Gold for gallantry in saving life at sea to Commander Francis Herbert Heaveningham Goodhart, D.S.O., R.N.

The account of the services, in respect of which the medal has been conferred, is as follows:-

Owing to an accident, one of H.M. submarines sank and became fast on the bottom in 38 feet of water, parts of the vessel becoming flooded. After several hours the only prospect of saving those remaining on board appeared to be for someone to escape from the submarine in order to concert measures with the rescuers, who were by this time present on the surface. Commander Goodhart, after consultation with the Commanding Officer, volunteered to make the attempt. Accordingly, after placing in his belt a small tin cylinder with instructions for the rescuers, Commander Goodhart went into the conning tower with the Commanding Officer. The conning tower was flooded up to their waists, and the high-pressure air was turned on; the clips of the conning tower were knocked off and the conning tower lid was soon wide open. Commander Goodhart then stood up in the dome, took a deep breath, and made his escape, but, unfortunately, was blown by the pressure of air against part of the superstructure, and was killed by the force of the blow.

F. H. H. GOODHART
Source: RN Submarine Museum

The Commanding Officer, whose intention it had been to return inside the submarine after Commander Goodhart's escape, was involuntarily forced to the surface by the air pressure, and it was thus rendered possible for the plans for rescuing those still inside the submarine to be carried out.

Commander Goodhart displayed extreme and heroic daring in attempting to escape from the submarine in order to save the lives of those remaining on board, and thoroughly realised the forlorn nature of his act. His last remark to the Commanding Officer was: "If I don't get up, the tin cylinder will."

GOODWIN, George Everett.

No. V-30924.
Rank: Sto 2.
Unit/Force: RCNVR.
Other decorations: Nil.
Date of deed: December 12, 1942.
Date of Gazette: March 23, 1945.
Place/date of birth: Winnipeg, Manitoba, March 16, 1917.
Place/date of death: St John's, Newfoundland, December 12, 1942.
Place of memorial: St John's (Mt Pleasant) Cemetery, Newfoundland, Section C, Plot 23, Grave 1.
Town/county connections: Winnipeg, St John's.
Remarks: Son of E. and F. E. Goodwin, Vancouver, BC. Husband of Mildred of Macgregor, Manitoba. Enlisted RCNVR March 11, 1942 at Winnipeg. Served Canada and Newfoundland. Also awarded Defence Medal, Canada Volunteer Service Medal with Clasp and War Medal 1939-45.

Citation
The KING has been pleased to approve a recommendation from His Excellency the Governor-General of Canada, that the Albert Medal be awarded posthumously to George Everett Goodwin, Stoker Second Class, R.C.N.V.R., for supreme gallantry in rescuing occupants of the Knights of Columbus Hostel, St John's, Newfoundland, on the occasion of its destruction by fire on the 12th December, 1942.

Notwithstanding the fact that he could have saved his own life, and that he himself was very badly burned, this rating assisted in removing two girls from the building, thereby saving their lives. He was then overcome by flames and lost his life.

GRIER, Henry.

Rank: Surgeon.
Unit/Force: AMD att. 10th Foot.
Other decorations: Nil.
Date of deed: August 28, 1880.
Date of Gazette: January 14, 1881.
Place/date of birth: August 29, 1854.
Place/date of death: Guildford, Surrey, April 29, 1930.
Place of memorial: Not known.
Town/county connections: Cork, Dublin, Guildford.
Remarks: Educated at Queen's College, Cork and Carmichael School, Dublin. LRFPS (Glasgow) 1875 and MKQCP 1882. Joined army as surgeon February 3, 1878. Lt Col after 20 years' service and went on half pay November 20, 1903. Served South Africa 1899-1901 as IC General Hospital (local Col). Mentioned in Despatches LG April 18, 1901. Awarded QSA with two clasps. Retired from army February 20, 1908.

Citation
THE Queen has been graciously pleased to confer the "Albert Medal of the Second Class" on - SURGEON HENRY GRIER, Army Medical Department.

The following is the account of the services in respect of which the decoration has been conferred:-
On the 26th of August, 1880, Lieutenant Graham, 10th Regiment, was dying of diphtheria, when SURGEON GRIER performed upon him the operation of tracheotomy: and, observing that no attempt at inspiration followed, applied his lips without a moment's hesitation to the wound, and, by suction, at the imminent risk of his own life, restored to the patient the power of breathing. Lieutenant Graham's life was thus saved for the time, although, unfortunately, on the following day the disease extended to his lungs, and he died.

I.T GRIFFITH
Source: Family

GRIFFITHS, Ivor Thomas.

Rank: SBA.
Unit/Force: RN. HMS *Illustrious*.
Other decorations: Nil.
Date of deed: March 12, 1944.
Date of Gazette: July 11, 1944.
Place/date of birth:
Corris, Merionethshire, April 4, 1922.
Place/date of death:
Indian Ocean, off Ceylon,
March 12, 1944.
Place of memorial: Plymouth Naval Memorial, Panel 91, Column.
Town/county connections:
Corris, Merionethshire; Cyffylliog nr Ruthin, Denbighshire.
Remarks: Married (wife: Glenys) with two sons. Worked in Braich Goch slate quarry, Corris, on leaving school, then as attendant at Denbigh Hospital. Joined RN October 29, 1941 and served mainly in *Drake* and *Raleigh*. Described as 6'0" in height with dark brown hair, brown eyes and a healthy complexion on enlistment. Both his sons served in the Royal Navy. Also awarded 1939-45, Burma and Italy Stars and War Medal 1939-45.

Citation
The KING has been graciously pleased ... to approve the following awards:-
For bravery in attempting to save life at sea:
The Albert Medal (Posthumous)
Temporary Sub-Lieutenant (A) George McHardy, R.N.V.R. (East Finchley, N.2).
Sick Berth Attendant Ivor Thomas Griffiths, D/MX.93880 (Gyff-ylliog, near Ruthin, Denbighshire).
When an aircraft crashed while landing on H.M.S. Illustrious and came to rest with the engine on the flight deck and the tail on top of a pom-pom gun, petrol began to pour from the wreck and within two minutes an explosion was followed by fire.

Within those two minutes Sub-Lieutenant McHardy, who had himself only just landed on, and Sick Berth Attendant Griffiths, who was a member of a party detailed for medical duties on the flight deck, climbed on to the aircraft in an attempt to free the pilot, although both were well aware of the extreme risk they were running. They were killed by the explosion that followed.

GUNNER, Walter George.

No. 5975.
Rank: TPR.
Unit/Force: 1 DG.
Other decorations: Nil.
Date of deed: August 19, 1917.
Date of Gazette: April 26, 1918.
Place/date of birth: Not known.
Place/date of death: Not known.
Place of memorial: Not known.
Town/county connections: Not known.
Remarks: Went to France August 16, 1914. Transferred to Army Pay Corps April 11, 1917, under No. 12969. Presented with AM by His Majesty the King at Buckingham Palace on October 31, 1918. Also awarded 1914 Star, British War and Victory Medals.

Citation
The KING has been pleased to award the Albert Medal ... in recognition of gallantry displayed in ... endeavouring to save life:-
Trooper Walter George Gunner, 1st Dragoon Guards, attached Army Pay Corps.

On the 19th August last a tramcar full of passengers was descending a hill at Dover, and got out of control. The driver, finding that the brakes would not act, jumped off the front platform, and Private Gunner promptly took the driver's place on the platform and made every effort to stop the car by the application of the brakes. Unfortunately, in spite of Private Gunner's courage and presence of mind, he was unsuccessful in stopping the car, which ran to the bottom of the hill at great speed and overturned. Private Gunner lost both his feet as a result of the accident.

HABIB KHAN.

Rank: L-Nk.
Unit/Force: Bengal S & M.
Other decorations: Nil.
Date of deed: April 16, 1898.
Date of Gazette: November 18, 1898.
Place/date of birth: Not known.
Place/date of death: Not known.
Place of memorial: Not known.
Town/county connections: Not known.

Citation
THE Queen has been graciously pleased to confer the "Albert Medal of the Second Class" on:
Lieutenant Ranald Hume Macdonald, Royal Engineers;
Lance-Naik Habib Khan, Bengal Sappers and Miners;
Sapper Sheikh Abdul Samand, Bengal Sappers and Miners;
Sapper Kallan Khan, Bengal Sappers and Miners;
in recognition of their gallantry in saving the life of Sepoy Karm Dad, of the 27th Bengal Infantry, who with certain native Officers and men of that regiment, had been overwhelmed in an avalanche at the summit of the Lowarai Pass on the 16th April, 1898.

HALLARAN, Charles Francis George Thomas.

Rank: Cdr.
Unit/Force: RN (Retired). HMS *Springbank.*
Other decorations: Nil.
Date of deed: March 21, 1941.
Date of Gazette: September 9, 1941.
Place/date of birth: c1898.
Place/date of death: Bangor Bay, N. Wales, March 21, 1941.
Town/county connections: Not known.
Place of memorial: Belfast City Cemetery, N. Ireland. Section D, Grave 125 (Glengling extension).
Remarks: Son of Col and Mrs William Hallaran and husband of Elizabeth Joyce Hallaran of Worcester.

Citation
The KING has been graciously pleased ... to approve the following awards:-
The Albert Medal (Posthumous)
Commander Charles Francis George Thomas Hallaran, Royal Navy (Retired).
On a very dark night a motor boat came alongside Commander Hallaran's ship to take off the Pilot. A swell made this boat roll and pitch heavily, and a Stoker was thrown overboard between it and the ship's side. He was seen to be in difficulties, and was in danger of being crushed as the swell kept heaving the boat against the ship. Commander Hallaran climbed into the boat, jumped into the sea, and swam round to help him. He got the Stoker back to the boat, but as he did so he was thrown against it. His skull was fractured and he was drowned before he could be got back on board.

HALSTEAD, Arthur.

Rank: Lt.
Unit/Force: 10 Bn W Riding Regt.
Other decorations: MC (LG August 25, 1917).
Date of deed: July 31, 1917.
Date of Gazette: January 1, 1918.
Place/date of birth: c1894.

Place/date of death: France, August 1, 1917.
Place of memorial: Longuenesse Souvenir Cemetery, France, Plot 4, Row C, Grave 83.
Town/county connections: Halifax, Yorkshire.
Remarks: Aged 23 at death. Went to France August 25, 1914. Enlisted in ASC as Pte SS/464. Awarded 1914 Star and Bar, British War and Victory Medals. Commissioned July 6, 1916. The AM was sent by post to his mother, Mrs Sarah Ann Halstead, of 8 Buxton Street, Leemount, Halifax, Yorkshire.

Citation

The KING has been graciously pleased to award the Decoration of the Albert Medal in Gold in recognition of the gallant action of Second Lieutenant Arthur Halstead, M.C., late of the 10th Battalion of the West Riding Regiment, in saving life in France, in July last, at the cost of his own life. The circumstances are as follows:-

On the 31st July, 1917, during instruction in the throwing of live bombs, a bomb was accidentally dropped. Lieutenant Halstead placed himself between the bomb and the soldier who had dropped it in order to screen him, and tried to kick the bomb away, but it exploded, fatally wounding him. The soldier was slightly wounded, and there can be little doubt that Lieutenant Halstead's gallant action saved the soldier's life.

HAMBLY, Cyril.

No. D/JX.133146.
Rank: LS.
Unit/Force: RN. HMS *Kandahar.*
Other decorations: Nil.
Date of deed: December 19, 1941.
Date of Gazette: June 9, 1942.
Place/date of birth: c1913.
Place/date of death: December 20, 1941.
Place of memorial: Plymouth Naval Memorial, Panel 46, Column 1.
Town/county connections: Marhamchurch, Cornwall.
Remarks: The son of James Frederick and Miriam Hambly of Marhamchurch.

Citation

The KING has ... been graciously pleased ... to approve the following awards:-
The Albert Medal (Posthumous)
Acting Yeoman of Signals George Patrick McDowell, D/JX.143268
Leading Seaman Cyril Hambly, D/JX.133146.

When H.M.S. Kandahar was sinking, the heavy seas made it impossible for the rescuing destroyer to go alongside, and she was ordered to lie off and pick up survivors as they abandoned ship. Nets were hung over her side to help those below on rafts, or in the sea, to climb on board. Yeoman of Signals McDowell and Leading Seaman Hambly swam across to the destroyer, but though they themselves had the strength to reach the deck of the ship as she plunged in the heavy swell, with great devotion they chose to stay in the water to help those whose force was spent. In this way they saved many men, until they lost their strength and were drowned.

HANDLEY, Frederick.

Rank: CDR.
Unit/Force: IOD.
Other decorations: Nil.
Date of deed: August 30, 1906.
Date of Gazette: September 26, 1911.
Place/date of birth: Sukkur, Scinde, India, March 23, 1860.
Place/date of death: Not known.
Place of memorial: Not known.
Town/county connections: Ashton-under-Lyne, Lancashire.
Remarks: Enlisted as Pte 2523 in Manchester Regt at Ashton-u-Lyne, Lancs, on February 23, 1880. Joined 2 Bn on February 24, 1880. Sgt January 11, 1892. Transferred to 2 Bn Connaught Rangers as No 6302 on October 1, 1897. Transferred to IOD as Sub-Cdr October 22, 1900. Cdr July 3,1903. Asst Commissary and Hon Lt September 1, 1906. Invalided to India. Maj and Commissary, October 18, 1919. Retired March 3, 1920. Still in Army List in January 1942. Married December 2, 1899, at Woolwich to Katherine Florence (née Davies). 3 sons (1 died in infancy) and 2 daughters. Awarded 1914-15 Star, British War, Victory and LS&GC Medals. Apart from his service in Mesopotamia (November 1914 to Octber 1917), his entire service was spent in India. He seems to have remained in India after retirement from the army.

Citation
See citation for ANDERSON, C. A.

HANKEY, Thomas Barnard.

Rank: 2 Lt.
Unit/Force: 12 Bn KRRC.
Other decorations: MC (LG September 16, 1916).
Date of deed: October 15, December 4 and 6, 1915.
Date of Gazette: May 19, 1916.
Place/date of birth: c1887.
Place/date of death: Faringdon, nr Swindon, August 13, 1969.
Place of memorial: Not known.
Town/county connections: Faringdon.
Remarks: To France July 22, 1915. MID LG January 4, 1917 and May 15, 1917. Chevalier of Légion d'Honneur. Presented with AM by His Majesty the King at Buckingham Palace January 28, 1919. Also awarded 1914-15 Star, British War and Victory Medals. He was later a Major and was the only member of the AM Association to hold the AM in Gold.

Citation
The KING has been graciously pleased to award the Decoration of the Albert Medal to the undermentioned Officer ... serving in France in recognition of (his) gallantry in saving life:-

Albert Medal of the First Class.
Second Lieutenant Thomas Barnard Hankey, 12th Battalion, King's Royal Rifle Corps. was in charge of a party under instruction in throwing live grenades. A man who was throwing a grenade with a patent lighter became nervous when the lighter went off and dropped the grenade at his feet. Second Lt. Hankey at once picked up the grenade and threw it out of the trench. There were four men in this section of the trench.

On the 4th December, 1915, while Second Lieutenant Hankey was in charge of a party under instruction in throwing live grenades, a man pulled the pin from a grenade and threw the grenade straight into the parapet. Second Lieutenant Hankey at once picked up the grenade and threw it over the parapet. There were four men in the throwing pit at the time.

On the 6th December, 1915, Second Lieutenant Hankey was in charge of a party under instruction in throwing live grenades

T.B. HANKEY
Source: Unknown

from a catapult. A live grenade was placed in the pocket of the catapult, the fuse was lighted, and the lever released. The grenade for some reason was not thrown by the catapult, and fell out of the pocket on to the ground. Second Lieutenant Hankey, who was standing on the other side of the catapult to that on which the grenade lay, rushed at the grenade, seized it, and threw it away. The fuse was a short five-second fuse, and the grenade exploded on hitting the ground 15 yards away. There were eight men near the catapult at the time, and ten others not far away.

HARKBIR THAPA.

No. 8557.
Rank: RFN.
Unit/Force: 2/8 GR.
Other decorations: Nil.
Date of deed: May 31, 1935.
Date of Gazette: November 19, 1935.
Place/date of birth: Not known.
Place/date of death: ?Nepal, November 25, 1949.
Place of memorial: Not known.
Town/county connections: Nepal.
Remarks: One of the awards for the Quetta earthquake. Presented at Loralai on May 4, 1936.

Citation

His Majesty The KING has been graciously pleased to award the Albert Medal ... for services rendered in connection with the recent earthquake in Baluchistan:-
Rifleman Harkbir Thapa, 2nd Battalion, 8th Gurkha Rifles.

On the morning of the 31st May, Rifleman Thapa was detailed as part of a rescue party which was going to dig out some living people behind the Police Lines. On the way to the work he heard noises in a building and obtained permission from the N.C.O. to try to get these people out. At about 6.30 a.m., the Adjutant visited the area to ascertain how work was progressing. He found Rifleman Harkbir Thapa had worked his way with his hands through the debris under a tottering roof, and was nearing two people who were alive but buried. As there was clearly every chance of the roof collapsing on top of him as he removed the debris, the Adjutant assisted him by propping up the roof as far as possible. Rifleman Harkbir Thapa continued his work and brought out two children alive. He undoubtedly saved those two children at the risk of his own life. On 2nd June this Rifleman's conduct was again brought to notice. On this occasion he formed part of a detachment working in Hudda Village. The upper storey of a crumbling house was being cleared, part of the roof had fallen through the floor into the lower storey, thus rendering the floor most dangerous. A living child was discovered in the lower storey. This man and one other volunteered to dig through a corner of the floor opposite to where it had crumbled. They did so with khukries and their hands and got through to the lower storey and rescued the child. They did this at considerable risk to their own lives, as the walls were in danger of falling and the floor might have collapsed at any moment.

HARPER, Leonard.

Rank: Lt.
Unit/Force: Ches Regt (Territorial Force Reserve).
Other decorations: Nil.
Date of deed: August 5, 1917.
Date of Gazette: September 6, 1918.
Place/date of birth: Not known.
Place/date of death: Not known.
Place of memorial: Not known.
Town/county connections: Northwich, Cheshire.
Remarks: A manager in the Brunner-Mond ICI works at Rudheath, Northwich. Did not serve abroad. Presented with his AM by His Majesty the King at Buckingham Palace on September 26, 1918.

Citation

The KING has been pleased to award the Albert Medal to Lieutenant Leonard Harper, Cheshire Regiment, T.F.R., in recognition of his gallantry in saving life in August of last year. The circumstances are as follows:-

On the 5th August, 1917, a melting-pot, used for refining high explosive at an explosives factory, was being freed from a deposit of sediment which had accumulated. During the absence of Lieutenant Harper (one of the managers of the factory) a foreman attempted to break away the sediment, which was of a highly explosive nature, with an iron bar. The mixture fused, giving off fierce flames and thick fumes. On his arrival, Lieutenant Harper at once crawled with a hose underneath the pot, which was raised about three feet from the ground, and directed water at the flames immediately above him.

It was not until five or six hoses had been brought to bear on the pot for some time that the burning mixture was cooled down. Meanwhile there was imminent risk of an explosion, which would certainly have killed Lieutenant Harper and must have involved other buildings near by where 25 tons of high explosives were stored. Had such an explosion occurred, great loss of life and material damage must inevitably have resulted.

HARVEY, William Fryer.

Rank: Surg-Lt.
Unit/Force: RN. HMS *Champion*.
Other decorations: Nil.
Date of deed: June 28, 1918.
Date of Gazette: October 29, 1918.
Place/date of birth: April 14, 1885.
Place/date of death: Letchworth, Herts. June 4, 1937.
Place of memorial: Not known.
Town/county connections: Leeds; Selly Oak, Birmingham; Letchworth.
Remarks: Educated Bootham School, York and Balliol College, Oxford. MA 1910. BCh after further medical study in Leeds. Joined Quaker Training Camp at Jordans in August 1914 and went with first detachment of the Friends Ambulance Unit to Flanders. On graduating in medicine, he took a commission as Temporary Surgeon-Lieutenant RN on July 10, 1917. He was invalided out of the Service on March 31, 1919 due to deterioration of his health consequent upon the act which won him the AM. He acted for a time as Warden of Fircroft Working Men's College, Selly Oak, Birmingham but had to give this up owing to a breakdown of health. He was a noted writer of ghost stories.

Citation
The KING has been graciously pleased to approve the award of the Albert Medal for gallantry in saving life at sea to
Surg.-Lieut. William Fryer Harvey, R.N.
The account of the services in respect of which this decoration has been conferred is as follows:-
On the 28th June, 1918, two of H.M. torpedo-boat destroyers were in collision, and Surg.-Lieut. Harvey was sent on board the more seriously damaged destroyer in order to render assistance to the injured. On hearing that a stoker petty officer was pinned by the arm in a damaged compartment, Surg.-Lieut. Harvey immediately went down and amputated the arm, this being the only means of freeing the petty officer. The boiler-room at this time was flooded, and full of fumes from the escaping oil. This alone constituted a great danger to anyone in the compartment, and Surg.-Lieut. Harvey collapsed from this cause after performing the operation, and had to be hauled out of the compartment. Moreover, at any time the ship might have broken in two and all hands were fallen in on deck, wearing lifebelts, at the time, in order to be ready for this eventuality. Surg.-Lieut. Harvey displayed the greatest gallantry and disregard of his personal safety in descending into the damaged compartment and continuing to work there amidst the oil fumes at a time when the ship was liable to sink.

M. HEALY
Source: Family

HEALY, Michael.

No. 5130.
Rank: SGT.
Unit/Force: 2 Bn R Munster Fus.
Other decorations: DCM (LG September 22, 1916), MM (LG August 10, 1916), Bar to MM (LG October 22, 1916).
Date of deed: March 1, 1917.
Date of Gazette: January 4, 1918.
Place/date of birth: Ballinamuck, Co Waterford, c1892.
Place/date of death: Chuignolles, France, March 2, 1917.
Place of memorial: Bray Military Cemetery, France, Plot 2, Row B, Grave 53. Welsh Chapel and War Memorial, Pontardawe. Town/county connections: Dungarvan, Co Waterford; Pontardawe, Glamorgan.
Remarks: Enlisted at Pontardawe, S. Wales, where he lived with relations and worked in the steel works. One of only two AMs to be decorated four times. Also awarded 1914-15 Star, British War and Victory Medals. His mother, Mrs Annie Healy, was presented with the AM, DCM and MM and Bar at the same time by His Majesty the King at Buckingham Palace on February 9, 1918.

Citation
The KING has been graciously pleased to award the Decoration of the Albert Medal in recognition of the gallant action of Sergeant Michael Healy, Royal Munster Fusiliers, in saving life in France, in March last, at the cost of his own life. The circumstances are as follows:-
Sergeant Michael Healy, Royal Munster Fusiliers.

In France, on the 1st March, 1917, during bombing practice, a live bomb failed to clear the parapet, and rolled back into the trench, which was occupied by the thrower, an officer, and Sergeant Healy. All three ran for shelter, but Sergeant Healy, fearing that the others would not reach shelter in time, ran back and picked up the bomb, which exploded, and mortally wounded him.

Sergeant Healy had previously performed other acts of distinguished gallantry, for which he had been awarded the Distinguished Conduct Medal, the Military Medal, and a bar to the Military Medal.

HEARNE, Henry.

No. 9242.
Rank: CPL.
Unit/Force: RFC. 12 Squadron RFC.
Other decorations: Nil.
Date of deed: January 3, 1916.
Date of Gazette: May 19, 1916.
Place/date of birth: Not known.
Place/date of death: Not known.

Place of memorial: Not known.
Town/county connections: Not known.
Remarks: Went to France October 31, 1915. Also awarded 1914-15 Star, British War and Victory Medals. Presented with AM by His Majesty the King at Buckingham Palace on January 23, 1918, by which time he was a Flt Sgt.

Citation

The KING has been graciously pleased to award the Decoration of the Albert Medal to the undermentioned Officer, Non-commissioned Officer and men of His Majesty's Forces serving in France in recognition of their gallantry in saving life:-
Albert Medal of the First Class.
Major Cyril Louis Norton Newall, 2nd Gurkha Rifles (attached to the Royal Flying Corps).
Albert Medal of the Second Class.
Corporal Henry Hearne, Royal Flying Corps.
1st Class Air Mechanic Harrie Stephen Harwood, Royal Flying Corps.
2nd Class Air Mechanic Alfred Edward Simms, Royal Flying Corps.

On the 3rd January, 1916, at about 3 p.m., a fire broke out inside a large bomb store belonging to the Royal Flying Corps, which contained nearly 2,000 high explosive bombs, some of which had very large charges, and a number of incendiary bombs which were burning freely. Major Newall at once took all necessary precautions, and then, assisted by Air Mechanic Simms, poured water into the shed through a hole made by the flames. He sent for the key of the store, and with Corporal Hearne, Harwood and Simms entered the building and succeeded in putting out the flames. The wooden cases containing the bombs were burnt, and some of them were charred to a cinder.
Note: Harrie Harwood became a GC in 1971.

HENDERSON, John William.

No. 4308.
Rank: CSGT.
Unit/Force: 1 KOSB.
Other decorations: Nil.
Date of deed: April 24, 1910.
Date of Gazette: November 15, 1912.
Place/date of birth: Not known.
Place/date of death: Not known.
Place of memorial: Not known.
Town/county connections: Not known.
Remarks: Thought to have become a WOII with No. 15849. To France July 9, 1915. Also awarded QSA, KSA, E&W Africa Medals, 1914-15 Star, British War, Victory and LS&GC Medals. Demobilised February 16, 1919. Presented with AM by GOC 8(Lucknow) Division at Lucknow, January 1, 1913.

Citation

The KING has been pleased to approve of the Albert Medal of the Second Class being conferred upon Colour-Sergeant John William Henderson, 1st Battalion, King's Own Scottish Borderers, in recognition of his gallantry in saving life on the occasion of an explosion at the Laboratory, Delhi Fort, on the 24th April, 1912, when at imminent risk to his own life from further shell explosions he entered the premises and rescued a Lascar, after which he returned to the danger zone to render further aid if possible.

HENDRY, James Claude Scott.

No. Not known.
Rank: PO Mech.
Unit/Force: RNAS. Seaplane School, Calshot, RNAS.
Other decorations: Nil.
Date of deed: March 11, July 28, November 19, 1914.
Date of Gazette: Not Gazetted. See Remarks.
Place/date of birth: Not known.
Place/date of death: Not known.
Place of memorial: Not known.
Town/county connections: Not known.
Remarks: One of three Service awards (all RN) which were not Gazetted. The following citation is taken from the HO file. Royal Mint records note all three awards as having been ordered and supplied.

Citation
March 11, 1914. Helped pilot with both in water clinging to wreckage of seaplane. July 28, 1914. Assembly Flight at Spithead, only with great difficulty could he be persuaded to share with the pilot one float of seaplane left undamaged by enforced descent. Early morning November 19, 1914, north of Yarmouth as Observer and Operator piloted by Flt. Lt. Ian Davis. Machine capsized by premature explosion of a bomb dropped by the pilot who was stunned by the explosion. Hendry was thrown out and fell some 150 ft. into the sea, Davis fell in plane. In spite of the fall in winter time Hendry at once swam to the pilot and released him, a very difficult and dangerous undertaking for the machine was rapidly sinking and the officer was imprisoned under water unconscious and drowning, at the risk of being entangled in the wreckage and dragged to the bottom. He swam directly to a trawler and left her boat to pick up Davis who was kept afloat by the air in his clothing. He then directed the trawler to proceed and moor alongside Crossley Hospital.
Note: This award was approved by His Majesty the King *on April 15, 1915.*

HENRY, James Dixon.

No. Not known.
Rank: AB.
Unit/Force: RN. Tug *Sunderland.*
Other decorations: Nil.
Date of deed: November 8, 1916.
Date of Gazette: July 9, 1918.

Place/date of birth: Not known.
Place/date of death: Not known.
Place of memorial: Not known.
Town/county connections: Not known.
Remarks:

Citation

The KING has ... been graciously pleased to approve of the award of the Albert Medal to;
Lieutenant Edward Henry Richardson, R.N.R.,
2nd Engineer Christopher Watson,
A.B. James Dixon Henry, and
A.B. Malcolm Thompson,
for gallantry in saving life at sea.

The following is the account of the services in respect of which the decoration has been conferred:-

On the 8th November, 1916, a series of fires and explosions occurred at Bakarista, Port of Archangel, on merchant ships and on the wharves. The S.S. "Baron Driesen" had blown up at 1 p.m. and part of the S.S. "Earl of Forfar" forty minutes later. The latter ship, with a cargo of explosives, was on fire, and might have blown up at any moment, and explosions were continually taking place in the immediate vicinity. The ship was alongside the main fire on shore, and burning embers were constantly showered over her.

Lieutenant Richardson, 2nd Engineer Watson, and Able Seamen Henry and Thompson, of the Tug "Sunderland", nevertheless volunteered to board the "Earl of Forfar" and effected the rescue of a considerable number of wounded and helpless men who would otherwise have perished.

They displayed the utmost gallantry and disregard of their own personal safety in saving the lives of others.

HIGGS, Henry Joseph.

Rank: Lt.
Unit/Force: RE. Engr Trg Centre RE.
Other decorations: OBE (LG June 3, 1919).
Date of deed: February 17, 1916.
Date of Gazette: November 28, 1916.
Place/date of birth: London, 1886.
Place/date of death: Newark, Notts, February 23, 1936.
Place of memorial: Not known.
Town/county connections: Newark, Notts; Southwell, Notts.
Remarks: Son of Joseph Higgs of Indiana, USA. Educated St Paul's School and Magdalen College, Cambridge. BA (Cantab), MIMechE, AMICE. Served WWI France 1914-17. GHQ Staff Palestine 1917-19. Wounded Neuve Chapelle. MID thrice. Became Lt Col. After war worked for Egyptian Civil Svc (Irrigation Dept) and later was Man Dir of Ransomes & Marles Bearing Co Ltd, Newark. Married Gladys Winifred, dau. of James Rawlings JP of Hartlepool. Also awarded 1914 Star and Bar, British War and Victory Medals.

H. J. HIGGS
Source: *Newark Advertiser*

Citation

The KING was pleased, on Saturday, the 25th instant, at Buckingham Palace, to present to Lieutenant Henry Joseph Higgs, Royal Engineers, the Albert Medal of the First Class, which had been conferred upon him by His Majesty for gallantry in saving life, as detailed below:-
At Newark, on 17th February last, whilst instruction in the use of bombs was taking place, some members of the class, after lighting the fuzes, dropped their bombs, through nervousness. Lieutenant Higgs picked up the bombs, the fuzes being more than half burned at the time, and threw them over the parapet. The bombs exploded when just clear of the parapet.

On the 11th April last, an officers' class was being practised in the throwing of live grenades from behind a breastwork. One officer, when throwing a grenade, struck his arm against another officer, who was standing too close to him, so that the grenade was jerked out of his hand and fell between the class (numbering 30 officers) and the breastwork. Lieutenant Higgs dashed forward, seized the bomb, and threw it over the breastwork; it exploded in the air in front of the breastwork.

In addition, on several other occasions, ten or twelve in all, men when being practised in throwing the live grenades have dropped them, through nervousness, and Lieutenant Higgs has picked them up and thrown them over the parapet, thus avoiding serious accidents.

HINDES, Frederick Joseph.

Rank: Lt.
Unit/Force: RN. HMS/M *Truculent.*
Other decorations: Nil.
Date of deed: January 12, 1950.
Date of Gazette: February 7, 1950.
Place/date of birth: September 16, 1923.
Place/date of death: Thames Estuary, January 12, 1950.
Place of memorial: Not known.
Town/county connections: Not known.
Remarks: Joined RN as Acting Sub-Lt September 1, 1944. Promoted Lt February 1, 1945.

F. J. HINDES
Source: Illustrated London News

Citation

The KING has been graciously pleased to approve the posthumous award of the Albert Medal to the undermentioned for gallantry in attempting to save life at sea:-

Lieutenant Frederick Joseph HINDES, Royal Navy.

On the 12th January 1950, H.M. Submarine TRUCULENT was in collision with the Swedish Tanker DIVINA in the Thames Estuary and sank almost immediately. Lieutenant Hindes, who was First Lieutenant of the submarine, was down below at the time of the collision. By his calm demeanour and clear orders he maintained perfect discipline and was able to ensure that the greater part of those on board moved safely to the engine room and after end of the vessel before she sank. He then divided the men, probably about sixty, between the two compartments and himself took charge of the escape arrangements in the after end. When all was ready he opened the escape hatch but, despite having told one hand to hold on to him, he was blown violently out of the boat and was not seen again. Yet the sense of order which Lieutenant Hindes had instilled survived him and it is probable that all those in the after end got clear of the submarine.

HINE, Francis Walter.

No. P/MX47321.

Rank: CERA.

Unit/Force: RN. HM S/M Truculent

Other decorations: DSM (LG October 13, 1942).

Date of deed: January 12, 1950.

Date of Gazette: February 7, 1950.

Place/date of birth: Taunton, Somerset, August 29, 1912.

Place/date of death: Thames Estuary, January 12, 1950.

Place of memorial: Not known.

Town/county connections: Taunton, Somerset; Strood, Kent; Rainham, Kent.

Remarks: Married with two daughters. Joined RN as a Boy on July 30, 1928. Joined S/M service in February 1934 and spent the rest of his service in S/MJ, apart from eighteen months as a POW from August 1943 to May 1945. He was also awarded the 1939-45, Atlantic and Africa Stars, War Medal and LS&GC Medal. His citation should be read as following on from that of Lt HINDES (q.v.).

F. W. HINE
Source: Family

Citation

Chief Engine Room Artificer Francis Walter HINE, D.S.M., P/MX47321.

After the men had been divided and the water tight door between the after end and the engine room had been closed, Chief Engine Room Artificer Hine took charge of the escape arrangements for the men in the engine room. This duty he performed faultlessly, taking care that the limited number of escape sets were allotted to the weakest swimmers and ensuring that the least experienced men were carefully reminded of the correct drill. Chief Engine Room Artificer Hine was the last man to leave the engine room and it is known that he reached the surface but was not picked up.

The conduct of all who went down in the submarine was in full accord with the great traditions of the Royal Navy but the splendid example set by Lieutenant Hindes and Chief Engine Room Artificer Hine was beyond praise.

HOARE, Keith Robin.

Rank: Lt-Cdr.
Unit/Force: RNVR. HMS *Lookout.*
Other decorations: DSO (LG July 23, 1918) and Bar (LG August 28, 1918), DSC (LG April 6, 1918 - no citation).
Date of deed: April 11, 1918.
Date of Gazette: August 20, 1918.
Place/date of birth: 1889.
Place/date of death: Carlisle, February 6, 1959.
Place of memorial: Carlisle Crematorium.
Town/county connections: Hamble, Hants; Keswick, Cumbria.
Remarks: Son of C. A. R. and Beatrice Hoare of Hamble, Hants. Educated Northwood Park and Loretto, Scotland. Married to Brenda, daughter of A. Bardsley. The Bar to his DSO was for Zeebrugge; there is no citation. In later life, he was a director of the Honister Slate Mine in Borrowdale, Cumbria. Also held 1914-15 Trio (MID), Defence and War Medals.

Citation
The KING has been graciously pleased to approve of the award of the Albert Medal for Gallantry in Saving Life at Sea to
Lieutenant-Commander Keith Robin Hoare, D.S.O., D.S.C., R.N.V.R., and Lieutenant Arthur

K. R. HOARE
Source: Family

Gerald Bagot, D.S.C., R.N.V.R.
   The account of the services in respect of which the Decoration has been conferred is as follows:-
   On the 12th April, 1918, an explosion took place in the engine-room of H.M. Motor Launch 356, and the forward tanks burst into flame. The Officer and some of the crew were blown overboard by the explosion, and the remainder were quickly driven aft by the flames, and were taken off in a skiff. By this time the flames were issuing from the cabin hatch aft, and there was much petrol burning on the surface of the water. It was then realised by the crews of adjacent vessels that the aft petrol tanks and the depth charge were being attacked by the fire, and might explode at any moment. At the moment when others were running away, Lieutenant Hoare and Sub-Lieutenant Bagot jumped into their dinghy, rowed to the wreck, got on board, and removed the depth charge, thereby preventing an explosion which might have caused serious loss of life amongst the crowd of English and French sailors on the quay.
   Note: Lieut Bagot exchanged his AM for the GC in 1972.*

HORN, Alfred.

No. T/28896.
Rank: DVR.
Unit/Force: ASC. 3 Cav Div Aux Horse Tpt Coy ASC.
Other decorations: Nil.
Date of deed: June 30, 1918.
Date of Gazette: November 8, 1918.
Place/date of birth: Not known.
Place/date of death: Belloy-sur-Somme, France, June 30, 1918
Place of memorial: Crouy British Cemetery, France, Plot 3, Row C, Grave 25.
Town/county connections: Armley, Leeds.
Remarks: Husband of Emily Ann Horn, 5 Elsworth Place, Armley, Leeds, who was presented with AM by His Majesty the King at Buckingham Palace July 31, 1919. Also awarded 1914 Star, British War and Victory Medals. His full name was Alfred Edward Montague.

Citation
See citation for BROOKS, V.

HOSKYN, Charles Reginald.

Rank: Capt.
Unit/Force: RAMC. 22 CCS RAMC.
Other decorations: OBE (LG June 1, 1964).
Date of deed: November 24, 1916.
Date of Gazette: January 1, 1918.
Place/date of birth: Pakistan, 1880.
Place/date of death: St Cross Hospital, Rugby, March 3, 1965
Place of memorial: Not known.
Town/county connections: Rugby, Warwickshire.

Remarks: Educated Bedford School. Studied medicine at Barts and graduated MB, BS in 1909. Became a GP in Rugby in 1910, serving there until 1911, when appointed assistant surgeon to the Hospital of St Cross, Rugby. He remained there until 1946, except for service in WWI. Made Freeman of Rugby for outstanding work as doctor and humanitarian. Married with a son (also a Dr., who predeceased him) and a daughter. Also awarded 1914-15 Star, British War and Victory Medals.

Citation

The KING has been graciously pleased to award the Decoration of the Albert Medal to the undermentioned Officer ... of His Majesty's Forces serving in France ... in recognition of (his) gallantry in saving life:-
Captain Charles Reginald Hoskyn, Royal Army Medical Corps.

In France on the 24th November, 1916, as a result of a serious railway accident, a man was pinned down by the legs under some heavy girders. The wreckage was on fire, and the flames had already reached the man's ankles. Captain Hoskyn crawled into a cavity in the flaming wreckage, and after releasing one of the man's legs, amputated the other, whereupon the man was drawn out alive, Captain Hoskyn retaining hold of the main artery until a tourniquet could be put on.

HOUGHTON, Frederick Leonard.

Rank: Lt.
Unit/Force: 3 Bn R Warwicks Fus.
Other decorations: MC (LG January 1, 1918). No citation.
Date of deed: July 27, 1917.
Date of Gazette: January 1, 1918.
Place/date of birth: Not known.
Place/date of death: Not known.
Place of memorial: Not known.
Town/county connections: Not known.
Remarks: Later Captain. Presented with AM by His Majesty the King at Buckingham Palace at BP June 28, 1918.

Citation

The KING has been graciously pleased to award the Decoration of the Albert Medal to the undermentioned officer(s)... of His Majesty's Forces serving in France or elsewhere in recognition of his gallantry in saving life:-
Second Lieutenant Frederick Leonard Houghton, The Royal Warwickshire Regiment.

On the 27th July, 1917, during bombing instruction, a bomb hit the parapet and fell back into the trench which was occupied by Lieutenant Houghton, a non-commissioned officer and the man who had thrown the bomb. The non-commissioned officer shouted to the man to take cover, which he could easily have done, but the man remained crouching near the bomb. Lieutenant Houghton had already placed himself in safety; but on hearing the shouts of the non-commissioned officer, he ran back into the trench, seized the bomb, and threw it over the parapet, where it at once exploded. Had not Lieutenant Houghton returned from safety into the danger, the man would almost certainly have been killed.

HUKAM DAD.

No. 7111.
Rank: L-Nk.
Unit/Force: 5 Bn 8 Punjab (Burma) Regt.
Other decorations: Nil.
Date of deed: May 31, 1935.
Date of Gazette: November 19, 1935.
Place/date of birth: Not known.
Place/date of death: Not known.
Place of memorial: Not known.
Town/county connections: Not known.
Remarks: A Quetta earthquake award. He was presented with the AM at Fort Salop on June 3, 1936.

Citation

His Majesty The KING has been graciously pleased to award the Albert Medal ... for services rendered in connection with the recent earthquake in Baluchistan:-
Lance-Naik Hukam Dad, 5th Battalion, 8th Punjab (Burma) Regiment.

In the early morning of 31st May, while employed in rescue work in the city, Lance-Naik Hukam Dad fought his way into the ruins of a burning house at considerable risk to his own life and rescued a woman who was imprisoned there. Two injured men had already perished in the flames, and it was only through the bravery and presence of mind of Hukam Dad that the woman was saved.

JOHNSON, Arthur.

No. DM.2/096744.
Rank: PTE.
Unit/Force: ASC. Att 364 Forestry Coy RE.
Other decorations: Nil.
Date of deed: June 30, 1918.
Date of Gazette: November 8, 1918.
Place/date of birth: Not known.
Place/date of death: Belloy-sur-Somme, France, July 1, 1918.
Place of memorial: Cruoy British Cemetery, France, Plot 3, Row C, Grave 26.
Town/county connections: Fulham, London.
Remarks: Went to France August 12, 1915. Also awarded 1914-15 Star, British War and Victory Medals. His AM was sent to his widow, Mrs L.A. Johnson of 38 Bayonne Road, Fulham, London, SW6 on August 2, 1918.

Citation

See citation for BROOKS, V.

JOHNSTON, George Edward.

No. 289129.
Rank: SPR.
Unit/Force: RE. 12 Lt Rly Tpt Crew Coy RE.
Other decorations: Nil.
Date of deed: April 30, 1918.
Date of Gazette: August 30, 1918.
Place/date of birth: c1893.
Place/date of death: Crombeke, Belgium, April 30, 1918.
Place of memorial: Haringhe Military Cemetery, Belgium, Plot 3, Row D, Grave 32.
Town/county connections: Colwick Valley, Notts.
Remarks: Also awarded British War and Victory Medals. AM was presented to mother, Mrs Ellen Johnston of 4 Oak Villas, Colwick Valley, Notts by His Majesty the King at Buckingham Palace on September 26, 1918.

Citation
See citation for BIGLAND, J. E.

JOYCE, Michael.

No. O.N.M1400.
Rank: ERA 3..
Unit Force: RN. HMS *Zulu.*
Other decorations: Nil.
Date of deed: November 8, 1916.
Date of Gazette: May 8, 1917.
Place/date of birth: Not known.
Place/date of death: Not known.
Place of memorial: Not known.
Town/county connections: Not known.

Citation
The KING has been graciously pleased to confer the Decoration of the Albert Medal of the Second Class on:-
Michael Joyce, Engine Room Artificer, 3rd Class (now Acting Chief Engine Room Artificer, 2nd Class), O.N.M1400.
Walter Kimber, Stoker Petty Officer (now Chief Stoker), O.N. 307820.
The following is the account of the services in respect of which the Decoration has been conferred:-
H.M.S. "Zulu" was mined on the 8th November, 1916. As a result of the explosion the bottom of the after part of the engine room was blown out, and the whole compartment reduced to a mass of debris and broken steam and water pipes.
Immediately after the explosion Joyce and Kimber proceeded to the engine room, the former having just come off watch. The latter had just left the boiler room, after he had seen that the

oil-burners were shut off and everything was in order, and had sent his hands on deck.

Hearing the sound of moans coming from inside the engine room, they both attempted to enter it by the foremost hatch and ladder.

As the heat in the engine room was intense and volumes of steam were coming up forward, they then lifted one of the square ventilating hatches further aft on the top of the engine room casing (port side) and climbed into the rapidly flooding compartment over the steam pipes, which were extremely hot.

Scrambling over the debris, they discovered well over on the starboard side Stoker Petty Officer Smith, with his head just out of the water.

A rope was lowered from the upper deck, and with great difficulty Smith, who was entangled in fractured pipes and other wreckage, was hauled up alive.

At the same time Stoker Petty Officer Powell was found floating in the water on the port side of the engine room. The rope was lowered again and passed around Powell, who, however, was found to be dead on reaching the deck.

The water was so high that further efforts to discover the remaining Artificer left in the engine room would have been useless, and the attempt had to be abandoned.

KABUL SINGH

No. 9670.
Rank: L-Nk.
Unit/Force: 4 Bn 19 Hyderabad Regt.
Other decorations: MC (1942).
Date of deed: May 31, 1935.
Date of Gazette: November 19, 1935.
Place/date of birth: Not known.
Place/date of death: Not known.
Place of memorial: Not known.
Town/county connections: Not known.
Remarks: Presented with AM at Quetta on May 9, 1936. Enlisted August 9, 1929. Subsequently commissioned Jemadar on October 17, 1941. POW Malaya, 1942. Retired c1950.

Citation
His Majesty The KING has been graciously pleased to award the Albert Medal ... for services rendered in connection with the recent earthquake in Baluchistan:-
Lance-Naik Kabul Singh, 4th Battalion, 19th Hyderabad Regiment.

On the morning of the 31st May, 1935, Lance-Naik Kabul Singh at great risk and personal danger to his life entered a tumbled down burning house in Bruce Road and succeeded in rescuing two women and three children.

KALLAN KHAN.

Rank: SPR.
Unit/Force: Bengal S & M.
Other decorations: Nil.
Date of deed: July 16, 1898.
Date of Gazette: November 18, 1898.
Place/date of birth: Not known.
Place/date of death: Not known.
Place of memorial: Not known.
Town/county connections: Not known.
Remarks:

Citation
See citation for HABIB KHAN.

C. A. KEEFER
Source: New Edinburgh News, Canada

KEEFER, Charles Allan.

No. 0-37880.
Rank: Lt.
Unit/Force:
RCNVR. HMS *Lulworth*.
Other decorations: Nil.
Date of deed: August 27, 1941.
Date of Gazette: February 17, 1942.
Place/date of birth:
Ottawa, Canada, September 2, 1910.
Place/date of death: 250m W of Slyne Head, Connemara, Ireland, August 27, 1941.
Place of memorial: Halifax Memorial, Nova Scotia, Panel 8.
Town/county connections:
Ottawa, Canada;
Remarks: Son of Mr & Mrs Allan Keefer of Ottawa. Was a junior executive with the Hudson Bay Co prior to enlistment. He lived at 35 McKay Street, Ottawa. Originally enlisted in 1929 and was appointed Midshipman on May 1, 1929. Promoted A/Sub-Lieut April 9, 1930. Resigned June 20, 1933. Re-enlisted for hostilities only on April 15, 1940 as Lieut. Served Canada and on the high seas. Also awarded 1939-45 and Atlantic Stars, Canadian Volunteer Service Medal with Clasp and War Medal. His Memorial Cross was sent to his mother, as NOK, on October 21, 1941, at 3 MacKinnon Road, Rockcliffe, Ontario.

Citation

The Albert Medal (Posthumous)

Lieutenant Charles Allan Keefer, R.C.N.V.R., H.M.S. Lulworth.

H.M.S. Lulworth went to the rescue of survivors from a torpedoed Merchantman. The night was dark, with heavy seas running, so that rescue work was slow and hazardous. As "Lulworth" was about to abandon search, two men and a woman were found clinging to the wreckage. The men were saved, but as the woman, who was unconscious, was being hauled on board, she slipped from her life-jacket, disappeared below the surface, and came up astern. Lieutenant Keefer at once dived into the sea to try to save her. He reached her, but both were swept away by the heavy seas, and though search was made for an hour, neither was seen again.

KELLY, Fred.

Rank: Lt.
Unit/Force: 6 (Res) Bn DWR.
Other decorations: Nil.
Date of deed: January 30, 1918.
Date of Gazette: April 26, 1918.
Place/date of birth: Not known.
Place/date of death: February 18, 1926.
Place of memorial: Not known.
Town/county connections: Not known.
Remarks: Also awarded British War and Victory Medals. Presented with his AM by His Majesty the King at Buckingham Palace May 25, 1918. He received the Silver War Badge.

Citation

The KING has been pleased to award the Albert Medal ... in recognition of gallantry displayed in saving ... life:-
Lieutenant Fred Kelly, 6th Battalion, Duke of Wellington's (West Riding) Regiment.

On the 30th January last, at a camp in England where rifle grenade practice was being carried out, one of the men struck the loophole with his bayonet and caused the fuse of the grenade to ignite. Lieutenant Kelly, who was in charge, shouted to the man to drop his rifle and get clear, but he lost his nerve and remained in the trench gripping the rifle. Lieutenant Kelly then seized the rifle, and with much difficulty got it out of the man's hands and threw it away. He then tried to push the man out of the emplacement, but before he could get him clear the bomb exploded, and they were both slightly wounded. But for Lieutenant Kelly's courage and resource the soldier would probably have been killed.

KEMPSTER, Albert Joseph.

Rank: SGT-MAJ.
Unit/Force: 2 Bn R Jersey Mil.
Other decorations: Nil.
Date of deed: September 29, 1910.

Date of Gazette: December 30, 1910.
Place/date of birth: Not known.
Place/date of death: Not known.
Place of memorial: Not known.
Town/county connections: Jersey, CI.
Remarks: Presented with the AM by His Majesty the King at Buckingham Palace on February 23, 1911.

Citation

The KING has been pleased to approve of the Albert Medal of the Second Class being conferred upon Sergeant Major Albert Joseph Kempster, of the 2nd Battalion Royal Jersey Militia, for gallantry in saving life as detailed below:-

On the 28th September, 1910, a carriage containing two ladies and two children was being driven near Pontac, in the Island of Jersey, when one of the horses stumbled and the driver was thrown into the road owing to the reins breaking when he tried to pull up. The horses became frightened and bolted at full speed, travelling at a furious pace towards St. Heliers. The horses and carriage passed Sergeant-Major Kempster, who was cycling in the same direction, and he promptly gave chase, and, getting alongside the carriage, succeeded in the very difficult feat of obtaining a foothold on the carriage step and transferring himself from his bicycle to the carriage.

Climbing along the pole of the carriage the Sergeant-Major managed to get hold of the broken reins and succeeded in bringing the frightened horses to a standstill. Had it not been for his presence of mind and determined courage the occupants of the carriage might have met with serious and possibly fatal injuries, for in about another minute the runaways would have reached the closed gates of a railway crossing.

KIMBER, Walter.

No. O.N.307820.
Rank: SPO.
Unit/Force: RN. HMS *Llewellyn*.
Other decorations: Nil.
Date of deed: November 8, 1916.
Date of Gazette: May 8, 1917.
Place/date of birth: Not known.
Place/date of death: Not known.
Place of memorial: Not known.
Town/county connections: Not known.
Remarks:

Citation
See citation for JOYCE, M.

W. LASHLY
Source: "An Unknown Few"

LASHLY, William.

No. 148009.
Rank: Ch Sto.
Unit/Force: RN.
Other decorations: Nil.
Date of deed: February 9-19, 1912.

Date of Gazette: July 29, 1913.
Place/date of birth: Hambledon, Hants, December 25, 1867.
Place/date of death: Hambledon, Hants, 1940.
Place of memorial: Lashly Glacier and Mountains, Antarctica.
Town/county connections: Hambledon, Hants.
Remarks: Second son of a farmworker. Left school at 13 to work as a gardener until January 1, 1889, when he joined the RN. He served with RN until October 1913, when he enrolled in the RFR. Recalled for war service and served again from August 2, 1914 to February 10, 1919. He was married with one daughter. On retirement from RN, worked for BOT until final retirement in 1932. Also awarded 1914-15 Star, British War, Victory, LS&GC (RN) and Polar Medals, the latter with clasps Antarctic 1902-04, Antarctic 1910-13. Featured, along with PO Tom Crean, in an issue of "The Hornet" comic, No. 433 - December 25, 1971: very fitting, as it was his birthday!

Citation
See citation for CREAN, T.

LAWRENCE, Joseph.

No. M2/050433.
Rank: PTE.
Unit/Force: ASC. GHQ Tps Sup Column Wksp.
Date of deed: May 2, 1916.
Date of Gazette: August 29, 1916.
Place/date of birth: Not known.
Place/date of death: Not known
Place of memorial: Not known.
Town/county connections: Not known.
Remarks: Also appears to have served in the Royal Warwickshire Regiment as Sgt 33359 and became a Cpl in the ASC. To France February 28, 1915. Also awarded 1914-15 Star, British War and Victory Medals. Discharged to Class Z Reserve March 22, 1919. Presented with AM by His Majesty the King at Buckingham Palace February 14, 1917.

Citation
See citation for ANDERSON, A.

LEACH, Grey de Leche.

Rank: Lt.
Unit/Force: 1 Bn SG.
Other decorations: Nil.
Date of deed: September 3, 1916.
Date of Gazette: December 11, 1917.
Place/date of birth: Leatherhead, Surrey, March 1, 1894.

Place/date of death: Morlancourt, France, September 3, 1916.
Place of memorial: Corbie Communal Cemetery Extension, Plot 2, Row B, Grave 1.
Town/county connections: Leatherhead, Surrey.
Remarks: Enlisted in 1/5 E Surreys (TF) August 10, 1914. Also awarded British War and Victory Medals. Son of C.F. Leach of Vale Lodge, Leatherhead. AM presented to his father by His Majesty the King at Buckingham Palace on February 9, 1918.

Citation

The KING has been pleased to award the Albert Medal in Gold in recognition of the conspicuous gallantry and self-sacrifice of Second Lieutenant Grey de Leche Leach, late of the 1st Battalion of the Scots Guards. The circumstances are as follows:-

In France, on the 3rd September, 1916, Lieutenant Leach was examining bombs in a building in which two non-commissioned officers were also at work, when the fuse of one of the bombs ignited. Shouting a warning, he made for the door, carrying the bomb pressed close to his body, but on reaching the door he found other men outside, so that he could not throw the bomb away without exposing others to grave danger. He continued, therefore, to press the bomb to his body until it exploded, mortally wounding him.

Lieutenant Leach might easily have saved his life by throwing the bomb away or dropping it on the ground and seeking shelter, but either course would have endangered the lives of those in or around the building. He sacrificed his own life to save the lives of others.

LECKY, Halton Stirling.

Rank: Lt.
Unit/Force: RN. HMS *Widgeon.*
Other decorations: CB (LG 1919).
Date of deed: August 25, 1900.
Date of Gazette: June 28, 1901.
Place/date of birth: Portrush, Ireland, 1878.
Place/date of death: London, June 2, 1940.
Place of memorial: Not known.
Town/county connections: Portrush, Co Antrim; Upper Norwood, London.
Remarks: Only son of Cdr S. T. S. and Mrs Elizabeth Susan Lecky. Educated at Eastman's RN Academy, Stubbington. To *Britannia* 1892. Married in 1908 Agnes, fourth daughter of Douglas Richmond Close of Uffculme, Devon. Two sons, six daughters. Sub Lt 1898. Retired as Capt 1925. Also awarded QSA (Natal clasp), 1914-15 Star, British War and Victory (MID) Medals, Greek Order of Redeemer (5th Class), Légion d'Honneur (5th Class), Order of Crown of Italy (4th Class), Lloyds' Silver Medal, RHS Silver Medal and Messina Earthquake Medal 1908.

Citation

HIS Majesty has been pleased to confer upon - Lieutenant HALTON STIRLING LECKY, R.N., the Albert Medal of the Second Class, on the recommendation of the Lords Commissioners of the Admiralty, in recognition of his gallantry in saving life at sea in the following circumstances:-
On the 25th August, 1900, His Majesty's ship "Widgeon", anchored in Kosi Bay, fifty miles

south of Delagoa Bay, in order to land stores and troops. The work of disembarkation was carried out by surf boats manned by Malays under the superintendence of Sub-Lieutenant LECKY, who had been sent on shore for the purpose.

Heavy breakers in lines of three to five, according to the tide, rolling in about fifty yards apart, made the work very risky.

One boat loaded with stores and with Second Lieutenant Arnold Gray, Thorneycroft's Mounted Infantry, Trooper Frederick Trethowen, Steinacker's Horse, and Private J. H. Forbes,

H.S. LECKY
Source: Navy & Army Illustrated.

Thorneycroft's Mounted Infantry, on board, capsized about three hundred yards from the shore. The five Malays forming the boat's crew, and Private Forbes, by dint of hard swimming, with the assistance of the boat's oars, managed to reach the land after severe buffeting from the heavy seas. Lieutenant Gray was unable to swim, but, with Trooper Trethowen, clung to the boat, which drifted slowly keel upwards in a northerly direction almost parallel with the shore, carried by the set of a strong current. Huge breakers continually swept over the boat, and the men had great difficulty in retaining their hold. Sharks were observed near the boat both before and after the accident. The boat was now about one hundred and fifty yards from the shore. Sub-Lieutenant LECKY, seeing the critical position the two men were in, tore off his clothes and, plunging into the surf, endeavoured to swim to their assistance. He was twice thrown back on the beach by the heavy seas, but afterwards succeeded in bringing first Lieutenant Gray and then the other safe to the shore. The rescued men were quite unconscious, having been nearly thirty minutes in the water.

Lieutenant LECKY and his servant, Private Botting, Royal Marine Light Infantry, then applied the usual methods for restoring animation, and both men eventually recovered consciousness - Lieutenant Gray after a lapse of two and a half hours.

LITHGOW, Hugh Lancaster.

Rank: Maj.
Unit/Force: RFA. 44 Bty RFA.
Other decorations: Nil.
Date of deed: February 25, 1908.
Date of Gazette: May 13, 1910.
Place/date of birth: May 15, 1868.
Place/date of death: Weymouth, Dorset, August 21, 1945.
Place of memorial: Not known.
Town/county connections: Weymouth, Dorset.
Remarks: RMA Woolwich 1886-8. 2Lt RA February 17, 1888. Maj October 31, 1903. Retired August 30, 1911.

Citation
His late Majesty King Edward the Seventh was pleased to signify His pleasure that the Albert Medal of the Second Class be awarded to Major Hugh Lancaster Lithgow, R.F.A., and to Sergeant-Major Charles Stephens, R.F.A., for gallantry in endeavouring to save life as detailed below:-

On the 25th February, 1908, a violent explosion of blank gun cartridges occurred in the store of the 44th Battery, Royal Field Artillery, at Kirkee, India, and while the building was full of smoke, and it was impossible to tell whether a further explosion might follow, Major Lithgow and Sergeant-Major Stephens, hearing that Battery Quarter-Master Sergeant Dennis was in the burning building, at once went to his rescue through the dense smoke, and succeeded in bringing him out, though unhappily he was so seriously hurt that he succumbed to the injuries sustained.

The Medals have now been presented - Major Lithgow's Decoration by Major-General E.A.H. Alderson, C.B., Commanding the 6th (Poona) Division, at a Parade held at Poona on the 1st January, and Sergeant-Major Stephens' Decoration at Cahir, on the 18th April, by the Major-General Commanding the 6th Division, Irish Command.

LOWRY, Arthur Cole.

Rank: Lt.
Unit/Force: RN. HMS *Empress of India.*
Date of deed: September 18/19, 1900.
Date of Gazette: December 18, 1900.
Place/date of birth: Not known.
Place/date of death: Gosport, Hants, December 3, 1903
Place of memorial: Not known.
Town/county connections: Not known.
Remarks: Also held Bronze, Silver and Gold (Stanhope) Medals of the RHS.

Citation

HER Majesty has been pleased to confer upon -

Lieutenant ARTHUR COLE LOWRY, R.N., the Albert Medal of the Second Class, on the recommendation of the Lords Commissioners of the Admiralty, in recognition of his gallantry in saving life at sea in the following circumstances:-

At 9.15 P.M., on September 18th, 1900, while Her Majesty's ship "Empress of India" was entering the Doro Channel, Cape Fassa, Isle of Andros, a steamer was observed firing signals of distress, and on nearer approach, about 10.45 P.M., was found to be anchored off a lee shore, and riding by a hawser only. She proved to be the Steamship "Charkich" of London, bound from Piraeus to Constantinople, commanded by an Austrian, with a crew of forty to fifty hands, and carrying upwards of thirty passengers. Lieutenant LOWRY communicated with the ship in the cutter, and, learning that the shaft was broken, asked the Captain what he could do for him, and whether he wished his crew taken off. The Captain asked for a hawser to take him in tow, but by the time the cutter had returned with it, the ship had drifted too close to the shore for this plan to be feasible. Immediately afterwards she disappeared from view. It was evident by the sudden extinction of lights that she had taken ground.

All efforts to find the vessel by search-light proved useless, and as the wind and sea made it impossible to search the coast with boats, the "Empress of India" stood off at 12.50 A.M. until daybreak, when the masts of the "Charkich" were seen standing out of the water. Three men were on the foremast, and three others on detached rocks close to the wreck. A heavy sea was running with a cross current, and much wreckage was about. Lieutenant LOWRY at once went in the cutter, and endeavoured under oars to float a line and life-buoy to the foremast to windward of the wreck. He failed owing to the cross current, but one man swam from the mast to the buoy, and was hauled into the boat. Having tried again for some time to get the buoy to the mast, with no success, and the men seeming unable to move, Lieutenant LOWRY jumped overboard about 7 A.M. and swam to the wreck with a life buoy and line. As he reached the rigging, he lost the line which fouled some wreckage, and he was cut off.

Throughout the forenoon efforts were made to establish communication with the wreck. The cutter first made another attempt, but was struck by a heavy sea and half filled with water. Both sea boats were then sent in with oil to throw on the water, rockets and grass lines, but all in vain.

The "Empress of India" then proceeded to Pargo Bay and landed a party to try and reach the wreck from the shore. On her return it was found that the back of the wreck had broken. One of the men had got ashore on a large piece of wreckage. Lieutenant LOWRY, with the other man, was still in the fore-rigging, which might now give way at any moment. His own life belt would possibly have enabled him to reach the shore, but he would not leave his companion, who had none.

Another attempt was made about 3 P.M., both by the shore party and by Lieutenant Vereker in the cutter, to reach the wreck. Lieutenant LOWRY directed the cutter from the mast of the wreck, and succeeded at last in throwing a line into her. With the aid of this the rescue was accomplished, Lieutenant LOWRY assisting the last man into the boat before leaving the wreck. Meanwhile one of the three men on the detached rocks managed to reach the shore. The others were washed off and drowned.

LYELL, Walter Howden.

Rank: Lt.
Unit/Force: 3 Res Bn Gordon Hldrs.
Other decorations: Nil.
Date of deed: May 4, 1916.
Date of Gazette: July 4, 1916.
Place/date of birth: Guthrie, Forfarshire, January 16, 1898.
Place/date of death: Rangoon, Burma, April 28, 1923.
Place of memorial: Guthrie Parish Church.
Town/county connections: Guthrie, Forfarshire; Rangoon, Burma.
Remarks: 5th son of A. Lyell, JP, of Gardyne Castle, Guthrie. Educated Montrose Academy and Haileybury College, Herts. Joined Inns of Court as cadet and was commissioned into Gordon Highlanders Special Reserve. Wounded three times and went to Malay States on demob. Worked for forestry dept of Steele Bros, Rangoon at time of death from black water fever. Believed to be related to Lord Lyell. To France August 21, 1916. Also awarded British War and Victory Medals.

Citation
The KING has been graciously pleased to award the Decoration of the Albert Medal to Second Lieutenant Walter Howden Lyell, 3rd Battalion, Gordon Highlanders, in recognition of (his) gallantry in saving life at bombing practice.

On the 4th May, 1916, Lieutenant Lyell was in command of a party under instruction in throwing hand grenades. One of the men threw a grenade on to the parapet directly in front of the party, thus placing them in great danger. Lieutenant Lyell at once ran up, and, picking up the bomb, threw it over the parapet.

... Explosion followed immediately the bomb had been thrown away.

LYNCH, Edward.

Rank: Sto.
Unit/Force: RN. HMS *Thrasher*.
Other decorations: Nil.
Date of deed: September 29, 1897.
Date of Gazette: December 21, 1897.

E. LYNCH
Source: Navy Illustrated

Place/date of birth: Not known.
Place/date of death: Not known.
Place of memorial: Not known.
Town/county connections: Not known.

Citation

HER Majesty the Queen has been graciously pleased to confer the Decoration of the Albert Medal of the First Class on -

EDWARD LYNCH, Stoker of Her Majesty's ship "Thrasher".

The following is the account of the services in respect of which the Decoration has been conferred:-

At 3 A.M., on the 29th September, 1897, the torpedo destroyer "Thrasher", with the "Lynx" and "Sunfish" in company, left St. Ives on passage to Falmouth. In the thick and foggy weather which was subsequently met, the "Thrasher", followed by the "Lynx", grounded at Dodman's Point, causing serious injury to the boliers, and the bursting of the main feed pipe. A falling tide caused the "Thrasher" to heel quickly over to about 60 degrees. The ship's company was therefore landed on the rocks, a few men being kept on board, with boats ready to land them.

There were six Petty Officers and men in the stokehold. Of these the Chief Stoker happened to be coming on deck by the starboard hatchway at the moment of striking, and escaped. This hatchway became distorted by the doubling up of the deck, preventing further egress. Stokers EDWARD LYNCH and James H. Paul were compelled to escape by the port hatchway close to a break in the steam pipe. The hatchway through which they passed was partially closed up, and Paul was unable to follow LYNCH, who then kneeling or lying on the deck, reached down into the escaping steam and drew James Paul, who was on the ladder, up on to the upper deck.

LYNCH was shortly after observed to be badly scalded about the head, arms, and upper portion of the body in this rescue, the skin hanging off his hands and arms. Oil and wood were applied to alleviate the pain, but LYNCH called attention to Paul, whom he wished attended to first, saying that he himself was not much hurt, but Paul was very bad. Neither man had said anything or called any attention to his injuries until this time, although quite five minutes had elapsed since the accident. The surgeon who attended LYNCH and Paul reports that the former, though very badly scalded and in great pain, would not allow his assistant or himself, for a considerable time, to do anything for him, saying, "I am all right; look after my chum."

The manly conduct of LYNCH induced the surgeon to make inquiries concerning the rescue of Paul from the stokehold, and he found that LYNCH with difficulty released himself from the hatchway (much narrowed by the accident), lay down and leaning into the scalding steam, caught Paul and dragged him up through the hatch, and in this way received his own wounds, which are such as to show that, in rescuing his comrade, he must have plunged the forepart of his own body into what was practically a boiling cauldron.

It transpired also that LYNCH in a most heroic manner had previously sacrificed his own opportunity of quitting the stokehold, in order to aid his comrade Paul in escaping. Paul subsequently succumbed to his injuries, and LYNCH, for a long time, was not expected to recover.

McCARTHY, Edward.

No. 3152.
Rank: PTE.
Unit/Force: 2 Bn POW Leinster Regt.
Other decorations: MM (LG February 23, 1918).
Date of deed: January 6, 1919.
Date of Gazette: July 18, 1919.
Place/date of birth: Not known.
Place/date of death: January 7, 1919.
Place of memorial: Köln Southern Cemetery, Germany, Plot 1, Row B, Grave 5.
Town/county connections: ?Dublin, Ireland.
Remarks: To France September 20, 1914. Also awarded 1914 Star, British War and Victory Medals.

Citation
The KING has been pleased to award the Albert Medal ... in recognition of gallantry displayed in saving life:-
Private Edward McCarthy, M.M., late of the Prince of Wales' Leinster Regiment (Royal Canadians). (Posthumous award).

On the 6th January, 1919, two horses harnessed to a limber, having been left unattended at Wermels-Kirchen, took fright and ran away. While they were going at great speed down the village street Private McCarthy rushed forward and seized the reins. He would doubtless have succeeded in stopping the horses had the reins held, but they broke, and he was thrown under the limber, which passed over his body, inflicting injuries from which he subsequently died. He succeeded, however, in diverting the limber from two children, who would otherwise undoubtedly have been killed.

McCARTHY, James.

No. 8674.
Rank: CPL.
Unit/Force: 1 Bn R Irish Regt.
Other decorations: Nil.
Date of deed: January 24, 1918.
Date of Gazette: May 14, 1918.
Place/date of birth: Clonmel, Co Tipperary, January 15, 1885.
Place/date of death: Palestine, January 24, 1918.
Place of memorial: Jerusalem War Cemetery, Plot F, Grave 37.
Remarks: To France December 19, 1914. Also awarded 1914-15 Star, British War and Victory Medals, all of which are now in the National Army Museum, London. His father was also a soldier. The AM was presented to his mother, Mrs Johanna McCarthy at Clonmel on May 25, 1918 by Maj Gen B. J. C. Doran CB, Comd South Dist, Mrs McCarthy being too poor to attend Buckingham Palace.

Citation

The KING has been pleased to award the Albert Medal in Gold in recognition of the gallantry of Corporal James McCarthy, 1st Battalion, Royal Irish Regiment, in saving life in January last at the cost of his own life. The circumstances are as follows:-

On the 24th January, 1918, in Palestine, Corporal McCarthy was cleaning grenades in his quarters, when the fuse of one became ignited. He carried it out to throw it into a safe place, but, finding a number of men standing around, he realised that he could not throw it anywhere without injuring his comrades. He clasped the grenade in both hands and held it close to his side. The grenade exploded, killing Corporal McCarthy, who by his devoted courage saved his comrades from serious injury.

McCREATH, Andrew Berghaus.

Rank: Lt.
Unit/Force: 7 NF, att KOSB (Egyptian Mil Force).
Other decorations: Nil.
Date of deed: July 26, 1917.
Date of Gazette: January 1, 1918.
Place/date of birth: Norham-on-Tweed, c1889.
Place/date of death: Egypt, December 11, 1917.
Place of memorial: Cairo War Memorial Cemetery, Plot O, Grave 62.
Town/county connections: Berwick-upon-Tweed.
Remarks: 5th son of Henry H. McCreath JP of Berwick-on-Tweed. Educated at Grammar School, Berwick and worked for Barclays Bank before WWI. To Egypt January 26, 1917. Also awarded British War and Victory Medals. AM presented to mother by His Majesty the King at Buckingham Palace on September 18, 1918.

A. B. MCCREATH
Source: Regimental Journal

Citation

The KING has been graciously pleased to award the Decoration of the Albert Medal to the undermentioned Officer ... in recognition of (his) gallantry in saving life:-
Lieutenant Andrew Berghans (sic) McCreath, Northumberland Fusiliers, attached The King's Own Scottish Borderers (Egyptian Military Force).

On 26th July, 1917, during an inspection of grenades, one of the grenades fell on the ground and detonated, and Lieutenant McCreath, hearing warning shouts, ran up and picked up the bomb. In order to get rid of it without endangering others, he had to run until he found an empty dug-out into which to throw it. As he was about to throw it away the detonator exploded; fortunately, the ammonal was wet (although Lieutenant McCreath did not know this), and no further explosion took place.

MacDONALD, Ranald Hume.

Rank: Lt.
Unit/Force: RE. Bengal S & M.
Other decorations: Nil.
Date of deed: July 16, 1898.
Date of Gazette: November 18, 1898.
Place/date of birth: February 22, 1869.
Place/date of death: Egham, Surrey, January 20, 1935.
Place of memorial: Not known.
Town/county connections: Egham, Surrey.
Remarks: Served in RE from 1889 to 1922, including WWI. Married 1905 Margaret Eleanor McLeod. Youngest son of Lord Newburgh. Comsd December 11, 1889. Ret as Lt Col.

Citation
See citation for HABIB KHAN.

McDOWELL, George Patrick.

No. D/JX143268.
Rank: A/YoS.
Unit/Force: RN. HMS *Kandahar.*
Other decorations: Nil.
Date of deed: December 19, 1941.
Date of Gazette: June 9, 1942.
Place/date of birth: c1919.
Place/date of death: December 19, 1941.
Place of memorial: Plymouth Naval Memorial.
Town/county connections: Not known.
Remarks: Aged 22 at death. Son of Hugh and Elizabeth McDowell.

Citation
See citation for HAMBLY, C.

McHARDY, George.

Rank: T/Sub-Lt (A).
Unit/Force: RNVR. HMS *Illustrious.*
Other decorations: Nil.
Date of deed: March 12, 1944.
Date of Gazette: July 11, 1944.
Place/date of birth: c1922.
Place/date of death: March 12, 1944.

Place of memorial: Madras War Cemetery, India, Plot 6, Row A, Grave 2.
Town/county connections: East Finchley, Middlesex.
Remarks: Son of Robert and Janet McHardy of East Finchley and husband of Ingeborg.

Citation
See citation for GRIFFITHS, I. T.

MACKINNON, Neil

Rank: Lt.
Unit/Force: 14 HLI.
Other decorations: Nil.
Date of deed: May 27, 1916.
Date of Gazette: August 29, 1916.
Place/date of birth: Not known.
Place/date of death: Not known.
Place of memorial: Not known.
Town/county connections: Not known.
Remarks: Also served as officer on the General List and in the King's African Rifles. Does not appear to have received any medals for WWI service.

Citation
The KING has been graciously pleased to award the Decoration of the Albert Medal of the Second Class to Lieutenant Neil Mackinnon, 14th Battalion, Highland Light Infantry, in recognition of his gallantry in saving life at Blackdown on the 27th May last.

At bombing practice, one of the men under instruction failed to clear the parapet with his bomb, which rolled down into the mud at the bottom of the trench. Lieutenant Mackinnon at once sprang forward to seize the bomb, but was impeded by the thrower, who was endeavouring to get clear; he succeeded, however, in securing the bomb after groping for it in the mud, and in throwing it clear of the trench just before it exploded.

There were two men in the trench at the time besides Lieutenant Mackinnon and the thrower, and undoubtedly a serious accident was averted by the Lieutenant's courage and coolness.

McLAUGHLIN, James.

No. 201391.
Rank: PTE.
Unit/Force: 1/5 A&SH attached 157 Lt Trench Mor Bty.
Other decorations: Nil.
Date of deed: August 2, 1918.
Date of Gazette: October 15, 1918.
Place/date of birth: Not known.
Place/date of death: Not known.
Place of memorial: Not known.

Town/county connections: Govan.

Remarks: Discharged October 28, 1918. Lived at 35 Logie Street, Govan. Does not appear to have been awarded any other medals for WWI. Presented with his AM by His Majesty the King at Buckingham Palace on December 21, 1918.

Citation

The KING has been pleased to award the Albert Medal ... in recognition of gallantry displayed in saving life:-

On the 2nd August, 1918, Private McLaughlin, in the course of his duty, was examining a Stokes Mortar shell in a gunpit in which there were nine other men and about 150 Stokes shells, when the striker of the shell gave way and ignited the fuse, timed to explode in thirteen seconds. McLaughlin warned the others, and, taking the shell with him, ran from the pit by the narrow rear exit and along a sap which he had difficulty in reaching, as the ground was slippery. It was necessary to traverse this sap for some distance to ensure that the inevitable explosion did not affect the men or the shells in the gunpit. The shell exploded as McLaughlin was throwing it clear and blew off his hand. It is stated that his action undoubtedly saved the lives of all the men in the gunpit.

McMAHON, Maurice.

Rank: Lt (A/Lt-Cdr).

Unit/Force: RNR. HMS *Iphigenia*.

Other decorations: DSO (LG June 4, 1917). No citation.

Date of deed: November 8, 1916.

Date of Gazette: January 1, 1918.

Place/date of birth: Not known.

Place/date of death: Liverpool, October 25, 1919.

Place of memorial: Yew Tree RC Cemetery, Liverpool, Plot IIIA, Grave 14.

Town/county connections: Liverpool.

Remarks: On strength of HMS *President* at time of death. Husband of J. M. McMahon, 97 Ampthill Road, Aigburth, Liverpool. He was aged 43 at the time of his death.

Citation

The KING has been pleased to approve of the award of the Albert Medal to

Lieutenant (Acting Lieutenant-Commander) Maurice MacMahon, R.N.R., for gallantry in saving life at sea.

The following is the account of the services in respect of which the decoration has been conferred:-

On the 8th November, 1916, a series of fires and explosions occurred at Bakarista, Port of Archangel. After the merchant ships had been got away from the wharves, cries and moans were heard from the direction of a 100-ton floating crane moored between the S.S. "Earl of Forfar" and the quay. The "Earl of Forfar" was on fire fore and aft, and it was obvious that an attempt to save life must be accompanied by the greatest risk, the ship having explosives on board and the quay abreast it burning furiously with intermittent explosions from small arm ammunition.

Lieutenant-Commander MacMahon, without a moment's hesitation, volunteered to carry out rescue work, although other rescue parties considered that they had already done all that was humanly possible.

In order to reach the floating crane it was necessary to cross the "Earl of Forfar", the after part of which had blown up, whilst the forepart was on fire and the forecastle was a mass of smouldering debris. Hearing moans from under the debris of the forecastle, Lieutenant-Commander MacMahon, with the aid of the crew of a tug, cleared away the wreckage and discovered the man with one arm, one leg, and collar-bone fractured. This man was extricated and passed into the tug. Lieutenant-Commander MacMahon then proceeded on to the floating crane by means of a single plank and rescued from beneath the debris of the crane the carpenter of the "Earl of Forfar" and two Russian subjects, part of the crane's crew.

McQUE, William.

No. 2041.
Rank: CPL.
Unit/Force: 3 KRRC.
Other decorations: Nil.
Date of deed: March 17, 1891.
Date of Gazette: June 26, 1891.
Place/date of birth: Ilkeston, Derbyshire, June, 1866.
Place/date of death: Not known.
Place of memorial: Not known.
Town/county connections: Ilkeston, Derbyshire; Hythe, Kent.
Remarks: A collier on enlistment, described as 5' 7" tall, weighing 126 lbs, with hazel eyes, brown hair and a fresh complexion. Married to Lilian Carslake at Sandgate Parish Church, Hythe, Kent on December 11, 1895. Discharged at Mallow, Co Cork on June 30, 1905 with exemplary character and was employed by the Corps of Commissionaires. He was a Colour Sergeant on discharge with the Queen's South Africa Medal (clasps Belfast, Cape Colony, Orange Free State, Talana, Defence of Ladysmith, Laing's Nek), the LS&GC, RHS Medal and Italian Humane Society's Medal, MID in South Africa.

Citation
HER Majesty the Queen has been graciously pleased to confer the Decoration of the Albert Medal of the Second Class on -
WILLIAM SEED, Chief of Police, Gibraltar, and
WILLIAM McQUE, Corporal, 3rd Battalion, King's Royal Rifles.
The following is an account of the services in respect of which the Decoration has been conferred:-
On the occasion of the sinking of the British steam ship "Utopia", through collision, off Gibraltar, on the 17th March, 1891, when 551 lives were lost, a number of boats were put out by the vessels of the Channel Squadron to the assistance of the shipwrecked persons.
The launch of Her Majesty's ship "Immortalité", while engaged in the work of rescue, fouled her screw, became uncontrollable, and was beaten on to the shore near the breakwater, where she eventually became a total wreck. Two of her crew were drowned, two others swam safely ashore, and the remainder, with eight emigrants from the "Utopia", were rescued in an exhausted condition by officers and men of the Port Department and of the King's Royal Rifles.
Among the rescuers, WILLIAM SEED, Chief of Police, and Corporal WILLIAM McQUE, of the Rifles, particularly distinguished themselves.

Although the night was intensely dark, with a strong gale blowing and a strong current and heavy sea dashing on the break-water (which is a low line of jagged rocks, giving no foothold outside the wall of fortifications), they plunged into the waves with ropes, and, although washed back on the rocks, renewed their attempt until they succeeded in reaching the launch, which was eighty yards off shore, when the rescue was effected.

MADDOX, James Edward.

Rank: Lt.
Unit/Force: 24 Ches Regt.
Other decorations: MM (LG December 9, 1916).
Date of deed: September 27, 1918.
Date of Gazette: April 25, 1919.
Place/date of birth: Not known.
Place/date of death: Not known.
Place of memorial: Not known.
Town/county connections: Not known.
Remarks: Also awarded British War and Victory Medals. He also served as No. 10773 Pte (LCpl) in the Shropshire LI and became Sgt. Commissioned July 31, 1917. To France May 22,

Citation
The KING has been pleased to award the Albert Medal ... in recognition of gallantry displayed in saving life:-
Lieutenant James Edward Maddox, M.M., 24th Battalion, Cheshire Regiment.

On 27th September, 1918, Lieutenant Maddox was instructing a class in throwing live bombs. One of the men, after withdrawing the pin from a Mills No. V Mark 1 Grenade, accidentally dropped the grenade in the trench, and then apparently through fright, fell on it. Lieutenant Maddox, with great presence of mind, immediately pulled the man off the grenade, seized it, and threw it over the parapet, where it exploded almost immediately.

By his prompt and courageous action Lieutenant Maddox undoubtedly saved the man's life.

MAGNUSSEN, James Werner.

Rank: TPR.
Unit/Force: NZMR.
Other decorations: Nil.
Date of deed: May 4, 1917.
Date of Gazette: March 8, 1918.
Place/date of birth: Gíteborg, Sweden, January 12, 1892.
Place/date of death: Off Italian coast, May 4, 1917.
Place of memorial: Not known.
Town/county connections: Gíteborg, Sweden; Auckland, NewZealand.
Remarks: Not a British subject at the time of his death. Resident in Auckland when

enlisted for service in WWI. Also awarded 1914-15 Star, British War and Victory Medals. The first NZ Albert Medallist. On board HMT *Transylvania* when she was torpedoed in the Mediterranean.

Citation

The KING has been graciously pleased to award the Decoration of the Albert Medal in recognition of the gallant action of Trooper James Werner Magnusson, New Zealand Mounted Rifles, in saving life on the occasion of the loss of a Transport.

Magnusson, who was on the deck of the Transport, saw an injured soldier struggling in the water, and immediately dived overboard, although there was a very rough sea, swam to his assistance, and succeeded in placing him in a boat. Magnussen (sic) then returned to the sinking ship and rejoined his unit. His life was lost.

P. MALCOLM
Source: Strand Magazine

MALCOLM, Pulteney.

Rank: Lt.
Unit/Force: 4 GR.
Other decorations: CBE (1932), DSO (LG September 2, 1902),MVO (1913).
Date of deed: June 10, 1887.
Date of Gazette: September 25, 1888.
Place/date of birth: August 16, 1861.
Place/date of death: April 20, 1940.
Place of memorial: Not known.
Town/county connections: Chester, Cheshire.
Remarks: Son of Gen Sir George Malcolm GCB, Bombay Army. Educated Summerfields, Oxford; Burney's, Gosport; Wellington College and Sandhurst. Entered army Aug 11, 1880 (2 Bn RF at Candahar). Major, Aug 11, 1900. Transferred to IA 1886 and posted to 2/4 GR. Served India until retirement on August 11, 1904. Head Constable Kingston-upon-Hull, 1904-10 and Chief Constable of Cheshire from 1910. Served WWI on Staff of New Armies. Hon Lt Col May 29, 1917. Married in 1888 Emily, eldest daughter of T. R. Bowen. Their only surviving child, Capt Pulteney Malcolm, commanding King's Coy Gren Gds, was KIA in France on August 25, 1918. He was also awarded the 1854 (bars Chin Lushai 1889-90), IGS 1895 (Rel of Chitral 1895, Tirah 1897-8, Waz 1901-02), 1914-15 Star, British War and Victory Medals (MID). He was mentioned in despatches four times in his career.

Citation

THE Queen has been graciously pleased to confer the "Albert Medal of the Second Class" upon Lieutenant Pulteney Malcolm, 4th Goorkha Regiment, in recognition of the conspicuous gallantry displayed by him on the 10th June, 1887, in attempting to save the life of a comrade who had fallen over a precipice near Dalhousie, East India.

MANGAL SAIN.

Rank: TPTR.
Unit/Force: 2 Indian Lancers (Gardner's Horse), IA.
Other decorations: Nil.
Date of deed: March 15, 1919.
Date of Gazette: July 11, 1919.
Place/date of birth: Not known.
Place/date of death: Not known.
Place of memorial: Not known.
Town/county connections: Not known.
Remarks: Although this rescue was launched from on shore, a Sea medal was awarded.

Citation

The KING has been graciously pleased to confer the Decoration of the Albert Medal upon Trumpeter Mangal Sain, 2nd Lancers, Indian Army.

On the 15th March last, while some Turkish prisoners-of-war were bathing at Beirut under a guard of British soldiers, one of them got into difficulties. Two members of the escort went to his assistance but failed to rescue him. On hearing of the man's danger, Mangal Sain at once swam out through the surf and eventually with great difficulty brought him ashore.

Shortly afterwards two British soldiers who were bathing were seen to have been caught in a current and to be in danger of drowning, and Mangal Sain, although still exhausted on account of his rescue of the first man, again swam out to the assistance of the two others. He succeeded in bringing one man ashore, and, although he was completely done up, he immediately started without hesitation to the rescue of the other soldier. He was, however, called back, as it was seen that the man had drifted so far out that it was impossible to save him.

Both men who were rescued were in the last state of collapse and must inevitably have been drowned had it not been for the gallantry displayed by Mangal Sain, who incurred great risk in rendering the services, owing to the violent surf and the dangerous currents beyond.

K. F. MARIEN
Source: Family

MARIEN, Kerry Francis.

Rank: Mid.
Unit/Force: RAN. HMAS *Voyager*.
Other decorations: Nil.
Date of deed: February 10, 1964.
Date of Gazette: March 19, 1965.
Place/date of birth: Wyong, NSW, Australia, May 7, 1944.
Place/date of death: Off Nowra, NSW, Australia, February 10,
Place of memorial: Not known.
Town/county connections: Wyong, NSW, Australia.
Remarks: Eldest of five sons. Father a journalist.

Educated Marist Brothers' College, Kogarah, NSW. Joined HMAS *Cresswell* 1960. Awarded Colours for tennis.

Citation
NOTE: As with EM (E) Condon (q.v.), there is no citation for this award in the London Gazette. The AM was awarded posthumously for attempting to save his shipmates after the collision between HMAS Voyager and HMAS Melbourne.

MARSHALL, Frederick George.

No. 290850.
Rank: Mech.
Unit/Force: RN. HMS *Vengeance.*
Other decorations: Nil.
Date of deed: February 27, 1915.
Date of Gazette: Not gazetted. Approved by HMK May 13, 1915.
Place/date of birth: Not known.
Place/date of death: Not known.
Place of memorial: Not known.
Town/county connections: Not known.
Remarks: There is evidence from Royal Mint records that this medal was ordered and supplied. Presented by His Majesty the King at Buckingham Palace on October 1, 1915.

Citation
On the evening of February 27th, 1915, Mechanicien Marshall was in charge of the stokehold of HMS Vengeance when it was filled with dense clouds of soot and steam, flinging him across the stokehold so that only with difficulty could he find his way to a ladder leading to the upper deck.

He helped two men up the ladder and twice endeavoured with a sponge in his mouth to reach the stop valve, without success owing to smoke, steam and heat. To protect himself against these, he emptied a sack of potatoes and put it across his mouth and nose but this was not enough and he had to put the sack over his head and shoulders. Thus blindfolded, with the utmost difficulty, he forced his way through the screen door, which was opened by stokers but it was blown to by the great weight of steam from inside. He went down a short ladder and groped along a grating 17 feet long to the stop valve of the injured boiler which he promptly shut off, saving the men remaining in the stokehold.

MARSHALL-A'DEANE, Walter Roger.

Rank: Cdr.
Unit/Force: RN. HMS *Greyhound.*
Other decorations: DSO (LG July 8, 1941), DSC (LG July 11, 1940). No citation for either.
Date of deed: May 22, 1941.
Date of Gazette: November 4, 1941.
Place/date of birth: Not known.

W. G. MARSHALL-A'DEANE
Source: S. Siddall Esq.

Place/date of death: May 22, 1941.
Place of memorial: Portsmouth Naval Memorial, Panel 45, Column 1.
Town/county connections: Not known.
Remarks: Son of Richard and Gertrude E. Marshall. Husband of a Miss A'Dean of New Zealand. Also held 1939-45, Atlantic and Africa Stars and War Medal.

Citation

The Albert Medal (Posthumous).
Commander Walter Roger Marshall-A'Deane, D.S.O., D.S.C., Royal Navy.

When his ship, H.M.S. Greyhound, was bombed and sunk, Commander Marshall-A'Deane was among the survivors picked up by H.M.S. Kandahar. Later in the day H.M.S. Fiji was sunk and H.M.S. Kandahar again went to the rescue. Commander Marshall-A'Deane, despite the ordeal he had already been through that day, dived overboard in the gathering darkness to rescue the men in the water. He was not seen again.

This was the last proof of his great gallantry. Commander Marshall-A'Deane had already in this war been appointed Companion of the Distinguished Service Order, won the Distinguished Service Cross, and twice been mentioned in Despatches.

MATTISON, Albert Charles.

Rank: WO (Bo'sun).
Unit/Force: RCN. HMCS *Niobe*.
Other decorations: Nil.
Date of deed: December 6, 1917.
Date of Gazette: February 18, 1919.
Place/date of birth: Not known.
Place/date of death: December 6, 1917.
Place of memorial: Halifax Memorial, Nova Scotia.
Town/county connections: Not known.
Remarks: Enlisted August 24, 1914. Served Canada and on the high seas. Also awarded 1914-15 Star, British War and Victory Medals.

Citation
See Citation for BEARD, E. E.

MEREDITH, William Herbert.

No. 15441.
Rank: LCPL.
Unit/Force: 4 Gren Gds.
Other decorations: Nil.
Date of deed: November 5, 1918.
Date of Gazette: February 4, 1919.
Place/date of birth: Lye, Nr Stourbridge, Worcs, December 1892.
Place/date of death: Not known.
Place of memorial: Not known.
Town/county connections: Stourbridge, Worcs; Battersea, London.
Remarks: Enlisted in Worcestershire Regt before transferring to Gren Gds. Served France and Flanders and awarded 1914 Star and Bar, British War and Victory Medals and Silver War Badge. Discharged 8th August, 1918.

Citation
The KING has been pleased to award the Albert Medal…in recognition of gallantry in saving life:- Lance-Corporal William Herbert Meredith, late of the Grenadier Guards.

On the 5th November, 1916, Lance-Corporal Meredith was instructing a class in the firing of live rifle grenades. One of the party fired a grenade, but the charge was insufficient to project the grenade, which fell back, with the ignited fuze, into the barrel of the rifle. The man held on to the rifle, instead of throwing it down, whereupon Meredith threw himself forward in front of the man and attempted to remove the grenade, but it exploded, blowing off three fingers of his right hand and wounding him in other places.

Meredith received the full force of the explosion, and undoubtedly saved the other man, who was only slightly wounded, from severe injury or death.

MILLAR, Charles Davie.

No. 218811.
Rank: LS.
Unit/Force: RN. HMS P.C. 51.
Other decorations: Nil.
Date of deed: June 29, 1918.
Date of Gazette: October 11, 1918.
Place/date of birth: Not known.
Place/date of death: Not known.
Place of memorial: Not known.
Town/county connections: Not known.
Remarks: Also awarded 1914-15 Star, British War and Victory Medals, 1939-45 and Atlantic Stars, Defence, War, RFR LS&GC and Messina Earthquake Medals.

Citation

The KING has been graciously pleased to approve the award of the Albert Medal to
Charles Davie Millar, Leading Seaman, O.N. 218811, in recognition of his gallantry in the
following circumstances:-

On the 29th June, 1918, an outbreak of fire occurred on board Motor Launch No. 483 whilst
refuelling alongside the jetty at Pembroke Dock, the fire being caused by the ignition of an
overflow of petrol from the hose.

Leading Seaman Millar, H.M.S. "P.C. 51", who was walking up and down the forecastle of
his ship, on seeing the flames break out on the upper deck of the motor launch, immediately slid
over the bows of his craft on to the motor launch, rushed aft, and removed the primers of the
depth charges. He then forced his way through the flames and kicked the hose overboard, getting
his clothes ignited as he did so. Having extinguished his burning clothing by jumping
overboard, he climbed inboard again and assisted in getting the motor launch in tow.

This man displayed initiative and disregard of danger, and by his prompt action he probably
averted a serious accident. Had the depth charges detonated, very great damage would have been
done and lives undoubtedly lost.

R. A. J. MONTGOMERIE
Source: OMRS Journal

MONTGOMERIE, Robert James Archibald.

Rank: A/Sub-Lt.
Unit/Force: RN. HMS *Immortalité*.
Other decorations: CB (1892), CMG (1904), CVO (1907).
Date of deed: April 6, 1877.
Date of Gazette: June 19, 1877.
Place/date of birth: September 11, 1855.
Place/date of death: September 1, 1908.
Place of memorial: Not known.
Town/county connections: Not known.
Remarks: Entered RN aged 14 and promoted Acting Sub-Lieut September 20, 1875. Served in Egyptian and West African campaigns. ADC to KEVII in 1904. Promoted Rear Admiral August 6, 1907. Also awarded Egypt Medal 1882 (bars Tel-el-Kebir, Nile 1884-85), E&W Africa Medal (bar Witu 1890), Khedive's Star 1882, RHS Silver Medal and Stanhope Gold Medal (both for the rescue which won him the AM). Married Alethe Marian Charrington August 18, 1866.

Citation

THE Queen has been graciously pleased to confer the Albert Medal of the Second Class on:-
Acting Sub-Lieutenant ROBERT JAMES ARCHIBALD MONTGOMERIE, R.N., of Her
Majesty's Ship "Immortalité".

The following is an account of the Act in respect of which the decoration has been conferred:-
At 3.10 on the morning of the 6th April, 1877, the "Immortalité", being under all plain sail,

moving 4¹/₂ knots with the wind, two points abaft the starboard beam, the port gangway look-out reported a man overboard, who proved to be Thomas Hocken. Mr MONTGOMERIE, who was on the bridge, working a star meridian altitude at the chart table, on hearing the cry, ran over to the lee side, saw the man in the water, and jumped after him. He made for Hocken, asking if he could swim, to which Hocken answered, "Yes, sir," but did not seem to be moving vigorously. Mr. MONTGOMERIE then got hold of him, hauled him on his back, and towed him to where he (MONTGOMERIE) supposed the life-buoy would be, but seeing no relief, he told Hocken to keep himself afloat while he took his clothes off. While he was in the act of doing so, Hocken, evidently sinking, caught hold of him by the legs, and dragged him down a considerable depth. Mr. MONTGOMERIE, however, succeeded in getting clear, and swam to the surface, bringing the drowning man with him. Hocken was now insensible, and too great a weight to support any longer; and finding that his only chance of saving himself was to leave Hocken, Mr. MONTGOMERIE reluctantly gave up the hope of saving him, and struck out for the ship. In the meantime the ship's course was stopped, and two boats were lowered, by one of which Mr. MONTGOMERIE was picked up. The latitudes in which the occurrence took place abound with sharks; and though there was a half-moon, the sea was sufficiently disturbed to render small objects, even boats, difficult to discern. Had not Mr. MONTGOMERIE been a most powerful swimmer, he would have had little chance of life.

MORGAN, William Marychurch.

Rank: 2 Lt.
Unit/Force: 15 RWF.
Other decorations: MC (LG November 25, 1916).
Date of deed: February 14, 1916.
Date of Gazette: May 19, 1916.
Place/date of birth: Not known.
Place/date of death: Jeffreston, Nr Tenby, S. Wales, October 23, 1944.
Place of memorial: Jeffreston Churchyard.
Town/county connections: Jeffreston, Tenby, S. Wales.
Remarks: Son of Rev. W. Morgan of Jeffreston. Served as Pte 1553 in 1 HAC. To France September 18, 1914. Also awarded 1914 Star and bar, British War and Victory Medals. Served WWII reaching rank of Lt Col in IA. Commissioned March 13, 1915.

Citation
The KING has been graciously pleased to award the Decoration of the Albert Medal to the undermentioned Officer ... in recognition of (his) gallantry in saving life:-
Albert Medal of the Second Class.
Second Lieutenant William Marychurch Morgan, 15th Battalion, Royal Welsh Fusiliers.

On the 14th February, 1916, during grenade instruction in a trench, a man let fall a grenade, which sank in the mud, so that only the smoke from the burning fuse could be seen. Lieutenant Morgan, who was outside the danger zone, at once sprang forward and groped in the mud for the grenade. The difficulty of finding it added greatly to the danger. He picked up the grenade and threw it over the parapet just in time, thereby saving several men from death or serious injury.

NEALE, John.

Rank: Lt.
Unit/Force: RNVR.
Other decorations: Nil.
Date of deed: August 25, 1916.
Date of Gazette: January 25, 1918.
Place/date of birth: Not known.
Place/date of death: Not known.
Place of memorial: Not known.
Town/county connections: Not known.
Remarks: He came from Oxshott, Surrey. AM presented by His Majesty the King at Buckingham Palace on April 6, 1918.

Citation
The KING has been pleased to award the Decoration of the Albert Medal to Lieutenant John Neale, Royal Naval Volunteer Reserve, in recognition of his gallantry in saving life at Esher in August, 1916. The circumstances are as follows:-

On the 25th August, 1916, Lieutenant Neale was conducting certain experiments which involved the projection from a Stokes Mortar of a tube containing flare powder. An accident occurred rendering imminent the explosion of the tube before leaving the mortar which would almost certainly have resulted in the bursting of the mortar with loss of life to bystanders. Lieutenant Neale, in order to safeguard the lives of the working party, at once attempted to lift the tube from the mortar. It exploded while he was doing so with the result that he was severely injured, but owing to the fact that he had partly withdrawn the tube from the mortar no injury was caused to others.

NEILSON, William.

Rank: 2 Lt (T/Capt).
Unit/Force: 7 Cameronians, attached 10 KRRC.
Other decorations: Nil.
Date of deed: February 24, 1917.
Date of Gazette: August 27, 1918.
Place/date of birth: Not known.
Place/date of death: November 21, 1917.
Place of memorial: Cambrai Memorial, France, Panel 5.
Town/county connections: Maryhill, Glasgow.
Remarks: Also awarded British War and Victory Medals. His AM was presented to his widow, Mrs Rosalie Neilson of Blacklands, Maryhill, Glasgow, by His Majesty the King at Buckingham Palace on November 11, 1918.

Citation
The KING has been pleased to award the Albert Medal ... in recognition of gallantry displayed in saving life in France:-

Second Lieutenant (temporary Captain) William Neilson, 7th Battalion, Scottish Rifles, attached 10th Battalion, King's Royal Rifle Corps.

On the 24th February, 1917, Captain Neilson was superintending men of his company at grenade-throwing at a Brigade Grenade School in France. A man threw a grenade from a trench while Captain Neilson was standing out of the trench behind him. The man slipped in the mud, and the grenade fell in the trench, in which several other men were standing. Captain Neilson jumped down, picked up the grenade out of the mud, and threw it over the parapet. The grenade exploded just after leaving his hand, and wounded him slightly in several places. By his promptitude and courage he undoubtedly saved his men from injury.

Captain Neilson died of his wounds in November, 1917.

NEVITT, Albert.

Rank: Lt.
Unit/Force: 62 Res Bn RWF.
Other decorations: MC (LG May 16, 1916).
Date of deed: September 4 and 24, 1916.
Date of Gazette: January 4, 1918.
Place/date of birth: Not known.
Place/date of death: Not known.
Town/county connections: Not known.
Remarks: To France prior to March 21, 1916. Also awarded British War and Victory Medals. Also served as Pte 16225 in RWF and Capt in King's Own Royal Lancaster Regt (Adjt 8 Service Bn). Presented with AM by His Majesty the King at Buckingham Palace on March 9, 1918.

Citation

The KING has been graciously pleased to award the Albert Medal to the undermentioned Officer ... in recognition of (his) gallantry in saving life:-

Lieutenant Albert Nevitt, M.C., Royal Welsh Fusiliers.

On the 4th September, 1916, bombing instruction was taking place in a trench occupied by Lieutenant (then Second Lieutenant) Nevitt, another officer, and two men. One of the men threw a bomb which hit the parapet, and fell back into the trench, where it was deeply embedded in mud and water. Lieutenant Nevitt at once groped for the bomb. He failed to find it at the first attempt, but made a second and successful attempt, seized the bomb, and threw it over the parapet, where it at once exploded.

On the 24th September, 1916, bombing instruction was taking place under the command of Lieutenant Nevitt. Another officer and three men were present in the trench. A bomb fell back from the parapet into the trench, whereupon the men rushed for the entrance, nearly knocking Lieutenant Nevitt down. In the confusion Lieutenant Nevitt lost sight of the bomb, but he searched for it, and, having found it, threw it clear, when it at once exploded. Only one of the men had succeeded in escaping from the trench when the bomb exploded.

On both occasions Lieutenant Nevitt's courage and presence of mind undoubtedly saved the lives of others.

C. L. N. NEWALL

NEWALL, *Cyril Louis Norton.*

Rank: Maj.
Unit/Force: 2 GR att RFC.
Other decorations: GCB (1938), OM (1940), CBE (1919).
Date of deed: January 3, 1916.
Date of Gazette: May 19, 1916.
Place/date of birth: February 15, 1886.
Place/date of death: November 30, 1963.
Place of memorial: Not known.

Town/county connections: Clifton-on-Dunsmore, Warwickshire.
Remarks: Born February 15, 1886. Son of Lt Col William Potter Newall IA. Educated Bedford School and Sandhurst. Commissioned R Warwickshire Regt 1905. Transferred to 2 Gurkhas 1909. To RFC in 1914 and RAF in 1919. Promoted Marshal of the RAF 1940 and was Governor-General of NZ from 1941-46. Married 1925 Olive Tennyson Foster; 1 son, 2 daughters. Also held K St J, IGS 1908 (NWF 1908), 1914-15 Star, British War and Victory Medals (MID), War Medal 1939-45, NZ War Service Medal, Jubilee 1935, Coronation 1937, Coronation 1953, Légion d'Honneur (Officier), Order of Crown of Italy (Officer), Order of Leopold (Officer), Croix de Guerre (Belgium). Created 1st Baron Newall of Clifton-on-Dunsmoor.

Citation

Albert Medal of the First Class.
Major Cyril Louis Norton Newall, 2nd Gurkha Rifles (attached to the Royal Flying Corps).
See citation for HEARNE, H.

NICHOLL, Thomas.

No. 19081.
Rank: SGT (FLT SGT)
Unit/Force: Royal Flying Corps. 101 Sqn RFC.
Other decorations: Nil.
Date of deed: February 26, 1918.
Date of Gazette: June 7, 1918.
Place/date of birth: Not known.
Place/date of death: Not known.
Place of memorial: Not known.
Town/county connections: Not known.
Remarks:

Citation
The KING has been pleased to award the Albert Medal to Sergeant (Flight-Sergeant) Thomas Nicholl, Royal Flying Corps, in recog-nition of an act of gallantry which he performed in France on the 26th February, 1918, under the following circumstances:-

Two bombs exploded under an aeroplane, burning the machine entirely and causing considerable loss of life. Owing to the explosion a phosphorous bomb attached to another machine standing near to it was ignited. Flight-Sergeant Nicholl with great presence of mind, and regardless of the danger to himself, unhooked the burning bomb and carried it to a place of safety. By his prompt action Flight-Sergeant Nicholl, whose hands were badly burned, saved the second machine and prevented further serious damage and loss of life which would probably have been caused.

NUNN, Edward.

No. 15703.
Rank: AB.
Unit/Force: RN. HMS *Trident.*
Other decorations: Nil.
Date of deed: September 16, 1918.
Date of Gazette: January 31, 1919.
Place/date of birth: Not known.
Place/date of death: Not known.
Place of memorial: Not known.
Town/county connections: Not known.
Remarks:

Citation
See citation for BELBEN, G. D.

OATLEY, George.

Rank: Gunner's Mate.
Unit/Force: RN.
Other decorations: Nil.
Date of deed: February 16, 1880.
Date pof Gazette: April 30, 1880.
Place/date of birth: London, October 29, 1842.
Place/date of death: 1933.
Place of memorial: Not known.
Town/county connections: London.
Remarks: Joined RN as a Boy on June 3, 1859. Promoted PO 1st Class December 12, 1876 and went to Coastguard. To pension September 19, 1883. Also held China Medal '57, LS&GC (RN), RHS Bronze Medal, Lloyd's Medal for Bravery in Bronze and a Swedish Gold Medal for Saving Life.

Citation
HER Majesty the Queen has been graciously pleased to confer the "Albert Medal of the Second Class" on -
MR. GEORGE OATLEY, Gunner's Mate in the Royal Navy, and Drill Instructor of the Royal Naval Reserve at Peterhead.
The following is an account of the services in respect of which the decoration has been conferred:-
On Monday, the 16th February, during a very heavy gale, a vessel, which proved to be the Swedish schooner "Augusta", was observed by the Coast Guard at Peterhead showing signals of distress and labouring heavily in the trough of the sea.
On reaching the opening of the Peterhead South Bay, the vessel headed for the land. As it was clear that she would come ashore, the life saving apparatus was at once started, but by the time

G. OATLEY
Source: B. Delahunt

it reached the beach, the vessel had struck on the rocks near Boddam, about four miles south of Peterhead, and drifted towards the shore, where she lay exposed to all the fury of the gale. Two rockets were fired, and the second carried the line over the stern of the vessel, but the crew were quite ignorant of the working of the apparatus and were unable to avail themselves of the assistance. OATLEY thereupon took off his clothes and swimming through the breakers and broken water, reached the smooth water between the ship and the rocks, and was pulled on board by a rope thrown to him. He then proceeded to haul in the line and fix it to the rigging, after which the crew, five in number, were one by one drawn ashore. OATLEY, who contrary to the captain's wishes, was the last to leave the ship, was landed benumbed with cold and fatigue, and cut and bleeding from contact with the rocks. OATLEY is not of a strong constitution and was invalided five years ago with phthisis.

PAFFETT, Frederick.

Rank: Ch Sto.
Unit/Force: RN. HMS *Daring*.
Other decorations: Nil.
Date of deed: January 10, 1901.
Date of Gazette: January 20, 1903.
Place/date of birth: Not known.
Place/date of death: Not known.
Place of memorial: Not known.
Town/county connections: Not known.

Citation
HIS MAJESTY the KING has been graciously pleased to confer the decoration of the Albert Medal of the Second Class on Frederick Paffett, Chief Stoker, R.N., dated the 17th February, 1902.

The following is the account of the services in respect of which the decoration has been conferred:-

On the evening of June 10th, 1901, at about 9.30, His Majesty's ship "Daring", torpedo boat destroyer, was entering Portsmouth Harbour under easy steam, when an explosion suddenly took place in the after stokehold. A tube was blown out of the lower barrel of No. 2 boiler and the whole stokehold was filled with steam.

At the time of the accident there were five men in the stokehold - Chief Stoker Paffett and four stokers. Owing to the volume of steam it was impossible for them to see each other, but two men, though scalded and partly overcome by the great heat, managed to get up the ladder to the deck. Paffett, whose place of duty as Chief Stoker gave him the best opportunities of escape, was standing, when the accident occurred, with his hand on the port side ladder. He remained, however, in the stokehold and endeavoured to avert the consequences of the explosion in the only way possible, namely, by opening the steam valve of the starboard fan. With this object he went deliberately across the hold, groping for the valve which he could not see, the steam from the boiler striking full on his left arm which was shielding his face. But he found it impossible to reach the valve and it was only with difficulty that he was able to regain the ladder, badly scalded and almost unconscious. As he mounted the ladder he was able to save the life of Stoker Elliott, who was slipping down from above in a fainting condition. Paffett being a very powerful man, raised him on his left shoulder and lifted him to the deck; then, reaching the deck himself, aided by those above, he fell down completely overcome. He was much disfigured by burns and scalds; and has almost lost the use of his left arm.

PARGITER, Henry.

Rank: Sub-Cdr.
Unit/Force: IOD. Ferozepore Arsenal.
Other decorations: Nil.
Date of deed: August 31, 1906.
Date of Gazette: September 26, 1911.
Place/date of birth: Hampstead, London, January 17, 1871.
Place/date of death: Basra, Mesopotamia, September 29, 1916.
Place of memorial: War Cemetery, Basra, Mesopotamia. Plot III, Row N, Grave 16.
Town/county connections: Hampstead, London.
Remarks: Son of Joseph Pargiter. Employed as a baker prior to enlistment on April 17, 1889 as No. 72641 Dvr RA. Served UK and India before transferring to Bengal Unattached List as Sgt on April 11, 1897. Appointed Sub-Cdr November 7, 1904 and Cdr September 1, 1906. Married Maud Stanis (née Loonam) at Dinapore September 20, 1898. 1 son (died in infancy), 2 daughters. He died of cholera WOAS. Also awarded British War, Victory, Delhi Durbar and LS&GC Medals. His AM and other medals were stolen from his quarters in Kirkee when he was on leave from December 8-15, 1914. A duplicate was issued on June 3, 1915, at a cost of £2.5.0 (£2.25). He was presented with his AM at the Delhi Durbar by His Majesty the King on December 13, 1911.

Citation
See citation for ANDERSON, C. A.

PETHEBRIDGE, Charles Alexander.

No. W.2164.
Rank: Sto 2.
Unit/Force: RANR. HMAS Perth.
Other decorations: Nil.
Date of deed: September 22, 1944.
Date of Gazette: July 17, 1945.
Place/date of birth: Northcote, Victoria, Australia, March 23, 1923.
Place/date of death: 100m NE of Paracel Is, South China Sea, September 22, 1944.
Place of memorial: Plymouth War Memorial, Panel 92, Col 3.
Town/county connections: Northcote, Victoria, Australia.
Remarks: Son of J. A. and S. Pethebridge. Joined RANR at Williamstown Port Div on June 30, 1941. Also awarded 1939- 45 and Pacific Stars, War and Australia Service Medals. Only RANR member ever to win AM.

Citation
The KING has been graciously pleased to approve the following award:-
Albert Medal in Bronze (Posthumous).
Stoker Second Class Charles Alexander PETHEBRIDGE, R.A.N.R., W.2164.

For gallantry in saving life at sea at the cost of his own.

When the ship on which he was a passenger was torpedoed, Stoker Pethebridge got away with twenty others on a raft. During the ordeal which followed Pethebridge left this raft on several occasions, without a life-belt, to go to the help of those who through physical weaknesses could not prevent themselves from slipping into the sea,

The strain of this merciful work upon himself was such that he could not carry on, and during the night which followed the sinking of the ship, he himself disappeared.

PICKERSGILL, Henry.

No. 4368.
Rank: CSGT.
Unit/Force: 1 SG.
Other decorations: Nil.
Date of deed: November 12, 1890.
Date of Gazette: December 23, 1890.
Place/date of birth: Dudley, Staffordshire, c April, 1859.
Place/date of death: Not known.
Place of memorial: Not known.
Town/county connections: Dudley, Staffs; King's Norton, Birmingham.
Remarks: Baker and confectioner on enlistment into Scots Guards at Wednesbury, Staffs, on April 1, 1878. Married twice; (1) Elizabeth (née Burden) (decd) August 1, 1885 and (2) Annie May (née Harris) January 20, 1897. Served with Scots Guards till November 30, 1891 and then went to Royal Scots as Sgt Maj until discharge at Glencorse on March 31, 1908. Went to live at 12 Northfield Rd, King's Norton on discharge. Also awarded Egypt Medal 1882 (Clasps Tel-el-Kebir, Abu Klea, The Nile 1884-85), Khedive's Star and LS&GC. Noted for the MSM but it is not known whether he ever received it.

Citation
See citation for DAVIS, D.T.

PLACE, Alfred.

No. Dev/J.3080.
Rank: PO.
Unit/Force: RN.
Other decorations: Nil.
Date of deed: June 16, 1916.
Date of Gazette: January 1, 1918.
Place/date of birth: Not known.
Place/date of death: Blandford, Dorset, June 16, 1916.
Place of memorial: Leeds Hunslet Old Cemetery, Row U, Grave 2967.
Town/county connections: Not known.
Remarks: Also awarded 1914-15 Star, British War and Victory Medals.

A. PLACE
Source: Leeds Museum

Citation

The KING has been graciously pleased to award the Decoration of the Albert Medal in recognition of the gallantry of Petty Officer Alfred Place, late of the Royal Navy. The circumstances are as follows:-

At Blandford, on the 16th June, 1916, during grenade practice, a live bomb thrown by one of the men under instruction fell back into the trench. Petty Officer Place rushed forward, pulled back two men who were in front of him and attempted to reach the grenade with the intention of throwing it over the parapet. Unfortunately the bomb exploded before he could reach it and inflicted fatal injuries. By his coolness and self sacrifice Petty Officer Place undoubtedly saved the lives of three other men.

POOLEY, Ernest A.

No. MB.1627.
Rank: Ch Motor Mech.
Unit/Force: RNVR. HMML 431.
Other decorations: Nil.
Date of deed: April 22, 1917.
Date of Gazette: September 4, 1917.
Place/date of birth: Not known.
Place/date of death: Not known.
Place of memorial: Not known.
Town/county connections: Not known.

Citation

The KING has been graciously pleased to confer the Decoration of the Albert Medal on:-
Ernest A. Pooley, Chief Motor Mechanic, M.B.1627.
Herbert Powley, Deckhand, S.D.1193.
The following is an account of the services in respect of which the Decoration has been conferred:-

On the 22nd April, 1917, a violent explosion occurred on board H.M. Motor Launch 431 while she was lying alongside the jetty at the Base.

The after part of the vessel was wrecked, and it at once became known that Sub-Lieutenant Charles W. Nash, R.N.V.R., was buried beneath the wreckage.

Chief Motor Mechanic Pooley and Deckhand Powley, who were on board their own vessel lying at the jetty some fifty yards astern, immediately hurried to the motor launch, which was by that time burning fiercely. The flames were every instant drawing nearer to the spot where Sub-Lieutenant Nash lay buried, and it was clear that there was imminent danger of the after petrol tanks exploding at any moment. Regardless of the fact that this would mean certain death to them, Powley and Pooley jumped on board the vessel and succeeded in extricating Sub-Lieutenant Nash from beneath the wreckage and carrying him to the jetty. As they were leaving the boat the whole of the after part burst into flames, and, in all probability, had they been delayed for another thirty seconds all three would have perished.

Deckhand Powley, who led the way on board the burning motor launch, had subsequently to be sent to hospital suffering from the effects of fumes.

POWLEY, Herbert.

No. S.D.1193.
Rank: Deckhand.
Unit/Force: RNR. HMML 431.
Other decorations: Nil.
Date of deed: April 22, 1917.
Date of Gazette: September 4, 1917.
Place/date of birth: Not known.

Place/date of death: Not known.
Place of memorial: Not known.
Town/county connections: Not known.
Remarks:

Citation
See citation for POOLEY, E. A.

PURKIS, Alfred Edwin.

Rank: Sub-Cdr.
Unit/Force: IOD. Hyderabad Fort.
Other decorations: Nil.
Date of deed: April 7 & 15, 1906.
Date of Gazette: September 26, 1911.
Place/date of birth: October 31, 1876.
Place/date of death: Not known.
Place of memorial: Not known.
Town/county connections: Not known.
Remarks: Enlisted RA March 31, 1892. Transferred to Indian Unattached List June 16, 1902. Served WWI Mesopotamia 1917-19. Cdr July 12, 1917. Retired August 2, 1921. Also awarded British War, Delhi Durbar 1911 and LS&GC Medals.

Citation
The KING has been pleased to approve of (the) Albert Medal of the First Class being conferred upon the undermentioned ... in recognition of (his) gallantry in saving life on the occasion of fires caused by explosions of cordite at Hyderabad (Sind) ... in the year 1906:-
HYDERABAD EXPLOSIONS.
Albert Medal of the First Class.
Sub-Conductor Alfred Edwin Purkis.

On the 7th of April, 1906, and again on the 15th April, the Cordite Magazine at Hyderabad caught fire. On the first occasion Sub-Conductor Purkis, acting on his own initiative, entered the magazine with his Lascars while smoke was still issuing from the building, and, by pouring water on the smouldering cases of cordite, extinguished the fire. Had he not succeeded in so doing the loss of life, both in the Fort (which was fully occupied at the time) and in the City (the population, some 138,000 in number, not having received warning of the danger), must have been very serious. On the second occasion the senior Officer ordered the evacuation of the Fort, and Purkis was the last person to leave after having done evrything in his power to avert the explosion. Notwithstanding that the Fort was cleared and the City warned, lives were lost when the second fire occurred. On each occasion both gunpowder and cordite were involved.

PYSDEN, Edmund John.

No. O.N.271312.
Rank: Art Engr.
Unit/Force: RN. HMS *Sandhurst.*
Other decorations: Nil.
Date of deed: February 27, 1917.
Date of Gazette: September 4, 1917.
Place/date of birth: Sheerness, Kent, October 28, 1881.
Place/date of death: Not known.
Place of memorial: Not known.
Town/county connections: Sheerness, Kent.
Remarks: Enlisted RN October 15, 1903. Served WWI and promoted Acting Mate (E) June 7, 1917. Subsequently commissioned and retired as Lt Cdr in 1926.

Citation
The KING has been graciously pleased to confer the Decoration of the Albert Medal on Artificer Engineer (now Acting Mate (E)) Edmund John Pysden,
The following is the account of the services in respect of which the Decoration has been conferred:-
On the morning of the 27th February, 1917, one of the auxiliary stop valves in one of H.M. Ships accidentally burst, the boiler room immediately becoming filled with dense steam. In spite of the danger of burning and suffocation from steam, and of the fact that it was impossible to draw fires or at once to lift the safety valves, which rendered the possibility of a second and even worse accident highly probable, Mr Edmund John Pysden, Artificer Engineer, R.N., made several gallant attempts to enter the stokehold, and succeeded in bringing out two men who were lying insensible on the stokehold plates, and helped to bring out others. Several of the survivors would undoubtedly have lost their lives but for the rescues effected by this officer and others. Mr Pysden also eventually succeeded in opening the safety valve, which relieved the immediate danger of a further accident. Although he had a wet rag tied over his mouth, he swallowed a considerable quantity of live steam, and was partially incapacitated by its effects.
Notwithstanding the gallant efforts of Mr. Pysden and other members of the ship's company, three men lost their lives owing to the accident and nine were seriously injured.

RAGHU NANDAN SINGH

No. 723.
Rank: Sepoy.
Unit/Force: 2/150 Indian Inf.
Other decorations: Nil.
Date of deed: July 25, 1920.
Date of Gazette: July 15, 1921.
Place/date of birth: Not known.
Place/date of death: Not known.
Place of memorial: Not known.
Town/county connections: Not known.

Citation

The KING has been pleased to award the Albert Medal to No. 723 Sepoy Raghu Nandan Singh, 2nd/150th Indian Infantry, in recognition of his gallantry in saving life near Piaza Raghza in July of last year.

On the 25th July, 1920, whilst moving the picquet bomb store near Piaza Raghza, Sepoy Raghu Nandan Singh noticed that the fuze of a bomb was burning. He called to his comrades to take shelter and taking the bomb out of the box attempted to throw it clear of the picquet. The bomb hit the parapet and burst. By his prompt action, he undoubtedly saved the lives of his comrades by preventing the bomb exploding among and detonating the other bombs.

J. RAMSAY
Source: The Fleet Magazine

RAMSAY, John.

No. O.N.216817.
Rank: AB.
Unit/Force: RN. HMS *Vivid*.
Other decorations: Nil.
Date of deed: January 7, 1908.
Date of Gazette: July 28, 1908.
Place/date of birth:
Not known.
Place/date of death:
Not known.
Place of memorial:
Not known.
Town/county connections:
Not known.

Citation

The KING was pleased, on Tuesday, the 21st July, at Buckingham Palace, to present to John Ramsay, Able Seaman, of His Majesty's Ship "Vivid", the Albert Medal of the Second Class, conferred upon him by His Majesty's command for gallantry in saving life as detailed below:-

Early on the morning of the 7th January last, when the 12.57 A.M. down mail train was approaching Temple Meads Station, Bristol, a Marine, W. Howat, belonging to His Majesty's Ship "Donegal", fell from the platform.

Howat's perilous position was observed by Ramsay, who at once jumped down to his assistance. The approaching train was only about sixty feet distant at the time, but he succeeded, though at the imminent risk of his own life, in dragging the fallen man back to the platform as the train passed the spot.

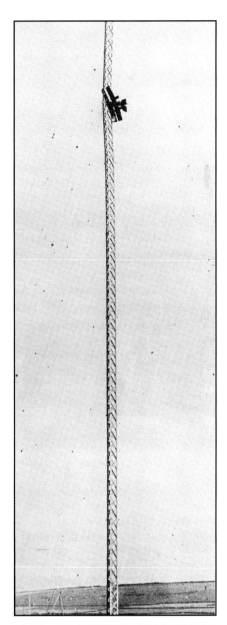

SEAPLANE STUCK IN POULSEN MAST
Source: Imperial War Museum

RATH, Nicholas.

Rank: Seaman.
Unit/Force: RNR. Horsea Island
Seaplane Station, RNAS.
Other decorations: Nil.
Date of deed: September 14, 1917.
Date of Gazette: December 14, 1917.
Place/date of birth: Not known.
Place/date of death: Not known.
Place of memorial: Not known.
Town/county connections:
Balbriggan, Co Dublin.
Remarks: Presented with AM by His Majesty
the King at Buckingham Palace February 16,
1918. Exploit featured in "Hornet" comic No.
474, October 7, 1972.

Citation

The KING has been pleased to award the Albert Medal in Gold to Nicholas Rath, Seaman, R.N.R., and the Albert Medal to Richard Knoulton, Ordinary Seaman, R.N., and George Faucett Pitts Abbott, Deckhand, R.N.R. (Trawler Section), in recognition of their gallantry in saving life in the following circumstances:-

On the 14th September, 1917, a seaplane collided with a Poulsen mast and remained wedged in it, the pilot (Acting Flight Commander E.A. de Ville) being rendered unconscious and thrown out of his seat on to one of the wings.

The three men above mentioned at once climbed up the mast for 100 feet, when Rath, making use of the boatswain's chair, which moves on the inside of the mast, was hoisted up by men at the foot of the mast to the place, over 300 feet from the ground, where the seaplane was fixed. He then climbed out on the plane, and held the pilot until the arrival of Knoulton and Abbott, who passed the masthead gantline out to him.

Having secured the pilot with the gantline Rath, with the assistance of Knoulton and Abbott, lifted him from the plane to the inside of the mast and lowered him to the ground.

The three men were very well aware of the damaged and insecure condition of the mast, which was bent to an angle where the seaplane had become wedged. One of the three supports of the mast was fractured, and, so far as the men knew, the mast or seaplane might at any time have collapsed.

Note: Knoulton and Abbott both survived to become GCs in 1971.

RATHBONE, William Leslie Coutts.

Rank: 2 Lt.
Unit/Force: 15 London Regt (TF)
Other decorations: MC (LG November 14, 1916).
Date of deed: May 6, 1916.
Date of Gazette: August 7, 1917.
Place/date of birth: Edmonton, London, c February, 1882.
Place/date of death: London, February 18, 1929.
Place of memorial: Not known.
Town/county connections: Not known.
Remarks: Served as Sgt 1210 15 London Regt before commissioning as 2Lt June 6, 1915. A/Capt December 27, 1917. Resigned commission March 12, 1921. To France March 17, 1915. Also awarded 1914-15 Star, British War and Victory Medals and the Life Saving Society Medal in Bronze. Trade on enlistment: Sorter with GPO. Served South African War. QSA Medal (Clasps Natal, Transvaal) as Pte 5815 Devon Regt. Married October 4, 1911, Annie Leslie (sic) Morrison. One son, William James, born April 3, 1914. Awarded TFEM (EVIIR) as Pte 1210 London Regt.

Citation
See citation for FELDWICK, A.E.

REEKIE, Stanley Martin.

Rank: 2 Lt.
Unit/Force: RF. Brigade Bombing Officer.
Other decorations: MM (LG - cannot be found).
Date of deed: July 19, 1918.
Date of Gazette: October 15, 1918.
Place/date of birth: Not known.
Place/date of death: Not known.
Place of memorial: Not known.
Town/county connections: Not known.
Remarks: To France July 30, 1915. Served as Pte - A/Sgt 13 Bn RF (No. GS/4780). Commissioned April 30, 1918. Also awarded British War and Victory Medals.

Citation
The KING has been pleased to award the Albert Medal ... in recognition of gallantry in saving life:-
Second Lieutenant Stanley Martin Reekie, M.M., Royal Fusiliers.
    At Newmarket, on the 19th July, 1918, a bomb thrown during practice failed to clear the parapet and rolled back into the pit. The man who had thrown it lost his head, and instead of running out of the pit ran into a corner away from the entrance. Second Lieutenant Reekie, the bombing officer, who was in a position of safety, saw that there was no time to get the man

out of the pit, and deliberately entered the pit and stood between the man and bomb, shielding him with his body. The bomb exploded and the officer was seriously wounded, but the man escaped injury.

RHODES, Charles Eric.

Rank: T/Surg-Lt.
Unit/Force: RNVR. HMS *Maidstone*.
Other decorations: Nil.
Date of deed: June 16, 1955.
Date of Gazette: November 1, 1955.
Place/date of birth: Whitworth, nr Rochdale, Lancs, April 3, 1928.
Place/date of death: Portland, Dorset, June 16, 1955.
Place of memorial: Not known.
Town/county connections: Rochdale, Lancs; Bramhall, Ches.
Remarks: A National Service Officer. Trained at London Hospital. Qualified MB, BS, London, 1952. Qualified MRCS, LRCP, 1952. House Physician London Hospital, House Surgeon Harold Wood Hospital, then to RNVR as T/Surg-Lt December 31, 1953 for Nat Svc. Appointed to HMS *Maidstone* February 8, 1954. Sports officer of depot ship and keen yachtsman. Married. Left three-week-old daughter.

Citation
The QUEEN has been graciously pleased to approve the posthumous award of the Albert Medal for gallantry in saving life at sea to:-
Temporary Surgeon Lieutenant Charles Eric RHODES, M.B., B.S., M.R.C.S., L.R.C.P., R.N.V.R.

An explosion occurred in H.M. Submarine SIDON in Portland Harbour on 16th June, 1955, which later caused the submarine to sink. Surgeon Lieutenant Rhodes was among the first to enter the SIDON after the explosion and, in spite of the total darkness and dense smoke, he brought out an injured man to safety. He then put on a Davis Submarine Escape Apparatus and re-entered the submarine with morphia to give further help to the injured. In doing so he greatly prejudiced his chance of escape. He was not a submarine officer and was not familiar with the use of the breathing apparatus or the lay-out inside a submarine. In spite of these handicaps and the pitch darkness his only thoughts were for those within the submarine; he had no hesitation in re-entering the SIDON and he succeeded in helping two more men to escape before the submarine sank. Surgeon Lieutenant Rhodes' gallant and selfless act in helping to save the lives of others cost him his own life.

RICHARDS, Albert Ernest.

No. PLY 21668.
Rank: MNE.
Unit/Force: RM. HMS *Flora*.
Other decorations: Nil.
Date of deed: September 25, 1928.
Date of Gazette: April 19, 1929.

Place/date of birth: Wendron, nr Helston, Cornwall, January 20, 1905.
Place/date of death: April 14, 1956.
Place of memorial: Not known.
Town/county connections: Wendron, Cornwall.
Remarks: Enlisted at Bristol September 25, 1923. Discharged October 15, 1945 as QMS with conduct described as Very Good. His only other medal was the RN LS&GC, awarded on September 26, 1938. His record states that he enlisted in the RMP on October 17, 1945. Married on January 23, 1930 at Plymouth. A gamekeeper before enlistment.

Citation

The KING has been graciously pleased to approve of the award of the Albert Medal to No. Ply/21668 Marine Albert Ernest Richards for gallantry in saving life.

The following is the account of the services in respect of which the decoration has been conferred:-

On the 25th September, 1928, blasting operations were in progress for the removal of rock on a site at St. Helena under the charge of No. Ply/14790 Sergeant Stewart Symons. Four charges had been laid, two in drilled holes and two in crevices in the rock. The drilled hole fuzes were each to be lit by a Marine and the crevice fuzes by Sergeant Symons. The hole fuzes and the upper crevice fuze were lit simultaneously, and the Sergeant was bending down to light the lower crevice fuze when the charge in the upper crevice exploded unexpectedly, blinding Sergeant Symons and knocking him helpless close to one of the drilled holes. The Marines who had lit the other fuzes had by this time run clear but Marine Richards, seeing that the Sergeant was disabled, turned back and helped him to his feet and dragged him clear of the subsequent explosions from the effects of which he shielded him with his own body.

Marine Richards was well aware that at least two further charges were due to explode within some thirty seconds, and his presence of mind and disregard of personal danger undoubtedly saved Sergeant Symons from death.

E .H. RICHARDSON
Source: J.P. O'Malley

RICHARDSON, Edward Henry.

Rank: Lt.
Unit/Force: RNR.
Other decorations: DSC.
Date of deed: November 8, 1916.
Date of Gazette: July 9, 1918.
Place/date of birth: Not known.
Place/date of death: Not known.
Place of memorial: Not known.
Town/county connections: Not known.
Remarks: Also had British War and Victory Medals (MID), Order of St Anne and Order of St Stanislas.

Citation
See citation for HENRY, J.D.

RICKETT, John.

Rank: AB.
Unit/Force: RN. HMS *Clio*.
Other decorations: Nil.
Date of deed: May 24, 1866.
Date of Gazette: December 24, 1867.
Place/date of birth: Not known.
Place/date of death: Not known.
Place of memorial: Not known.
Town/county connections: Not known.
Remarks: The first Serviceman to be awarded the AM.

Citation

THE Queen has been graciously pleased to confer the decoration of "The Albert Medal of the Second Class" on:-
JOHN RICKETT, A.B., of Her Majesty's ship "Clio".

The following is an account of the services in respect of which the decoration has been conferred:-

On the 24th May, 1866, whilst Her Majesty's ship "Clio" was lying at anchor off the Ajaiampo, on the coast of Mexico, a boy named Thomas (or Tom) Walton, belonging to her, fell into the sea from a stage outside the ship. He was unable to swim, and was sinking the third time, when JOHN RICKETT jumped into the water, brought him to the surface, got him to the ship's cable, and there supported him for ten or fifteen minutes, when the ship's boat reached them.

A man named Card assisted to hold the boy up from overhead.

There was a heavy sea on at the time, and the port was known to be infested with sharks, and just as the ship's boat came up, RICKETT, who was at the time still suffering from the effects of an attack of coast fever, and was in consequence very weak, relaxed his hold of the cable, and himself dropped into the water, from which he was picked up just in time to save his life. Both were insensible when taken into the boat.

ROBERTSON, Peter Gordon.

Rank: Lt.
Unit/Force: RN. HMS *Bastion*.
Other decorations: Nil.
Date of deed: December 19, 1965.
Date of Gazette: July 19, 1966.
Place/date of birth: Not known.
Place/date of death: Persian Gulf, December 19, 1966.
Place of memorial: Not known.
Town/county connections: Not known.
Remarks: The last Serviceman to be awarded the AM.

Citation

The QUEEN has been graciously pleased to approve the posthumous award of the Albert Medal for gallantry in saving life at sea to:-
Lieutenant Peter Gordon ROBERTSON, Royal Navy.

On 19th December 1965, during force 7 weather conditions, H.M.S. Bastion went to the assistance of an Iranian dhow in distress. The dhow subsequently foundered and in order to recover survivors it was necessary to launch a liferaft. This was manned by Lieutenant Robertson and a naval rating, both volunteers. The liferaft was cut adrift upwind and as it neared the survival area Lieutenant Robertson entered the water on a tended line and swam towards the nearest survivors. He secured one survivor, and at this stage H.M.S. Bastion stopped within 30 feet of him with the intention of picking them up. With complete disregard for his own safety however and thinking only of the other survivors, Lieutenant Robertson shouted that he was alright and that the ship should proceed to pick up other people in the water. The next time Lieutenant Robertson was sighted he appeared to have recovered another survivor but when the ship returned to his position some 10-15 minutes later it was discovered that Lieutenant Robertson's body was being used as a raft by three survivors and that his head was being held under the water. On being taken aboard he was found to be dead.

Throughout the whole proceedings Lieutenant Robertson was well aware of the dangers to his own life from panic stricken survivors. He showed the greatest gallantry and courage in being concerned solely and at all stages in saving the greatest number of lives.

ROBINSON, Arthur James.

No. 4365.
Rank: SGT.
Unit/Force: IOD. Ferozepore Arsenal.
Other decorations: Nil.
Date of deed: August 31, 1906.
Date of Gazette: September 26, 1911.
Place/date of birth: Emsworth, Hants, June, 1875.
Place/date of death: Not known.
Place of memorial: Not known.
Town/county connections: Emsworth, Hants.
Remarks: Pupil teacher on enlistment. Joined 3 (Mil) Bn R Sussex Regt as Pte 5984. Enlisted as Pte in R Sussex Regt at Chichester June 1, 1893. Served in S African War. Appt Cdr Jul 1, 1918 for services during WWI. Retd August 27, 1922. Married (1) February 18, 1909 at Jubbulpore Dora Ann (née Donnelly) 1 daughter. (2) April 29, 1922 at Eastchurch, Kent, Ethel Charlotte (née Ellis). Dora Ann died November 20, 1914. Also awarded IGS 1895 (2 bars), QSA (3 bars), KSA (2 bars), LS&GC Medals. Apparently no medal entitlement for WWI.

Citation
See citation for ANDERSON, C.A.

ROBINSON, Harold Victor.

Rank: AM 1.
Unit/Force: RNAS. Air Ship Station, Polegate, RNAS.
Other decorations: Nil.
Date of deed: December 20, 1917.
Date of Gazette: March 8, 1918.
Place/date of birth:
Place/date of death: Queensland, Australia, October 1969.
Town/county connections: Queensland, Australia.
Remarks: Believed to have been the last surviving holder of the Albert Medal in Gold.

Citation

The KING has been pleased to award the Albert Medal to Flight Lieutenant Victor Albert Watson, R.N., and the Albert Medal in Gold to Air-Mechanic, 1st Grade, Harold Victor Robinson and Boy Mechanic Eric Edward Steere, in recognition of their heroic conduct in the following circumstances:-

On the occasion of an accident to one of His Majesty's Air-ships, which resulted in a fire breaking out on board her, Flight Lieutenant Watson, who was the senior Officer on the spot, immediately rushed up to the car of the airship under the impression that one of the crew was still in it, although he was well aware that there were heavy bombs attached to the airship which it was impossible to remove owing to the nearness of the fire, and which were almost certain to explode at any moment on account of the heat. Having satisfied himself that there was in fact no one in the car, he turned away to render assistance else-where, and at that moment one of the bombs exploded, a portion of it shattering Lieutenant Watson's right arm at the elbow. The arm had to be amputated almost immediately.

Air Mechanic H.V. Robinson and Boy Mechanic E.E. Steere, on the occasion of an accident to one of His Majesty's airships which caused a fire to break out on board her, approached the burning ship without hesitation, extricated the pilot and two members of the crew, all of whom were seriously injured, and then unclipped the bombs from the burning car and carried them out of reach of the fire. As the bombs were surrounded by flames, and were so hot that they scorched the men's hands as they carried them, they must have expected the bombs to explode.

Note: Flight Lieutenant Watson survived to become a holder of the GC in 1971.

ROSS, Eglintoune Frederick.

Rank: Capt.
Unit/Force: 1 Dorset Regt.
Other decorations: Nil.
Date of deed: August 21, 1906.
Date of Gazette: August 26, 1913.
Place/date of birth: June 20, 1883.
Place/date of death: 1955.
Place of memorial: Not known.

Town/county connections: Not known.
Remarks: Commissioned August 12, 1902. Transferred to IA December 12, 1909. Served mainly with IA. Retd as Maj November 23, 1921. Presented with AM by Gov of Madras February 7, 1914.

Citation
See citation for BATTYE, B. C.

ROWLANDS, George Thomas.

No. 240005.
Rank: CPL.
Unit/Force: 4 (Res) Bn DCLI.
Other decorations: Nil.
Date of deed: October 21, 1918.
Date of Gazette: February 4, 1919.
Place/date of birth: Not known.
Place/date of death: Not known.
Place of memorial: Not known.
Town/county connections: Not known.
Remarks: Also awarded British War and Victory Medals. He was presented with his AM by HMK at BP on May 22, 1919.

Citation
*The KING has been pleased to award the Albert Medal ... in recognition of gallantry in saving life:-
Corporal George Thomas Rowlands, 4th Reserve Battalion, The Duke of Cornwall's Light Infantry.*
At Clonmany, County Donegal, on the 21st October, 1918, Corporal Rowlands was instructing a party in the firing of live rifle grenades when a grenade, the fuze of which had been started, fell into the firing bay. Rowlands shouted to the party to take cover, and ran out of the trench, but the man from whose rifle the grenade had fallen did not move, and Rowlands thereupon returned to the trench, picked up the grenade, and threw it over the parapet, when it immediately exploded. He undoubtedly saved the man's life at the risk of his own.

ROWLANDSON, Sidney Albert.

Rank: Lt.
Unit/Force. ASC. GHQ Tps Sup Col Wksp ASC.
Other decorations: Nil.
Date of deed: May 2, 1916.
Date of Gazette: August 29, 1916.
Place/date of birth: Not known.
Place/date of death: Not known.
Place of memorial: Not known.
Town/county connections: Not known.

Remarks: To France September 23, 1914. Served as Pte 3572 ASC. Comsd April 14, 1915 into ASC. Later T/Capt. Also awarded 1914 Star, British War and Victory Medals.

Citation
See citation for ANDERSON, A.

RUR SINGH.

No. 1485.
Rank: Hav-Maj.
Unit/Force: 48 Pioneers IA.
Other decorations: Nil.
Date of deed: October 18, 1921.
Date of Gazette: December 22, 1922.
Place/date of birth: Not known.
Place/date of death: Not known.
Place of memorial: Not known.
Town/county connections: Not known.
Remarks: Presented with AM at Kirkee November 27, 1922.

Citation
The KING has been pleased to award the Albert Medal to Havildar Major Rur Singh, 48th Pioneers, in recognition of his gallantry in saving and endeavouring to save life at Chagmalai in October of last year.

On October 18th, 1921, in the course of operations in Waziristan, a party of men were crossing the Shahur Tangi, and had reached some high ground in mid-stream, when they were cut off by a sudden rise of the water. The river rapidly became a roaring torrent; five of the men were swept away, and it seemed that the remainder were doomed. Havildar Major Rur Singh made several attempts to swim out with a rope, and eventually succeeded in reaching the men, but they were then exhausted and, the river rising still higher, the whole party was swept away. One man to whom the rope was handed by Rur Singh was pulled to the bank, while Rur Singh himself was washed ashore some distance down the stream alive, but considerably battered.

RUSSELL, Edward Peregrine Stuart.

Rank: Lt.
Unit/Force: RNVR. HMS *Eskimo.*
Other decorations: Nil.
Date of deed: May 9, 1942.
Date of Gazette: August 11, 1942.
Place/date of birth: c1917.
Place/date of death: Off Falmouth, Cornwall, May 9, 1942.
Place of memorial: Falmouth Cemetery, Section K, Row B, Grave 15.
Town/county connections: Camberley, Surrey.

Remarks: Son of Capt S. P. B. Russell RN and Eileen Russell of Camberley, Surrey. Also awarded 1939-45 and Atlantic Stars and War Medal.

Citation

The KING has been graciously pleased to approve the following ..:

The Albert Medal (Posthumous)

For great bravery and devotion to duty in trying to save life at sea:

Lieutenant Edward Peregrine Stuart Russell, R.N.V.R.

When H.M.S. Eskimo was on passage in heavy weather on 9th May, 1942, a man was washed overboard. Lieutenant Russell, seeing that he could not grasp the bearing lines thrown to him, dived overboard and tried to secure him, but the man sank before he could do this.

As Lieutenant Russell himself was being hauled on board he lost his hold of the bearing line, and drifted away. Another Officer tried to save him, but could not reach him, and by the time the ship could be stopped, he was dead.

He was not a strong swimmer, and had made a gallant attempt to save his shipmate.

F. J. RUTLAND
Source: "Rutland of Jutland"

RUTLAND, Frederick Joseph.

Rank: Lt.

Unit/Force: RNAS. HMS *Engadine.*

Other decorations: DSC (LG September 15, 1916), Bar to DSC (Edinburgh Gazette October 5, 1917). The first DSC was for Jutland.

Date of deed: June 1, 1916.

Date of Gazette: August 11, 1916.

Place/date of birth: October 21, 1886.

Place/date of death: London, January 28, 1949.

Place of memorial: Not known.

Town/county connections: Not known.

Remarks: Joined RN as Boy Entrant 1901. Qualified as naval diver 1912. Comsd 1913. Pilot October 1914, cert. no. 1085. Resigned commission 1923. Married twice: 1915 (1 son - Dr F. A. Rutland, Surg-Lt RNVR and 1923 (1 son, 1 daughter). The subject of the book "Rutland of Jutland" by Desmond Young (Cassell & Co, 1963). He committed suicide in a hotel room.

Citation

The KING has been graciously pleased to confer the Decoration of the Albert Medal of the First Class on -

Lieutenant Frederick Joseph Rutland, R.N. (Flight Lieutenant, Royal Naval Air Service).

The following is the account of the services in respect of which the Decoration has been conferred:-

During the transhipment of the crew of H.M.S. "Warrior" to H.M.S. "Engadine" on the morning of the 1st of June, 1916, succeeding the naval battle off the coast of Jutland, one of the severely wounded, owing to the violent motion of the two ships, was accidentally dropped overboard from a stretcher and fell between the ships. As the ships were working most dangerously, the Commanding Officer of the "Warrior" had to forbid two of his officers from jumping overboard to the rescue of the wounded man, as he considered that it would mean their almost certain death.

Before he could be observed, however, Lieutenant Rutland, of H.M.S. "Engadine", went overboard from the forepart of that ship with a bowline, and worked himself aft. He succeeded in putting the bowline around the wounded man and in getting him hauled on board, but it was then found that the man was dead, having been crushed between the two ships. Lieutenant Rutland's escape from a similar fate was miraculous. His bravery is reported to have been magnificent.

SANDILANDS, The Honourable Francis Robert.

Rank: Lt.
Unit/Force: RN. HMS *Audacious*.
Other decorations: Nil.
Date of deed: January 1, 1875.
Date of Gazette: March 16, 1875.
Place/date of birth: January 12, 1849.
Place/date of death; July 30, 1887.
Place of memorial: Not known.
Town/county connections: Coston, Leics.
Remarks: Son of Rev John Sandilands MA, Rector of Coston, Leics' and Helen, daughter of James Hope (Clerk to the Signet). He was grandson of 10th Baron Torphichen. Married June 4, 1885 Maude Bayard Wiggins. 1 son, who died in infancy. He also held the Order of Osmanieh 4th Class.

Citation

THE Queen has been graciously pleased to confer the Albert Medal of the Second Class on:-
LIEUTENANT THE HONOURABLE FRANCIS ROBERT SANDILANDS, R.N., of
Her Majesty's Ship "Audacious".
  The following is an account of the services in respect of which the decoration has been conferred:-
  In latitude 13 deg 44 min N., longitude 58 deg 29 min E., at one o'clock, A.M., of the 1st January, 1875, the ship being under steam, it being at the time dark, and the weather fine and clear, Frederick Cowd, Ship's Corporal of the First Class, fell over-board from the top-gallant forecastle, and passed aft, apparently unable to help himself.
  LIEUTENANT THE HONOURABLE FRANCIS ROBERT SANDILANDS, who had had the first watch, and was at the time on the bridge in conversation with the officer of the middle watch, immediately sprang after the drowning man, from a height of twenty-four feet, swam to him, and kept him above water. Owing to part of the slipping apparatus having been carried away, some delay was occasioned in getting the life-boat clear of the slings, but LIEUTENANT SANDILANDS never ceased his efforts to keep the man above water. Both were eventually picked up, the Ship's Corporal being insensible, and dying soon after being got on board the ship. LIEUTENANT SANDILANDS was unable to reach the life-buoys which had been let go, and he supported the man in the water from twelve to eighteen minutes, never quitting him until he was taken into the boat.

L.A. SAUSMAREZ AM RN
Source: Family

SAUSMAREZ, *Lionel Andros.*

Rank: Sub-Lt.
Unit/Force: RN. HMS *Myrmidon.*
Other decorations: Nil.
Date of deed: June 1, 1868.
Date of gazette: November 17, 1868.
Place/date of birth: Not known.
Place/date of death: Not known.
Place of memorial: Not known.
Town/county connections: Channel Islands.

Citation

THE Queen has been graciously pleased to confer the decoration of "The Albert Medal of the Second Class" on -

Sub-Lieutenant LIONEL ANDROS DE SAUSMAREZ, of Her Majesty's ship "Myrmidon".

The following is an account of the services in respect of which the decoration is conferred:-

At about 10.30 P.M. on the night of the 1st June, 1868, while Her Majesty's ship "Myrmidon" was lying in Banana Creek, River Congo, Western Africa, William Torrance, Able Seaman, fell overboard.

Mr. DE SAUSMAREZ was Officer of the Watch, and although a strong current was running at the time, and the river infested with sharks, he immediately jumped overboard, secured Torrance (who could not swim), swam with him to the pier, and supported him there until assistance came.

SCOTT, *Richard James Rodney.*

Rank: Lt-Cdr.
Unit/Force: RN. HMS *Myrtle.*
Other decorations: CB (1944).
Date of deed: July 15, 1919.
Date of Gazette: March 12, 1920.
Place/date of birth: Bath, April 21, 1887.
Place/date of death: Bath, November 28, 1967.
Place of memorial: Not known.

Town/county connections: Bath, Somerset.

Remarks: Son of R. J. B. Scott FRCS of Bath. Educated Bath College and HMS Britannia. Joined RN in 1902. Promoted Rear Admiral 1942. FOIC Portland 1944. JP Somerset 1947. DL Somerset 1950. Founder member of AM Association 1966. Married (1) Dorothy May, daughter of E. T. Sturdy (died 1925), (2) Ruth Margaret Macintyre, daughter of P. Macyntyre Evans CBE. 1 son from first marriage. MID 1939.

Citation

R. J. R SCOTT
Source: Family

The KING has been graciously pleased to approve of the award of the Albert Medal to Lieutenant-Commander Richard James Rodney Scott, R.N., for gallantry in endeavouring to save life at sea.

The following is an account of the services in respect of which the decoration has been conferred:-

On the 15th July, 1919, during minesweeping operations in the Baltic, four mines were swept up which H.M.S. "Myrtle", commanded by Lieutenant-Commander Scott, and another vessel were ordered to sink.

During the operations the two vessels were mined and H.M.S. "Myrtle" immediately began to sink.

So great was the force of the explosion that all hands in the engine room and after boiler room of the ship were killed with one exception, and many others of the crew were wounded.

After the wounded had been successfully transferred to another vessel, the forepart of H.M.S. "Myrtle" broke away and sank.

Lieutenant-Commander Scott, hearing that the fate of one of the crew of the "Myrtle" had not been definitely ascertained, gallantly returned alone to what was left of the ship, which was drifting through the minefield, rolling heavily and burning fiercely, and regardless of the extreme risk which he ran, made a thorough search for the missing man, unfortunately without success.

SCRASE-DICKINS, Spencer William.

Rank: Capt.
Unit/Force: 2 HLI.
Other decorations: CB (1916).
Date of deed: April 27, 1893.
Date of Gazette: August 18, 1893.
Place/date of birth: September 27, 1862.
Place/date of death: October 23, 1919.
Place of memorial: Not known.
Town/county connections: Coolhurst, Sussex.
Remarks: Second son of C. Spencer Scrase-Dickens of Coolhurst, Sussex. Served Egypt 1882, NWF 1897-1898 and WWI, becoming Brig-Gen. Also awarded Egypt Medal 1882 (1 bar), IGS 1895 (1 bar), Khedive's Star and Stanhope Gold Medal. MID WWI.

Citation
HER Majesty the Queen has been graciously pleased to confer the Decoration of the Albert Medal of the Second Class on -
Captain SPENCER W. SCRASE-DICKINS, 2nd Highland Light Infantry.
    The following is an account of the services in respect of which the Decoration has been conferred:-
    While the S.S. "Peshawur" was passing through the Red Sea on the 27th April, 1893, a Lascar, who was at work in one of the boats fell overboard. Captain SCRASE-DICKINS, who had been invalided home, and was lying half asleep in a chair on the deck, immediately jumped overboard and swimming to the Lascar, succeeded in keeping him afloat until they were both picked up by the ship's boat a mile and a half away from the vessel.
    The "Peshawur" was going at the time at the rate of 11$^{1/2}$ knots with a strong head wind, and the sea was moderately high, and known to be infested with sharks.

SCURFIELD, Bryan Gouthewaite.

Rank: Lt-Cdr.
Unit/Force: RN. HMS *Hunter.*
Other decorations: DSO (LG September 1, 1942) OBE (LG July 8th,1941. No citation for either.
Date of deed: May 13, 1937.
Date of Gazette: July 2, 1937.
Place/date of birth: c1902.
Place/date of death: April 11, 1945 (as a result of a bombing raid while a POW).
Place of memorial: Becklingen War Cemetery, Soltau, Germany, Plot 3, Row A, Grave 12.
Town/county connections: Not known.
Remarks: Son of Harold and Mary Louisa Scurfield. Married to Mary Katherine of Petersfield, Hants .His exploit was featured in the "Hornet" comic No. 214 (October 14, 1967). He was the brother-in-law of another AM, Geoffrey RACKHAM (subsequently GC).

Citation

The KING has been graciously pleased to approve of the award of the Albert Medal to Lieutenant-Commander B.G. Scurfield, R.N.

The following is the account of the services in respect of which the decoration has been conferred:-

On 13th May, 1937, H.M.S. "Hunter" sustained serious damage in an explosion off Almeria, Spain. Immediately the ship took on a heavy list, all lights were extinguished and there was no steam. Apparently she was about to sink.

Lieutenant-Commander Scurfield, who was aft, rushed forward. Passing the galley, he heard cries from the Petty Officer Cook, who had fallen into the boiler room. He jumped down through the smoke, oil fuel, steam and debris, and by extraordinary feats of strength removed the wreckage pinning the man down. The rating was passed up on deck, but did not long survive.

Lieutenant-Commander Scurfield then proceeded to the Torpedo-men's mess deck. This was flooded to a depth of $2^{1/2}$ feet in oil fuel; also battery gas had escaped from the switchboard room. The ladder having been blown away, he jumped down into the mess deck, not knowing whether it was intact, and passed up two men. Calling for assistance, he was joined by Lieutenant Humphreys and A.Bs. Collins, Thomas and Abrahams.

After the mess deck had been cleared, he led the party into the stoker petty officers' mess. The bulkhead had been shattered, and bedding and curtains were smouldering on top of the oil fuel. Bodies were pulled out from under the wreckage, and passed up on deck.

During the whole of this time, he might in the darkness have fallen into the oil fuel tanks below or into the sea. By his gallant behaviour he saved the lives of Stoker Petty Officers Lott, May and Fenley, Stoker Neil and A.B. Oliffe.

SEWELL, Herbert William.

Rank: Lt.
Unit/Force: RE. Staff for RE Svcs.
Other decorations: Nil.
Date of deed: June 6, 1917.
Date of Gazette: January 4, 1918.
Place/date of birth: Not known.
Place/date of death: Not known.
Place of memorial: Not known.
Town/county connections: Not known.
Remarks: To France December 29, 1914. Served also as 2290 Pte HAC. Comsd RE May 13, 1915. Also awarded 1914-15 Star, British War and Victory Medals (MID), Presented with AM by His Majesty the King at Buckingham Palace November 10, 1920. Cpl A. C. Bird ASC and LCpl W. Ogg RE both received the MSM for this incident.

Citation

The KING has been graciously pleased to award the Decoration of the Albert Medal to the undermentioned Officer ... in recognition of (his) gallantry in saving life:-

Lieutenant Herbert William Sewell, Staff for Royal Engineer Services.

In France, on the 6th June, 1917, during a fire at Calais, Lieutenant Sewell broke through *the roof of an engine-house which was in flames, and removed the weights of the safety valves. But for the officer's gallant action a serious explosion would have occurred, and he ran grave risk of being fatally scalded by the steam released by the removal of the weights.*

SEYMOUR, William.

No. 2202.
Rank: SGT.
Unit/Force: 2 NF.
Other decorations: Nil.
Date of deed: February 5, 1917.
Date of Gazette: November 9, 1917 & February 8, 1918.
Place/date of birth: Not known.
Place/date of death: Not known.
Place of memorial: Not known.
Town/county connections: Byker, Newcastle-upon-Tyne.
Remarks: To France July 20, 1915. Also awarded 1914-5 Star, British War and Victory Medals plus Silver War Badge. Presented with AM by His Majesty the King at Buckingham Palace April 13, 1918, by then a civilian, having been discharged as unfit. In 1936 reported AM lost in fire in 1922 in Winnipeg, Canada.

Citation
See citation for ALLAN, A. D. H.

SHACKLADY, Eric Arnold.

Rank: Lt.
Unit/Force: 3 Manchester Regt.
Date of deed: December 5, 1916.
Date of Gazette: January 1, 1918.
Place/date of birth: Liverpool, October 30, 1892.
Place/date of death: Wallasey, Cheshire, June 20, 1965.
Place of memorial: Landican Crematorium, Birkenhead.
Town/county connections: Liverpool, Wallasey.
Remarks: Son of James and Elizabeth Shacklady. Educated Liverpool Institute. Clerk in Royal Exchange Assurance 1909-1931. Insurance broker 1931-33. Joined Graves John & Westrup, Insurance Brokers 1933. Elected director 1951. Retired 1959. Joined 5 King's Regt August 7, 1914 as Pte 2248. To France February 21, 1915. Comsd April 13, 1915.Invalided to UK with trench fever. Accidentally wounded at bombing practice 1916. Admin duties 1917-19. Home Guard 1939-44 as Liaison Officer. Reserve 1952-56. Also awarded 1914-15 Star, British War, Victory and Defence Medals. Married to Lois Mary Withers October 30, 1917. 2 sons, both of whom served in WWII. Presented with AM by His Majesty the King at Buckingham Palace on January 16, 1918.

E. A. SHACKLADY
Source: Family

Citation

The KING has been graciously pleased to award the Decoration of the Albert Medal to the undermentioned Officer ... in recognition of (his) gallantry in saving life:-
Lieutenant Eric Arnold Shacklady, Manchester Regiment.

During bombing practice at Cleethorpes on the 5th December, 1916, a live grenade which was thrown by one of the men under instruction failed to clear the parapet. The bomb was picked up and thrown a second time, but again failed to clear the parapet. By this time the fuse had burnt nearly to the end, but Lieutenant Shacklady ran forward, picked up the grenade, and was about to throw it away when it exploded and blew off his hand. By this gallant action, in which he risked his life, Lieutenant Shacklady undoubtedly saved the life of the man who had thrown the grenade.

SHAIK MOHIDEN.

Rank: Tindal of Stokers.
Unit/Force: RIM. RIMS *Lawrence.*
Other decorations: Nil.
Date of deed: April 14, 1913.
Date of Gazette: October 31, 1913.
Place/date of birth: Not known.
Place/date of death: Not known.
Place of memorial: Not known.
Town/county connections: Not known.
Remarks: Presented with AM on board ship at Bombay, July 8, 1914.

Citation

The KING has been graciously pleased to confer the Decoration of the Albert Medal of the Second Class upon Shaik Mohiden, Tindal of Stokers, Royal Indian Marine.

The following is an account of the services in respect of which the Decoration has been conferred:-
On the 14th April, 1913, the Shatt-al-Arab Outer Bar gas buoy in the Persian Gulf was being charged with acetylene gas from the Royal Indian Marine Ship "Lawrence", and as the carbide, soaked in crude oil, was being passed down a canvas shute to the buoy, an explosion occurred. Shaik Mahomed, 1st Class Stoker, who was inside the cage of the buoy tending the chute, was knocked senseless, and as the chute caught fire both in and outside the cage, enveloping the manhole in flames, his life was in extreme danger. Shaik Mohiden, who was not on duty, saw the accident, and at once jumped from the power boom on to the buoy, dashed through the flames, 8 to 10 feet high, knocked the burning chute aside, and dragged Shaik Mahomed out of the cage. He then put him in the water on the weather side of the buoy and held him there till a boat came to his relief.

SHAIKH ABDUL SAMAND.

Rank: SPR.
Unit/Force: Bengal S & M.
Other decorations: Nil.
Date of deed: July 16, 1898.
Date of Gazette: November 18, 1898.
Place/date of birth: Not known.
Place/date of death: Not known.
Place of memorial: Not known.
Town/county connections: Not known.

Citation
See citation for HABIB KHAN.

SHOOTER, William.

No. 19556.
Rank: A/CSM.
Unit/Force: 15 Ches Regt.
Other decorations: Nil.
Date of deed: April 8, 1916.
Date of Gazette: January 4, 1918.
Place/date of birth: Not known.
Place/date of death: Not known.
Place of memorial: Not known.
Town/county connections: Brighouse, Yorks.
Remarks: Foreman stoker with Bradford Dyers Association at Brighouse, Yorks, before enlistment. Enlisted November 30, 1914. Discharged November 26, 1918. Substantive Sgt. Also awarded British War and Victory Medals. Presented with AM by His Majesty the King at Buckingham Palace September 18, 1918.

Citation
The KING has been graciously pleased to award the Decoration of the Albert Medal to the undermentioned ... Non-Commissioned Officer of His Majesty's Forces ... in recognition of (his) gallantry in saving life:-
Acting Company Sergeant-Major William Shooter, The Cheshire Regiment.
On the 8th April, 1916, while bombing instruction was being given in a trench occupied by two officers, Sergeant-Major Shooter, and a private, the private, who was about to throw a bomb from which he had withdrawn the safety pin, dropped it. Without giving any warning of what had occurred, he ran away. After about two seconds had elapsed, Sergeant-Major Shooter saw the bomb. He could easily have escaped round the traverse, but, in order to save the others, he seized the bomb and threw it away. It exploded in the air before Sergeant-Major Shooter could take cover, wounding him. By risking his life he undoubtedly saved the two officers who were with him in the trench from serious or fatal injury.

SIMMONS, Edward Arthur.

Rank: Lt.
Unit/Force: 14 Middx Regt, att 5 Middx Regt.
Other decorations: Nil.
Date of deed: November 1, 1918.
Date of Gazette: February 28, 1919.
Place/date of birth: Not known.
Place/date of death: Not known.
Place of memorial: Not known.
Town/county connections: Not known.
Remarks: To France October 2, 1915. Also served in 3 Bn Middx Regt. Also awarded 1914-15 Star, British War and Victory Medals. Presented with AM by His Majesty the King at Buckingham Palace May 5, 1919.

Citation
The KING has been pleased to award the Albert Medal to Lieutenant Edward Arthur Simmons, Middlesex Regiment, in recognition of his gallantry in saving life in November last.

On the 1st November, 1918, at Wouldham, a platoon was engaged in attack practice, in the course of which the rifle sections advanced under cover of a rifle bomb barrage. The riflemen had reached a point some twenty yards in advance of the bombers, when, owing to a defective cartridge one of the bombs fired from the right flank, where Lieutenant Simmons was stationed as bombing officer, fell about four yards in rear of the riflemen. Lieutenant Simmons, who was behind the bombers, at once rushed forward, and, as there was no time to pick up the bomb and throw it away, he kicked it away. It exploded immediately, and he received severe wounds.

Lieutenant Simmons undoubtedly saved some of the men from injury or death at the cost of injury to himself and at the risk of his own life.

SIMMS, Alfred Edward.

No. 5538.
Rank: AM 2.
Unit/Force: RFC. 12 Sqn RFC.
Other decorations: Nil.
Date of deed: January 3, 1916.
Date of Gazette: May 19, 1916.
Place/date of birth: September, 1898.
Place/date of death: Glastonbury, Som, October 14, 1969.
Place of memorial: Not known.
Town/county connections: Glastonbury, Som.
Remarks: Married; 3 sons, 1 daughter. Also awarded 1914-15 Star, British War and Victory Medals. He was presented with his AM by HMK at BP December 19, 1917, by which time he was Cpl. Member of AM Association.

Citation
See citation for HEARNE, H.)

SMITH, Frederick Stuart.

Rank: 2 Lt.
Unit/Force: RFC. 6 Sqn RFC.
Other decorations: Nil.
Date of deed: October 14, 1916.
Date of Gazette: January 1, 1918.
Place/date of birth: 1887.
Place/date of death: Cheltenham, Glos, July 10, 1970.
Place of memorial: Not known.
Town/county connections: Cheltenham, Glos.
Remarks: Presented with AM by His Majesty the King at Buckingham Palace April 13, 1918. Member of AM Association.

Citation
The KING has been graciously pleased to award the Decoration of the Albert Medal to the undermentioned Officer and Non-Commissioned Officer of His Majesty's Forces ... in recognition of their gallantry in saving life:-
Lieutenant Frederick Stuart Smith
Serjeant William Ernest Rhoades, both of the Royal Flying Corps.
At an aerodrome in France, on the 14th October, 1916, a bomb accidentally exploded in the mouth of a dug-out forming a bomb store, which contained a large number of bombs packed in wooden cases and a quantity of rockets. Two men were killed by the explosion, and another man, who was severely injured, was thrown down into the store. Dense volumes of smoke issued from the dugout, and there was great risk of a further explosion. Lieutenant (then 2nd Lieutenant) Smith, on hearing a call for help, immediately entered the dug-out, followed by Serjeant Rhoades, and succeeded in rescuing the wounded man, who would otherwise have been suffocated.
Note: Sergeant Rhoades survived to become a GC holder in 1971.

SMITH, Frederick William.

No. C/JX 127402.
Rank: A/CPO.
Unit/Force: RN. HMS *Grove*.
Other decorations: Nil.
Date of deed: June 12, 1942.
Date of Gazette: December 22, 1942.
Place/date of birth: c1911.
Place/date of death: June 12, 1942.
Place of memorial: Chatham Naval Memorial, Panel 52, Column 1.

Town/county connections: Gorleston-on-Sea, Norfolk.
Remarks: Widow lived in Gorleston. He was 31 at the time of his death.

Citation
The KING has been pleased to ... approve the following Awards ..:
    For great bravery in attempting to save life at sea:
                    The Albert Medal (Posthumous)
Acting Chief Petty Officer Frederick William Smith, C/JX. 127402.
    C.P.O. Smith's ship was torpedoed and abandoned. She was settling and likely at any moment to capsize, when somebody was heard calling from her bows. C.P.O. Smith swam back to her, taking a desperate risk to save a comrade, but he was too late, and his gallant action cost him his life.

SMITH, George.

    Rank: SGT.
    Unit/Force: IOD. Ferozepore Arsenal.
    Other decorations: Nil.
    Date of deed: August 31, 1906.
    Date of Gazette: September 26, 1911.
    Place/date of birth: Not known.
    Place/date of death: Not known.
    Place of memorial: Not known.
    Town/county connections: Not known.
    Remarks: Presented with AM by His Majesty the King at Delhi Durbar, December 13, 1911.

Citation
See citation for ANDERSON, C.A. (No. 5)

SMITH, Harry.

    Rank: Wt Engr.
    Unit/Force: RN. HMS *Rob Roy*.
    Other decorations: Nil.
    Date of deed: May 13, 1920.
    Date of Gazette: October 5, 1920.
    Place/date of birth: Not known.
    Place/date of death: Not known.
    Place of memorial: Not known.
    Town/county connections: Not known.
    Remarks:

Citation

The KING has been graciously pleased to approve of the award of the Albert Medal to Mr. Harry Smith, Commissioned Engineer, R.N., for gallantry in saving life at sea.

The following is the account of the services in respect of which the decoration has been conferred:-
On the 13th May last, while H.M. Torpedo Boat Destroyer "Rob Roy" was proceeding at utmost speed on a full-power trial, a fire broke out in the forward boiler-room.

With entire disregard of his own safety, Mr. Smith immediately went below to search for the two ratings who were still there, and to shut off the boilers under extreme difficulties owing to the heat, escaping steam and water, well knowing in doing so the danger he ran from the burning oil fuel and the unconsumed gases accentuated by the confined and congested space of a destroyer's boiler-room.

Owing to his prompt action and presence of mind, Mr. Smith localised the damage and saved the lives of all who were below.

SMITH, James.

No. P / 10494.
Rank: CPL.
Unit/Force: MFP.
Other decorations: Nil.
Date of deed: January 17, 1919.
Date of Gazette: July 8, 1919.
Place/date of birth: Not known.
Place/date of death: Not known.
Place of memorial: Not known.
Town/county connections: Not known.
Remarks: Enlisted December 1, 1911. Does not appear to have received any WWI service medals. Discharged August 16, 1919. Presented with his AM by His Majesty the King at Buckingham Palace November 31, 1919.

Citation
See citation for GIBSON, A.

SMITH, Robert Sydney Steele.

Rank: Prob-Surg.
Unit/Force: RNVR. HMS *Bergemot*.
Other decorations: Nil.
Date of deed: August 13, 1917.
Date of Gazette: November 20, 1917.
Place/date of birth: Not known.
Place/date of death: Believed 1952.
Place of memorial: Not known.
Town/county connections: Not known.

Citation

The KING has been graciously pleased to confer the Decoration of the Albert Medal on:-
Surgeon Probationer Robert Sydney Steele Smith, R.N.V.R.

The following is the account of the services in respect of which the Decoration has been conferred:-
Surgeon Probationer Robert Sydney Steele Smith, R.N.V.R., was Medical Officer of one of H.M. ships which was torpedoed by an enemy submarine.

When the enemy torpedo struck the ship Surgeon Probationer Smith was in the wardroom aft with the 1st Lieutenant. The explosion wrecked the wardroom and rendered the 1st Lieutenant unconscious. All other exits being blocked, Surgeon Probationer Smith piled the wrecked furniture under the skylight, and got the 1st Lieutenant through this on deck. He then attended to a Petty Officer who was lying on deck with a broken arm and leg, adjusted and blew up his life-belt, and after doing the same for the 1st Lieutenant got him overboard, as the ship was then foundering.

The 1st Lieutenant was by then partially conscious, but was again stunned owing to an explosion when the vessel foundered, and when he was picked up by the boat he was apparently dead. Surgeon Probationer Smith applied artificial respiration until the 1st Lieutenant showed signs of life; he afterwards attended to the injured in the boat so far as circumstances allowed, until they were picked up forty-three hours later.

SMITH, William Revell.

Rank: Lt.
Unit/Force: RFA. A Bty 107 Bde RFA.
Other decorations: CB (LG January 24, 1946), CBE (1944), DSO (LG July 11, 1940), MC (LG April 6, 1918), Bar to MC (LG October 4, 1919).
Date of deed: January 17, 1919.
Date of Gazette: July 8, 1919.
Place/date of birth: Melbourne, Australia, 1894.
Place/date of death: Southern Rhodesia, June 4, 1956.
Place of memorial: Not known.
Town/county connections: Melbourne, Australia; Marandellas, Southern Rhodesia.
Remarks: Only son of Herbert Smith, 1 Pont Street, London. Educated Charterhouse. Enlisted as Pte 1865 2 Co of London Yeo. To Egypt November 5, 1914. Maj Gen January 16, 1945. Retired 1949. Married 1920 Norma, only daughter of J.G. Flowerdew Lowson. 1 son, 1 daughter. Also awarded 1914-15 Star, British War and Victory Medals (MID), 1939-45 Star, France & Germany Star, Defence Medal, War Medal, CdeG (Fr), Cdr L of M (USA), Comd O of Crown (It), CdeG (Bel). He was presented with his AM by His Majesty the King at Buckingham Palace on July 31, 1919.

Citation
See citation for GIBSON, A.

SPALDING, Edward Thomas.

No. 55883.
Rank: AB.
Unit/Force: RN. HMS *Comet*.
Other decorations: Nil.
Date of deed: August 4, 1918.
Date of Gazette: February 21, 1919.
Place/date of birth: Not known.
Place/date of death: Not known.;
Place of memorial: Not known.
Town/county connections: Not known.

Citation

The KING has been graciously pleased to approve of the award of the Albert Medal for gallantry in saving life at sea to
Commander Henry de Beauvoir Tupper, R.N.,
Able Seaman Edward Thomas Spalding, O.N. J55883 (Ch.).

The account of the services in respect of which these decorations have been conferred is as follows:-

On the 4th August, 1918, H.M.S. "Comet", under the command of Commander Tupper, was seriously damaged in collision. The ship was badly holed on the starboard side, the deck and all compartments eventually filled with water as far as the engine-room bulkhead, and the stern was at any moment liable to fall off. On being informed that the hydraulic release depth-charge was set to "fire", Commander Tupper sent away a man in a whaler to remove the primer. It was only possible to remove the primer from one of the charges, leaving the other depth-charge about 15 feet under water, still at "fire". Commander Tupper then went away in a dinghy himself, and by repeated diving operations tried to render it safe. After a rest he returned to complete the operation, in which Able Seaman Spalding, who was a passenger on the ship at the time and was a good swimmer, volunteered to assist. Commander Tupper at first refused to allow Spalding to assist him, as the latter had no knowledge of depth-charges, and Commander Tupper did not consider it safe for him to go down. Ultimately Commander Tupper and Able Seaman Spalding swam to the spot beneath which the depth-charge was submerged, and alternately gave a turn to the iron bar which Commander Tupper had placed in the handle, until the primer was eventually unscrewed and taken out of the depth-charge, thus rendering it safe. This operation was of the most dangerous nature, as at any moment the stern of the ship might have dropped off before the depth-charge was removed and would have carried down both the officer and the man, who would inevitably have lost their lives. The explosion would also have destroyed the remaining portion of the ship, with loss of life to those of the crew who were on board.

SPRING, James.

Rank: PTE.
Unit/Force: 1 Vol Bn E Yorks Regt.
Other decorations: Nil.
Date of deed: December 10, 1887.
Date of Gazette: April 20, 1888.
Place/date of birth: Not known.
Place/date of death: Not known.
Place of memorial: Not known.
Town/county connections: Not known.

Citation
THE Queen has been graciously pleased to confer the "Albert Medal of the Second Class" upon Mr. James Spring,a Private in the 1st Volunteer Battalion, the East Yorkshire Regiment, in recognition of the conspicuous gallantry displayed by him in saving the life of James Sharp, in St. Andrew's Dock, at Hull, on the 10th December, 1887.

STARTIN, Sir James.

Rank: Cdre (Adm, RN, Retd).
Unit/Force: RNR.
Other decorations: KCB (1917).
Date of deed: June 10, 1918.
Date of Gazette: August 20, 1918.
Place/date of birth: May 20, 1855.
Place/date of death: September 25, 1948.
Place of memorial: Not known.
Town/county connections: Leamington, Warks; Hayling Island, Hants.
Remarks: Son of William Startin of Leamington. Educated RN School, New Cross. Entered RN 1869. Sub-Lt 1876. Admiral (Retired) 1915. Served Royal Yacht *Victoria & Albert* 1889-1891. ADC to KEVII 1906-07. Married (1) Alice 1891 (d 1923) 3 sons, 1 daughter. (2) Ethel 1924 (d 1943). Father of Capt R.A. Startin OBE AM RN (q.v.). Also awarded SA 1879 (1 clasp), Egypt 1882 (1 clasp) (Despatches), E&W Afr (1 clasp) (Despatches), China 1900, 1914-15 Star, British War and Victory Medals, Ld'H (officier), RHS Silver Medal, RHS Bronze Medal with Clasp and Khedive's Star.

Citation
The KING has been graciously pleased to approve of the award of the Albert Medal for Gallantry in Saving Life at Sea to
Commodore Sir James Startin, K.C.B., R.N.R. (Admiral, retired).
   The account of the services in respect of which the Decoration has been conferred is as follows:-
An explosion occurred on board H.M. Motor Launch 64, on the 10th June, 1918.

Immediately after the explosion Commodore Startin proceeded alongside M.L. 64, the engine-room of which was still burning fiercely. On learning that the engineer was below, he sprang down the hatch without the slightest hesitation, and succeeded in recovering the body practically unaided.

In view of the fact that the bulkhead between the engine-room and the forward tanks had been blown down by the force of the explosion, and that the fire was blazing upon the side and on the top of the forward tanks, which are composed of exceedingly thin metal and were consequently liable to burst at any moment, the action of Commodore Startin in entering the engine-room before the fire was subdued showed the utmost possible gallantry and disregard of personal safety. Had the engineer not been past human aid he would undoubtedly have owed his life entirely to the courage and promptitude of Commodore Startin.

STARTIN, Robert Arthur.

Rank: Lt.
Unit/Force: RN. HMS *Melpomene.*
Other decorations: OBE.
Date of deed: March 28, 1916.
Date of Gazette: May 9, 1916.
Place/date of birth: February 7, 1894.
Place/date of death: Crowborough, Sussex, September 14, 1967
Place of memorial: Not known.
Town/county connections: Crowborough, Sussex.
Remarks: Son of Commodore Sir James Startin, KCB, AM, RNR. The only instance of a father and son gaining the AM. He later became Capt RN.

Citation

The KING has been graciously pleased to confer the Decoration of the Albert Medal of the Second Class on -
Lieutenant Robert Arthur Startin, R.N.
The following is the account of the services in respect of which the Decoration has been conferred:-
During the violent gale and snowstorm on the night of the 28th March, 1916, the whaler of H.M.S. "Melpomene", with a crew of six men, was driven by the blizzard on to the mud about 3/4 of a mile up the river above the Parkstone Jetty, Harwich. Lieut. Startin, on hearing that the whaler was missing, set out alone to search along the river bed. After wading through deep mud, at times up to his armpits, for a distance of about 300 yards, he eventually found the whaler, half full of water, aground on the mud, with her crew lying helpless in the boat, having given up all hope of being rescued. He only succeeded in rousing them by beating them with his stick, one man having to be forcibly dragged all the way to the shore by Lieut. Startin and the coxswain of the boat. After dragging him for about an hour, a distance of about 40 or 50 yards had been covered, when a light was seen moving inshore. Lieut. Startin ordered the crew to remain where they were whilst he went to the light, which proved to be carried by a search party with a rope. This rope was taken backwards and forwards personally by Lieut. Startin from the shore to the boat's crew until each one had been rescued, this exhausting and dangerous task in the deep mud being performed under the most trying conditions. All the crew were thus saved, though one afterwards died from the effects of exposure.

STEERE, Eric Edward.

Rank: Boy Mech.
Unit/Force: RNAS.
Other decorations: Nil.
Date of deed: December 20, 1917.
Date of Gazette: March 8, 1918.
Place/date of birth: Not known.
Place/date of death: August, 1921 (R.38 disaster).
Place of memorial: Not known.
Town/county connections: Worthing, Sussex.
Remarks: AM lost in R.38 disaster and a duplicate was issued to his father, Mr J. B. Steere of 37 Gloucester Place, Worthing, Sussex.

Citation
See citation for ROBINSON, H. V.

STEPHENS, Charles.

No. 64238.
Rank: SGT-MAJ.
Unit/Force: RFA. 44 Bty RFA.
Other decorations: Nil.
Date of deed: February 25, 1908.
Date of Gazette: May 13, 1910.
Place/date of birth: Hetton, Co Durham, October 21, 1868.
Place/Date of death: Not known; thought to be during WWII.
Place of memorial: Not known.
Town/county connections: Hetton, Co Durham.
Remarks: A miner before enlistment. Enlisted RA October 21, 1887. Battery SM May 12, 1899. Bde SM 42 Bde RFA January 4, 1908. Discharged to pension January 3, 1913. Married August 4, 1890 Emma (née Stanley). 2 daughters (1 died in infancy), 1 son. Also awarded QSA (6 bars) (MID) and LS&GC Medals. He does not appear to have been recalled for WWI; but in any event, he received no medals for this.

Citation
See citation for LITHGOW, H. L.

A. STICKLEY (RIGHT)

STICKLEY, Alfred.

No. PO.131808.
Rank: Ch Sto.
Unit/Force: RN. HMS *Success.*
Other decorations: Nil.
Date of deed: June 11, 1904.
Date of Gazette: February 17, 1905.
Place/date of birth: Isle of Dogs, January 12, 1867.
Place/date of death: Not known.
Place of memorial: Not known.
Town/county connections: Isle of Dogs.
Remarks: Enlisted RN as Boy April 1, 1885. A bargeman prior to enlistment. Served RN until March 29, 1919, being discharged as Chief Stoker. Also awarded QSA (no bar), 1914-15 Star, British War, Victory, Coronation 1911 and LS&GC Medals.

Citation

HIS MAJESTY The King has been graciously pleased to confer the Decoration of the Albert Medal of the Second Class on -
ALFRED STICKLEY, Chief Stoker, R.N.

The following is the account of the services in respect of which the decoration has been conferred:-

On the morning of the 11th June, 1904, at about 11.30, His Majesty's Torpedo Boat Destroyer "Success" was steaming towards Lamlash, when it became apparent from deck, owing to the issue of steam from the funnel, that something was wrong in the after stokehold. Alfred Stickley, Chief Stoker, in accordance with the orders of the Engineer Officer, went below to ascertain the cause.

On reaching the stokehold he found that there was an escape of steam from the top drum of No. 4 Boiler, which shortly caused one of the furnace doors which had been left unlatched to be blown open. The stokehold was immediately filled with flame and steam, and the men present were burnt and scalded.

Stickley grasped the situation with promptness, showing the greatest presence of mind in the emergency, and ran great risks in endeavouring to minimise the consequences of the accident and prevent further injuries to the men.

In spite of the conditions in the stokehold, and his own severe exposure to the flames, he managed to open out the fans to their full extent, and made many gallant attempts to close the furnace door and open the drencher valve. Finding it was impossible to drive the flames back, he gave orders for the hatch to be opened, and himself remained below until the four men in the stokehold effected their escape. His face and neck were severely burned, and his hands and forearms very badly scalded. For over four months he has been on the sick list suffering from his injuries. His lungs escaped injury, as he had the presence of mind to put cotton waste into his mouth while he was in the stokehold.

STOKER, Albert Ernest.

No. 227692.
Rank: PO.
Unit/Force: RN. HMS *Trident.*
Other decorations: Nil.
Date of deed: September 16, 1918.
Date of Gazette: January 31, 1919.
Place/date of birth: Not known.
Place/date of death: Not known.
Place of memorial: Not known.
Town/county connections: Not known.

Citation
See citation for BELBEN, G. D.

STONES, Robert.

No. 29998.
Rank: AB.
Unit/Force: RN. HMS *Highflyer.*
Other decorations: Nil.
Date of deed: December 6, 1917.
Date of Gazette: March 26, 1918.
Place/date of birth: Not known.
Place/date of death: Not known.
Place of memorial: Not known.
Town/county connections: Not known.

Citation
The KING has ... been graciously pleased to approve of the award of the Albert Medal for gallantry in saving life at sea to
Leading Seaman Thomas N. Davis, O.N.J. 18334 (Dev.), and
Able Seaman Robert Stones, O.N.J. 29998 (Dev.).
The account of the services in respect of which these medals have been conferred is as follows:-
On the 6th December, 1917, the French steamer "Mont Blanc", with a cargo of high explosives, and the Norwegian steamer "Imo", were in collision in Halifax Harbour. Fire broke out on the "Mont Blanc" immediately after the collision, and the flames very quickly rose to a height of over 100 feet. The crew abandoned their ship and pulled to the shore. A few minutes later a tremendous explosion took place, and the tug "Musquash" was seen to be on fire forward. The fire was increasing, and there appeared to be a great danger of her getting adrift, and being carried down on to another vessel. As the "Musquash" had a gun and ammunition on board there was danger of a further explosion and consequent loss of life.

The Captain of H.M.S. "Highflyer" hailed a private tug and asked her to take the "Musquash" in tow, but as they were unwilling to board the "Musquash" to get her in tow, the tug was brought alongside H.M.S. "Highflyer". Leading Seaman Davis and Able Seaman Stones immediately volunteered, and having been transferred by the tug to the burning "Musquash", which had by this time broken adrift, they secured a line from her stern, by means of which she was towed into midstream. The line then parted, and Davis and Stones passed another line from the "Musquash" to the pumping lighter "Lee", which had now arrived. They then both went forward to the burning part, and succeeded in getting to the ammunition, which was by this time badly scorched, pulled it away from the flames and threw it overboard. They then broke open the door of the galley, which was on fire inside, to enable the "Lee" to play her hoses into it. They repeated the same thing with the cabin.

By their work they made it possible to subdue the fire and save further damage and loss of life. At any moment whilst they were on board the "Musquash" the ammunition might have exploded. Note: Thomas Neil Davis (later Lt-Cdr) survived to become a GC in 1971.

STREAMS, Albert Edward.

No. PLY. 21038.
Rank: MNE.
Unit/Force: RM. HMS *Devonshire*.
Other decorations: Nil.
Date of deed: July 26, 1929.
Date of Gazette:
November 19, 1929.
Place/date of birth:
Reading, Berks, June 5, 1903.
Place/date of death:
KIA Sicily, July 10, 1944.
Place of memorial:
Syracuse War Cemetery, Sicily, Plot III, Row B, Grave 5.
Town/county connections:
Reading, Berks.

Citation

The KING has been graciously pleased to approve of the award of the Albert Medal to No. Po./21038 Marine Albert Edward Streams for gallantry in saving life at sea.

The following is the account of the services in respect of which the decoration has been conferred:-

H.M.S. "Devonshire" was carrying out full calibre firing on 26th July, 1929, when at the first salvo there was a heavy

A. E. STREAMS
Source: Unknown

explosion which blew off the roof of one of the turrets.

Marine Streams was the only man in the gun house who was not either killed instantly or fatally injured. He was seriously shaken by the explosion and instinctively climbed to the top of the side plating to escape but, on arriving at the top he looked back and saw the conditions inside the turret, and deliberately climbed back into it amidst the smoke and fumes notwithstanding the grave risk of further explosions. He then helped to evacuate the one remaining man of the right gun's crew, and took charge and played a major part in evacuating the crew of the Fire Control cabinet. When all the wounded were out he collapsed. His bravery, initiative and devotion to duty were beyond praise.

SULLIVAN, John.

Rank: Ch Sto.
Unit/Force: RN.
Other decorations: Nil.
Date of deed: March 22, 1913.
Date of Gazette: Not Gazetted. Approved by HMK August 27, 1913.
Place/date of birth: Not known.
Place/date of death: Not known.
Place of memorial: Not known.
Town/county connections: Not known.
Remarks: There is evidence in Royal Mint records of the AM in this case having been supplied. Citation is from HO file HO45/10707/241483.

Citation

While one of His Majesty's Torpedo Boat Destroyers was taking in oil fuel by means of two hoses from the R.F.A. "Burma" at Invergordon, the forward hose jerked out throwing oil fuel on to the Lower Mess deck in the vicinity of a stove which was alight and open. Owing to the ignition of oil fuel spray and vapour thus present there was a flash, the results of which were severe injuries to several men, to render one, Stoker Bickerstaff, helpless, to set fire to some clothing and fuel on the deck with dense black smoke and suffocating fumes which rendered it impossible to see or remain below decks for any but the shortest period.

The hose also continued to discharge, flooding the deck with oil which was thus heated by the flash to a dangerous temperature so that with the burning clothing and the open stove there was no small risk of general ignition of the pool of oil on the deck and a serious fire. The proximity of the foremost magazine, separated from the Mess deck by a single bulkhead only, must have made the effects of an ignition very disastrous.

At the time of the flash Sullivan was tending the after hose. Hearing something amiss he went forward and groped his way through the fumes to the Lower Mess Deck where Bickerstaff was lying. He managed to bring him up to the hatchway. Following the rescue of Bickerstaff he returned below where he searched this time with a rope tied to him, held by his commanding officer - to see if anyone else was there and to get up the clothing he had seen burning. He felt his way round the mess tables but finding no one he put out a fire smouldering on one of the tables and came up for fresh air, with burning clothes in his arms. Afterwards he went below once more to close the bottom flap of the store. Bickerstaff succumbed later.

J. SUTHERLAND
Source: Daily Graphic

SUTHERLAND, James.

Rank: LS.
Unit/Force: RN. HMS Salmon.
Other decorations: Nil.
Date of deed: December 2, 1901.
Date of Gazette: January 20, 1903.
Place/date of birth: Not known.
Place/date of death: Not known.
Place of memorial: Not known.
Town/county connections:
Not known.

Citation

HIS MAJESTY the King has been graciously pleased to confer the Decoration of the Albert Medal of the Second Class on James Sutherland, Leading Stoker, R.N., dated the 1st June, 1902.

The following is the account of the services in respect of which the decoration has been conferred:-

On the night of December the 2nd, 1901, His Majesty's torpedo boat destroyer "Salmon" was entering the port of Harwich in company with the Chatham Instructional Flotilla, when a collision took place between her and the steamship "Cambridge".

It appeared that the "Salmon" was sinking from the injuries she had sustained, and the order was given for the men to go forward and leave the ship by means of ropes which had been passed over the bows of the "Cambridge".

At the moment of the collision James Sutherland Leading Stoker, was in the mess deck asleep.

He went on deck immediately but remained behind when the order was given, and went to the stokehold to open the hatches.

He opened one and was in the act of opening the other when it blew open in his face and a stoker named Scholfield was seen coming up.

Sutherland assisted him out. Scholfield tried to go back for Bartlett, a stoker who was afterwards discovered to have been killed by the steam which the shock of the collision had caused to escape in great quantities from the pipes. He was prevented, however, by Sutherland, who sent him on board the "Cambridge" and said he would look after Bartlett.

Sutherland then by the aid of a light lowered from the "Cambridge" went down into the stokehold.

When he got down there was much steam, although the full force of it had gone. The chief danger, however, was from drowning, as it was full of water, and the ship was in great danger of sinking.

Sutherland found a Chief Stoker named Church in the far end of the stokehold, got behind him and floated him along. A rope was passed down the hatchway, and Church, who was nearly unconscious, was got out.

Sutherland, after looking round to see if anyone else was there, went on deck, searched the forward mess deck and stokers' mess deck, and then went on board the "Cambridge."

TANNER, Christopher Champain.

C. C. TANNER AM RNVR
Source: Cheltenham College Archives

Rank: Chaplain.
Unit/Force: RNVR. HMS *Fiji*.
Other decorations: Nil.
Date of deed: May 23, 1941.
Date of Gazette: April 28, 1942.
Place/date of birth: Cheltenham, Glos, June 24, 1908.
Place/date of death: Off Crete, May 23, 1941.
Place of memorial: Portsmouth Naval Memorial, Panel 60, Column 3; Cheltenham College.
Town/county connections: Cheltenham, Glos; Farnham Royal, Surrey; Haslemere, Surrey: Gloucester.
Remarks: Son of Rev Maurice Tanner of Christowe, Cheltenham, Educated Cheltenham College and Pembraoke College, Cambridge. BA (Cantab) 1932. Deacon 1935. Priest 1936 (by Bishop of Oxford). Curate of Farnham Royal, Surrey, 1935-37, St Michael de Lode, Gloucester, 1937-39. Haslemere, Surrey, 1939. Only England rugby player to win AM in WWII. The only Service Chaplain ever to win the AM. Played Rugby Union for England. Married Elanor Rutherford, September 18, 1937. One daughter, born January 5, 1939. Memorial near Chapel, Cheltenham College.

Citation

The KING has been graciously pleased to approve the following ...
For bravery and tireless devotion in saving life:
The Albert Medal (Posthumous).
The Reverend Christopher Champain Tanner, Temporary Chaplain, R.N.V.R., H.M.S. Fiji, who, when H.M.S. Fiji was sunk in the Battle of Crete, stayed to save the wounded men from the sick bay, and was one of the last to leave the ship. While in the water he spent himself in helping men to rafts and floats, and, when the rescuing ship came up, in bringing over to her disabled men and such as could not swim.

At length only one man remained to be brought across. Despite his exhaustion Mr. Tanner made a last effort to save him. He brought him across and saw him safely on board. But when hauled up he himself died within a few minutes.

TEHAN, Alfred George.

No. 3215.
Rank: PTE.
Unit/Force: 12 L.
Other decorations: MM (LG March 19, 1918).
Date of deed: December 11, 1915.
Date of Gazette: May 19, 1916.
Place/date of birth: London.
Place/date of death: Not known.
Place of memorial: Not known.
Town/county connections: London.
Remarks: To France August 15, 1914. Later Sgt. Also awarded QSA (Clasps Cape Colony, SA 01, SA 02), 1914 Star and bar, British War, Victory, Defence and LS&GC Medals. Presented with AM by His Majesty the King at Buckingham Palace on November 9, 1918.

Citation
The KING has been graciously pleased to award the Decoration of the Albert Medal to the undermentioned ... in recognition of (his) gallantry in saving life:-
Albert Medal of the Second Class
Private Alfred George Tehan, 12th (Prince of Wales's Royal) Lancers.

On the 11th December, 1915, whilst at bomb practice, one of the bomb throwers detonated the cap of his bomb, thus lighting the fuse, preparatory to throwing it. The fuse was damp, and as he thought it had gone out he placed this bomb on the ground and went on bomb throwing. Private Tehan, who was also in the trench, suddenly heard a fizzing noise, and saw that the fuse of the bomb was burning. He seized it, though the fuse was already half burnt through, and threw it out of the trench, thereby probably saving the lives of himself and four other men in the traverse with him. The bomb burst just before reaching the ground.

THOMPSON, Malcolm.

Rank: AB.
Unit/Force: RN. Tug *Sunderland*.
Other decorations: Nil.
Date of deed: November 8, 1916.
Date of Gazette: July 9, 1918.
Place/date of birth: Not known.
Place/date of death: Not known.
Place of memorial: Not known.
Town/county connections: Not known.

Citation
See citation for HENRY, J. D.

THORNER, Harry.

Rank: 2 Lt.
Unit/Force: MGC. 90 Coy MGC.
Other decorations: Nil.
Date of deed: December 30, 1917.
Date of Gazette: June 7, 1918.
Place/date of birth: March 5, 1887.
Place/date of death: Nr Ypres, Belgium, December 30, 1917.
Place of memorial: The Huts Military Cemetery, Dickebusch, Plot 15, Row A, Grave 12.
Town/county connections: Not known.
Remarks: Unmarried. Served WWI in 10 Hy Bty RGA from August 14, 1914, with No. 42041. Transferred to MGC as T/2Lt December 1, 1916. Was Cpl in RGA. To Balkans July 19, 1915. Also awarded 1914-15 Star, British War and Victory Medals. His AM was presented to his brother, Thomas Thorner, of 68 Durlston Rd, Upper Clapton, London, NE by His Majesty the King at Buckingham Palace on June 1, 1918.

Citation

The KING has been pleased to award the Albert Medal in Gold in recognition of the gallant act of Temporary Second Lieutenant Harry Thorner, 90th Company, Machine Gun Corps, in saving life in France in December last at the cost of his own life. The circumstances are as follows:-

On the 30th December, 1917, Lieutenant Thorner was examining some Mills Hand Grenades in a small concrete dugout in France prior to taking them up to his machine gun position during an expected enemy raid. One of the grenades began to fizz when taken out of the box. There were twelve men in the dugout at the moment, and there was no possible means of disposing of the bomb. Realising what had happened Lieutenant Thorner shouted to his men to clear out whilst he himself held the bomb in his hand close to his body until it exploded and killed him. By this magnificent act of courage Lieutenant Thorner deliberately sacrificed his own life for others. Of the twelve men who were in the dugout all but two escaped without injury they were slightly wounded.

THORPE, James William.

No. D/SBR/X7813.
Rank: SBA.
Unit/Force: RN. HMS *Broke*.
Other decorations: Nil.
Date of deed: November 8, 1942.
Date of Gazette: April 20, 1943.
Place/date of birth: Bacup, Lancs, 1920.
Place/date of death: Off N. Africa, November 9, 1942.
Place of memorial: Plymouth Naval Memorial.

J. W. THORPE
Source: Family

Town/county connections: Bacup, Lancs.
Remarks: Eldest son of Walter and Lily Thorpe of Bacup. Two younger brothers. Educated Tunstead Church of England School, Shacksteads, Rossendale. Worked as a shoe designer and joined RNVR in 1938. Also awarded 1939-45, Atlantic and Africa Stars and War Medal.

Citation
The KING has been graciously pleased to approve the following...
For gallantry in saving life at sea:
The Albert Medal in Bronze (Posthumous).
Sick Berth Attendant James William Thorpe, D/SBR/X.7813.
In a hazardous operation off the North African Coast, H.M.S. Broke came under heavy fire. Many of her company were wounded. Sick Berth Attendant Thorpe showed great courage in tending the wounded and getting them to places of greater safety. He himself was then badly hit, but he spent his last strength in the care of others, working till he could no longer stand. He died of his wounds.

TOMAN, Richard Wright.

Rank: Engr.
Unit/Force: RN. HMS *Foam.*
Other decorations: Nil.
Date of deed: August 3, 1898.
Date of Gazette: November 18, 1898.
Place/date of birth: Not known.
Place/date of death: Not known.
Place of memorial: Not known.
Town/county connections: Not known.
Remarks:

Citation
HER Majesty the Queen has been graciously pleased to confer the Decoration of the Albert Medal of the Second Class on -
RICHARD WRIGHT TOMAN, Engineer of Her Majesty's Ship "Foam".
The following is the account of the services in respect of which the Decoration has been conferred:-
On the 3rd August, 1898, whilst Her Majesty's ship "Foam" was carrying out her full speed trial at Malta, the mean pressure cylinder burst; the revolutions of the engines at the time being 350 per minute.

There was no indication whatever of the impending explosion, which happened with great suddenness.

MR. TOMAN at once ordered every one to leave the engine room, and ran to the main throttle-valve, which is at the fore-end of the engine room, and endeavoured to shut it off, getting both arms and hands badly scalded in consequence. He then proceeded to shut off the main stop valves of boilers in the stokeholds.

Having done this with great promptitude, and so confining the steam to the boilers alone, he increased the chance of saving the life of anyone who might have been left below.

MR. TOMAN, thinking all the men were not up from the engine room, went down and searched in this volume of steam, which was at a pressure of 200 lbs. to the square inch when the cylinder burst, but was unable to find anyone.

He then tried to get on deck, but, owing to the excessive volume of steam, he twice fell halfway down the ladder. He eventually reached the deck, and at once proceeded to turn on the fire extinguishers to the boilers, his hands at the time being almost bare of skin.

The valve wheel was heated to such an extent as to be almost unbearable to hands in an ordinary condition.

As the engines were flying round immediately after the accident there was every danger of the connecting rod being driven through the bottom, but it was greatly lessened by the promptitude and pluck shown by MR. TOMAN in shutting off the main stop-valves, and so reducing the risk of the ship being sunk or seriously damaged, and the lives of all on board being probably lost.

MR. TOMAN, after having been driven out of the engine room and severely scalded, again went below into the engine room, which was filled with steam, to search for anyone who may not have been able to escape, and only successful in finally getting out of the engine room after two attempts.

MR. TOMAN was very much scalded on both arms and knees by the escape of steam, which necessitated his removal to hospital.

T. K. TRIGGS

TRIGGS, Tom Kenneth.

Rank: Lt-Cdr (A/Cdr).
Unit/Force: RN. HMS *Highflyer.*
Other decorations: Nil.
Date of deed: December 6, 1917.
Date of Gazette: March 26, 1918.
Place/date of birth: Not known.
Place/date of death: December 6, 1917.
Place of memorial: Plymouth Naval Memorial, Panel 20.
Town/county connections: Southsea, Hants.
Remarks: Son of Captain Tom B. Triggs. Appointed Midshipman January 1, 1900 (HMS *Glory*). Sub Lt February 10, 1903. Married to Anis Triggs of Western Parade, Southsea.

Citation
See citation for BECKER, W.

TUNN, John Patrick.

Rank: 2 Lt.
Unit/Force: 9 AIF..
Other decorations: Nil.
Date of deed: July 19, 1918.
Date of Gazette: October 15, 1918.
Place/date of birth:
Glasgow, July 8, 1892.
Place/date of death: Brisbane, Australia, October 12, 1955.
Place of memorial: Toowong Cemetery, Brisbane.
Town/county connections: Glasgow; Brisbane.
Remarks: Son of John and Catherine Tunn. Father was a pawn-broker. Educated St Mungo's Academy, Glasgow. Family emigrated to Australia about 1910. Tunn worked as a cabinet maker then began accountancy studies and in 1916 became clerk in State Government Insurance Office. Enlisted AIF May 19, 1916. To France May 28, 1917. Corporal October 1917. Commissioned May 20, 1918. Married Mary Louisa Sherman September 16, 1919. 2 sons, 2 daughters. Entitled to British War and Victory Medals.

J. P. TUNN
Source: "Reville"

Citation
The KING has been pleased to award the Albert Medal in recognition of gallantry displayed in saving life:-
Second Lieutenant John Patrick Tunn, 9th Battalion, Australian Imperial Force.

On the 19th July, 1918, as some Australian troops were advancing to an attack in France, one of the men tripped on some wire and a rifle grenade fell from his rifle to the ground with the pin out. Second Lieutenant Tunn, who was about 10 yards away, saw what had happened and ran back and picked up the grenade. In doing so he tripped on the wire and the grenade fell from his hand. He picked it up again, and as he did so it exploded and blew off his right hand, besides wounding him in the head. The men were unhurt.

TUPPER, Henry de Beauvoir.

Rank: Cdr.
Unit/Force: RN. HMS *Comet*.
Other decorations: Nil.
Date of deed: August 4, 1918.

Date of Gazette: February 21, 1919.
Place/date of birth: Not known.
Place/date of death: Not known.
Place of memorial: Not known.
Town/county connections: Not known.

Citation
See citation for SPALDING, E. T.

A. T. TURNER
Source: Globe & Laurel

TURNER, Alec Talbot.

Rank: Lt.
Unit/Force: RM. HMS *Ramillies*.
Other decorations: Nil.
Date of deed: March 2, 1939.
Date of Gazette: August 4, 1939.
Place/date of birth: Tonbridge, Kent, March 30, 1916.
Place/date of death: Off Gozo, March 2, 1939.
Place of memorial: Chapel, RM Barracks, Stonehouse, Plymouth
Town/county connections: Tonbridge, Kent.
Remarks: Son of A. Turner of Haslemere, Surrey. Comsd as Probationary 2nd Lt September 1, 1934. Also held NGS Medal with bar for Palestine.

Citation
The KING has been graciously pleased to approve the posthumous award of the Albert Medal to the late Lieutenant A.T. Turner, R.M.

The following is an account of the services in respect of which the Decoration has been conferred:-
On the 2nd March, 1939, when H.M.S. "Ramillies" was preparing to enter the Grand Harbour at Malta, the Royal Marines were employed in making the ladders ready to hoist out. Sergeant C.E. Young, Royal Marines, was in charge of the starboard foremost gangway davit when one of the davits broke loose and carried him overboard. Lieutenant A.T. Turner, R.M., who was standing some 12 yards further aft, saw what happened and without hesitation dived into the sea after Sergeant Young without even removing his india-rubber boots.

Lieutenant Turner was last seen about 40 yards swimming towards the Sergeant. The two life boats were lowered immediately, and got away very promptly. These were followed by the Ship, but despite a thorough search for several hours, neither Lieutenant Turner nor Sergeant Young were seen again.

The sea at the time was very rough with a strong following wind.

USHER, Albert Edward.

No. M2/188130.
Rank: PTE.
Unit/Force: ASC. 707 MT Coy ASC.
Other decorations: Nil.
Date of deed: October 22, 1916.
Date of Gazette: January 1, 1918.
Place/date of birth: Not known.
Place/date of death: Not known.
Place of memorial: Not known.
Town/county connections: Not known.
Remarks: Alss awarded British War and Victory Medals. Hewas presented with the AM by His Majesty the King at Buckingham Palace July 10, 1919.

Citation
See BEARNE, L. C.

VAISEY, Guy Maddison.

Rank: 2 Lt.
Unit/Force: 3 GLOSTERS, att 10 Bn.
Other decorations: Nil.
Date of deed: April 6, 1917.
Date of Gazette: August 27, 1918.
Place/date of birth: c 1890.
Place/date of death: France, April 19, 1918 (DOW).
Place of memorial: Pernes British Military Cemetery, Plot 1, Row C, Grave 25.
Remarks: Also served as Pte 18100 3 Canadian Inf Bn. Also awarded 1914-15 Star, British War and Victory Medals. AM was presented to his widow, Mrs E. J. Vaisey by His Majesty the King at Buckingham Palace September 4, 1918.

Citation
The KING has been pleased to award the Albert Medal ... in recognition of gallantry displayed in saving life in France:-
Second Lieutenant Guy Maddison Vaisey,
3rd Battalion (attached 10th Battalion), Gloucestershire Regiment.
On the 6th April, 1917, during bomb throwing practice at a Divisional Bomb School in France, one of the men under instruction, having extracted the pin from a Mills grenade, allowed the grenade to slip out of his hand. Lieutenant Vaisey, seeing what had happened, dashed round a traverse in the trench from which the practice was being conducted, picked up the grenade, and threw it clear of the trench; it exploded almost immediately.
The action was performed at great personal risk, as the thrower was in his way and was dazed with fright. Lieutenant Vaisey by his courage and prompt action undoubtedly prevented a fatal accident.
Lieutenant Vaisey died of his wounds in April last.

WADDAMS, Arthur Richard.

Rank: Lt.
Unit/Force: IARO, att 44 Merwara Inf.
Other decorations: Nil.
Date of deed: November 22, 1917.
Date of Gazette: August 30, 1918.
Place/date of birth: Gloucester, November 12, 1891.
Place/date of death: Mesopotamia, November 22, 1917.
Place of memorial: Basra War Cemetery, Iraq.
Town/county connections: Gloucester, London.
Remarks: Son of Christopher and Harriette Waddams of 14 Shakespear Road, London. Also awarded 1914-15 Star, British War and Victory Medals.

Citation
The KING has been pleased to award the Albert Medal ...in recognition of gallantry displayed in saving ... life:-
Lieutenant Arthur Richard Waddams, Indian Army Reserve of Officers.

In Mesopotamia, in November last, Lieutenant Waddams was instructing a class in firing rifle grenades. While a private of the 88th Burmans was under instruction, the rifle missed fire and the detonator of the grenade started working without the grenade leaving the rifle. Lieutenant Waddams, realising the danger, rushed forward, and, pushing back the soldier, seized his rifle with one hand and the grenade with the other, and tried to throw it over the wall before it exploded. Unfortunately, the grenade exploded in his hand and he received fatal injuries. The soldier whose life Lieutenant Waddams saved was only slightly injured.

WADE, Charles Herbert.

Rank: Lt.
Unit/Force: DLI. 88 Labour Coy.
Other decorations: Nil.
Date of deed: June 16, 1917.
Date of Gazette: January 4, 1918.
Place/date of birth: Not known.
Place/date of death: Not known.
Place of memorial: Not known.
Town/county connections: Sunderland.
Remarks: Was Pte 2587 DLI. To France April 17, 1915. Comsd October 26, 1915. To Labour Corps April 27, 1917. Capt July 28, 1920. Also awarded 1914-15 Star, British War and Victory Medals. Came from 19 Roseville Rd, Sunderland. Presented with AM by His Majesty the King at Buckingham Palace December 4, 1917.

Citation

The KING has been graciously pleased to award the Decoration of the Albert Medal to the undermentioned Officer ... in recognition of (his) gallantry in saving life:-

Lieutenant Charles Herbert Wade, 88th Labour Company, formerly Durham Light Infantry.

On the 16th June 1917, a party of men were loading trucks alongside an ammunition dump. The ammunition ignited and began to explode in all directions. The men rushed for shelter, but one of them was caught in the trucks. Lieutenant Wade at once ran forward into the blazing ammunition and released the man, and then called for volunteers to save the trucks which, with their assistance, he succeeded in doing.

WAINWRIGHT, David.

Rank: Lt.
Unit/Force: RN. HMS *Penarth*.
Other decorations: Nil.
Date of deed: February 4, 1919.
Date of Gazette: May 20, 1919.
Place/date of birth: Not known.
Place/date of death: Not known.
Place of memorial: Not known.
Town/county connections: Not known.

Citation

The KING has been graciously pleased to approve of the award of the Albert Medal for gallantry in saving life at sea to -

Lieutenant David Wainwright, R.N.

The account of the services in respect of which this decoration has been conferred is as follows:-

On the 4th February, 1919, H.M.S. "Penarth" struck a mine and immediately began to sink. Lieutenant David Wainwright, taking command of the situation, at once superintended the manning and lowering of the starboard gig, and later the launching of the Carley floats. Hearing there was a stoker injured in one of the stokeholds, he called for volunteers to show him the way, and at once made his way forward. There was by now a heavy list on the ship, and it was apparent she would not remain afloat much longer, the upper deck on the starboard side being already awash.

Lieutenant Wainwright made his way below unaided, and while he was in the stokehold the ship struck a second mine abaft of him. The forepart was blown off and sank, and he was forced to wait till the stokehold had filled before he could float to the surface up the escape.

He displayed the greatest gallantry and disregard of his own personal safety in going below at a time when the ship was liable to sink at any moment.

WALTON, Thomas Michael.

No. M/08147.
Rank: Mech SSGT.
Unit/Force: ASC. GHQ Tpt Sup Col Wksp ASC.

Other decorations: Nil.
Date of deed: May 2, 1916.
Date of Gazette: August 29, 1916.
Place/date of birth: Not known.
Place/date of death: Not known.
Place of memorial: Not known.
Town/county connections: Not known.
Remarks: To France December 13, 1914. Also awarded 1914-15 Star, British War, Victory Medals and GSM (bar Iraq). Later Major, TD. Presented with his AM by His Majesty the King at Buckingham Palace October 21, 1917 (as Lieut).

Citation
See citation for ANDERSON, A.

A. R. S. WARDEN
Source: W. S. Buoy

WARDEN, Arthur Richard Shaw.

Rank: Lt-Cdr.
Unit/Force: RN. Naval Transport Officer.
Other decorations: Nil.
Date of deed: October 26, 1915.
Date of Gazette: April 18, 1916.
Place/date of birth: Kamptee, E Indies, 1866.
Place/date of death: Not known.
Place of memorial: Not known.
Town/county connections: Not known.
Remarks: Son of Captain Warden RIM. Trained on TS Conway and indentured to Shaw, Savill Line January 18, 1884. Also awarded 1914 Star, British War, Victory and Special Constabulary Faithful Service Medals. MID (March 16, 1919). He was presented with his AM by His Majesty the King at Buckingham Palace April 16, 1916.

Citation
See citation for GIMBLE, E.

WARNE, Albert Edgar.

Rank: FLT SGT.
Unit/Force: RFC. Aeroplane Repair Sec, 24 Wg RFC.
Other decorations: Nil.
Date of deed: January 26, 1918.
Date of Gazette: April 26, 1918.

Place/date of birth: c1895.
Place/date of death: October 13, 1918. (Aircraft accident).
Place of memorial: Ugborough (St Peter) Churchyard, Devon.
Town/county connections: Grantham, Lincs.
Remarks: From Mill House, Grantham, Lincs. Son of Richard and Jane Warne of 1 Sunny Dale, Bittaford, Ivybridge, Devon. Presented with his AM by His Majesty the King at Buckingham Palace on June 22, 1918.

Citation

The KING has been graciously pleased to award the Albert Medal
... in recognition of gallantry displayed in ... endeavouring to save life:-
Flight-Serjeant Albert Edgar Warne, 24th Wing Aeroplane Repair Section, and
Flight Serjeant Horace Cannon, No. 50 Training Squadron.

On the 26th January last, while flying in England, a pilot when attempting to land lost control of his machine, which crashed to the ground from a height of about 150 feet, and burst into flames. Flight Serjeants Warne and Cannon went to the rescue of the pilot at great personal risk, as one tank of petrol blew up and another was on fire; moreover, the machine was equipped with a belt of live cartridges, which they dragged out of the flames. They managed to extricate the pilot, who was strapped to the burning plane, but he died shortly afterwards from his injuries and burns.
Note: Horace Cannon survived to become a GC holder in 1971.

WARWICK, Percy.

No. 18905.
Rank: LCPL.
Unit/Force: 1 Gren Gds, att 3 Gds Bde Grenade Coy
Other decorations: Nil.
Date of deed: September 19, 1915.
Date of Gazette: July 4, 1916.
Place/date of birth: Wakefield, Yorks, c January, 1885.
Place/date of death: Not known.
Place of memorial: Not known.
Town/county connections: Wakefield, Yorks.
Remarks: Apprentice on enlistment. Son of William Warwick. Enlisted August 1914. To France May 1, 1915. MID LG June 13, 1916. Discharged 1918. Married (1) Elizabeth Dawson November 21, 1916. (2) Lilly, November 17, 1947. Also awarded 1914-15 Star, British War and Victory Medals. Presented with AM by His Majesty the King at Buckingham Palace March 21, 1916.

Citation

The KING has been graciously pleased to award the Decoration of the Albert Medal of the Second Class to ... Lance-Corporal Percy Warwick, 1st Battalion, Grenadier Guards (who is serving in France), in recognition of (his) gallantry in saving life at bombing practice.

On the 19th September, 1915, a class of men attached to the Grenade Company of the 3rd

J. WEBB
Source: Mrs L. M. Warnes

Guards Brigade was being instructed in throwing live bombs from a saphead into a small trench twenty-five yards away. One of the men when his turn came was nervous and, after igniting his bomb, dropped it behind him. Warwick at once, with great presence of mind, picked the bomb from between the legs of several men and threw it out of the trench.

...Explosion followed immediately the bomb had been thrown away.

WATSON, Christopher.

Rank: 2nd Engr.
Unit/Force: RN. Tug *Sunderland*.
Other decorations: Nil.
Date of deed: November 8, 1916.
Date of Gazette: July 9, 1918.
Place/date of birth: Not known.
Place/date of death: Not known.
Place of memorial: Not known.
Town/county connections: Not known.

Citation
See citation for HENDRY, J. D.

WEBB, James.

No. 2511.
Rank: CPL.
Unit/Force: RAMC.
Other decorations: Nil.
Date of deed: January 2, 1916.
Date of Gazette: May 19, 1916.
Place/date of birth: Northampton, November 17, 1885.
Place/date of death: Northampton, March 19, 1961.
Place of memorial: Northampton.
Town/county connections: Northampton.
Remarks: A railwaymen with the London & North Western Railway prior to enlistment. Married May 27, 1911 and had 2 sons and 1 daughter. Both sons served in WWII, one being killed at Tobruk. Retired from railway service in 1950. To France August 21, 1914. Also awarded 1914 Star, British War and Victory Medals. Presented with his AM by His Majesty the King at Buckingham Palace August 15, 1917.

Citation
See citation for FOLEY, R.

WEEKS, Frederick William.

Rank: A/Lt.
Unit/Force: RNR. HMS *Halcyon*.
Other decorations: Nil.
Date of deed: January 18, 1917.
Date of Gazette: March 13, 1917.
Place/date of birth: Not known.
Place/date of death: Not known.
Place of memorial: Not known.
Town/county connections: Not known.

Citation
The KING has been graciously pleased to confer the Decoration of the Albert Medal of the Second Class on:-
Acting Lieutenant Frederick William Weeks, R.N.R.
The following is the account of the services in respect of which the Decoration has been conferred:-
On the night of Thursday, the 18th January, 1917, a member of the crew of one of his Majesty's Ships, when returning from leave, fell into the sea between the ship and the quay. The matter was at once reported to Acting Lieutenant Frederick William Weeks, R.N.R., to whom it was obvious that any attempt at rescue must be attended by considerable danger. The ship, which was kept clear of the side of the quay by spar fenders of only nine inches in diameter, was working to and fro with the slight swell entering the harbour. Moreover the man was incapable of helping himself; he was of heavy build and was wearing a uniform greatcoat. In view of the risk to the rescuer of being crushed between the ship and the quay, Lieutenant Weeks decided that he could not order a man down. He thereupon took a line and went down himself. By this time the man was almost unconscious. Lieutenant Weeks managed to obtain a hold of his hair and by this means kept him sufficiently above the water, whilst wedging himself with his back against the quay with his knees against the ship's side. During this time he was mostly under water, the temperature of which was thirty-nine degrees. He succeeded in securing a line round the man, who was hauled on deck. The man was unconscious and very nearly drowned when brought on deck, and there is no doubt that, but for Lieutenant Weeks' prompt measures, he would have lost his life.

WHITEHEAD, William.

No. 14410.
Rank: LCPL.
Unit/Force: 9 Manchester Regt.
Other decorations: Nil.
Date of deed: January 5, 1919.
Date of Gazette: April 25, 1919.
Place/date of birth: Not known.
Place/date of death: Not known.
Place of memorial: Not known.

Town/county connections: Not known.
Remarks: To France November 9, 1915. Also awarded 1914-15 Star, British War and Victory Medals. Presented with AM by His Majesty the King at Buckingham Palace June 28, 1919.

Citation

The KING has been pleased to award the Albert Medal in ... recognition of gallantry diaplayed in saving life:-
Lance-Corporal William Whitehead, 9th Battalion, Manchester Regiment.

On the night of the 5th January, 1919, Lance-Corporal Whitehead was in command of a guard on the River Meuse. One of the guard, in crossing a plank gangway from a barge where the guard-room was situated to relieve a sentry on the river bank, missed his footing and fell into the river, which was in flood. Lance-Corporal Whitehead immediately jumped into the river, but in the pitch darkness missed the drowning man. He swam to the shore, climbed out and ran down the bank until he reached the spot where the man had been carried by the swift-running stream, and again jumping in he succeeded in rescuing him.

Both rescuer and rescued were wearing equipment and greatcoats at the time, and Lance Corporal Whitehead undoubtedly risked his life in saving the life of his comrade who, when brought to the bank, was unconscious.

H. E. WILD
Source: "An Unknown Few"

WILD, Harry Ernest.

Rank: PO.
Unit/Force: RN.
Other decorations: Nil.
Date of deed: October 9, 1915 to March 20, 1916.
Date of Gazette: July 6, 1923.
Place/date of birth: Not known.
Place/date of death: Mediterranean Sea, March 10, 1918 (believed).
Place of memorial: Capuccina Naval Cemetery, Malta (believed).
Town/county connections: Not known.
Remarks: Also awarded Polar Medal (bars Antarctic 1914-16 and Antarctic 1917) and Messina Earthquake Medal 1908.

Citation

The KING has been pleased to award the Albert Medal in recognition of the gallant conduct of Mr. Ernest Edward Mills Joyce, ex-Petty Officer, R.N., Mr. William Rayment Richards, Mr. Victor George Hayward (deceased) and Petty Officer Harry Ernest Wild, R.N. (deceased) in saving and endeavouring to save life while serving as members of the Ross Sea Party of the Shackleton Trans-Antarctic Expedition of 1914-17.

The Expedition had for its object the crossing of the Antarctic Continent from the Weddell Sea to the Ross Sea, via the South Pole, a distance of about seventeen hundred miles. Sufficient supplies for the journey could not be carried, and it was therefore necessary to establish a chain of depots on the Ross Sea side as far southwards as possible. With this end in view, the ship *"Aurora"* was sent to McMurdo Sound at the southern extremity of the Ross Sea and, as it was intended that the vessel should winter there, a portion only of the stores and equipment was disembarked. McMurdo Sound was reached in January, 1915, but during a blizzard in May, the *"Aurora"* was blown out to sea and was unable to return, and the nine members of the Expedition who were on shore were left stranded. They recognised that failure to establish the depots would undoubtedly result in the loss of the main body and resolved, in spite of their grave shortage of equipment to carry out the allotted programme.

For this purpose a party under the command of Sub-Lieutenant A.L. Mackintosh, R.N.R., and consisting of the Reverend A.P. Spencer-Smith, Messrs Joyce, Richards, Hayward and Wild and three other members who assisted for a part of the outward journey left Hut Point, Ross Island, on October 9th. They took with them two sledges and four dogs, and 162 days elapsed before the surviving members of the party were back at Hut Point, the total distance covered being approximately 950 miles.

Mr. Spencer-Smith had to be dragged on a sledge for 42 days, mainly by hand labour, the distance covered being over 350 miles. When more than 100 miles remained to be covered the collapse of Lieutenant Mackintosh imposed an additional burden on the active members of the party who were all suffering from scurvy and snow blindness and were so enfeebled by their labours that at times they were unable to cover more than 2 or 3 miles in 15 hours.

Mr. Spencer-Smith died when only 19 miles remained to be covered, but Lieutenant Mackintosh was brought in safely to the base.

Note: By the time this citation appeared, Joyce had been killed in action and Hayward and Wild were both dead. Richards, whose Christian names were Richard Walter and not as above, went to live in Australia and survived to become a GC in 1971.

WILLIS, Patrick Henry.

No. D/J 19570.
Rank: PO.
Unit/Force: RN. HMS/M *Poseidon.*
Other decorations: Nil.
Date of deed: June 9, 1931.
Date of Gazette: July 24, 1931.
Place/date of birth: March 17, 1897.
Place/date of death: Merton, Surrey, 1953.
Place of memorial: Morden, Surrey.
Town/county connections: Merton, Surrey.
Remarks: Joined RN March 17, 1915. Served WWI. Joined submarines August 31, 1926 and joined *Poseidon* October 1, 1929. Rated CPO June 9, 1931. Married. 1 son, 1 daughter. Later became Chief Electrician at Merton Park Studios, Surrey. In 1931 a film was made of this incident entitled "Men Like These" (USA: "Trapped in a Submarine"). It was rated Cert A and lasted 46 minutes. It was described as a very good film. Willis is believed to have been the last surviving holder of the AM in Gold for Sea Service. Also held 1914-15 Trio and LSEGC (RN).

P. WILLIS
Source: "Recent Heroes of Modern Adventure"

Citation

The KING has been graciously pleased to approve of the award of the Albert Medal in Gold to Petty Officer (now Chief Petty Officer) Patrick Henry Willis, R.N., Official No. D/J.19570.

The following is the account of the services in respect of which the decoration has been conferred:-

On the 9th June, 1931, H.M. Submarine "Poseidon" collided with a merchant ship and eventually sank as a result of the severe damage sustained.

After the collision occurred and the order "Close watertight doors" had been given, Petty Officer Willis took charge of the hands in the fore part, calling upon them to close the door of the torpedo compartment with those inside as this step might mean the saving of the submarine. The operation was difficult, as the bulkhead had buckled, but by their united efforts the door was eventually closed, leaving only a slight leak. Whilst this work was in progress the ship lurched to starboard and sank with heavy inclination by the bows. The electric light leads were all cut at the moment of the collision and from that time until the final evacuation the imprisoned men were working with the occasional illumination of an electric torch. Willis first said prayers for himself and his companions and then ordered them to put on their escape apparatus, making sure that they all knew how to use it. He then explained he was going to flood the compartment in order to equalise the pressure with that outside the submarine, and how it was to be done, telling off each man to his station. He also rigged a wire hawser across the hatchway to form a support for men to stand on whilst the compartment was flooding. During the long period of waiting which ensued, Willis kept his companions in good heart, while one Able Seaman passed the time in instructing a Chinese Boy in the use of his apparatus. The other men worked cheerfully at the various valves and rigging the platform. After two hours and ten minutes when the water was about up to the men's knees, Willis considered the pressure might be sufficient to open the hatch. With considerable difficulty the hatch was opened sufficiently to release two men, but the pressure than reclosed the hatch, and it was necessary to make the pressure more equal by further flooding before a second attempt could be made. After another hour, by which time the men in the compartment were nearly up to their necks in water and the air lock was becoming very small, a second effort was made. This was successful and the hatch opened, and four other men came to the surface, including Petty Officer Willis.

It is abundantly clear that all the men imprisoned in the slowly flooding compartment in almost total darkness, faced a situation more than desperate, with courage and fortitude in accordance with the very highest traditions of the Service. The coolness, confidence, ability and power of command shown by Petty Officer Willis, which no doubt were principally responsible for the saving of so many valuable lives, are deserving of the very highest praise.

WILLOUGHBY, James Beautine.

Rank: Capt.
Unit/Force: RN. Principal Naval Transport Officer.
Other decorations: Nil.
Date of deed: March 3, 1869.
Date of Gazette: July 27, 1869.
Place/date of birth: Not known.
Place/date of death: Not known.
Place of memorial: Not known.
Town/county connections: Not known.

Citation

THE Queen has been graciously pleased to confer the decoration of "The Albert Medal of the Second Class" on:-

Captain JAMES BEAUTINE WILLOUGHBY, R.N., the Principal Transport Officer in Egypt.

The following is an account of the services in respect of which the decoration has been conferred:-

On the 3rd March, 1869, whilst the 1st Battalion of the 21st Regiment was disembarking, at Alexandria, from the Egyptian steamer "Bird of the Harbour", one of the soldiers, who was fully accoutred, fell overboard in a fit, and sank immediately.

Captain WILLOUGHBY at once jumped into the water after him, dived, and got hold of him; and after considerable difficulty and danger, saved him. When brought out of the water, the man was insensible.

The harbour of Alexandria is known to be dangerously infested with sharks; but in addition to the danger from sharks, Captain WILLOUGHBY ran great risk from the fact that the soldier fell between the pier and the vessel, and that, owing to the swell in the harbour, both Captain WILLOUGHBY and the soldier might have been crushed.

WILSON, William.

No. 5383.
Rank: CSGT.
Unit/Force: 1 SG.
Other decorations: Nil.
Date of deed: November 12, 1890.
Date of Gazette: December 23, 1890.
Place/date of birth: Govan, Lanarkshire, January 1862.
Place/date of death: Not known.
Place of memorial: Not known.
Town/counth connections: Govan, Lanarkshire; Cullybackey, Co Antrim, N. Ireland.
Remarks: A fitter on enlistment at Glasgow on July 30, 1881. Married Elizabeth (née Bishop) on July 14, 1885 at St Mary's Lambeth, London. 3 sons, 6 daughters. Discharged as a Colour Sgt on August 31, 1905 after 24 years 33 days service Also held Egypt Medal 1882 (Bar Tel-el-Kebir), Khedive's Star and LS&GC Medal.

Citation

See citation for DAVIS, D.T.

WOOD, Archibald Charles.

No. 361747.
Rank: CPL.
Unit/Force: RAF. 60 (Bomber) Sqn RAF.
Other decorations: Nil.
Date of deed: August 8, 1936.

Date of Gazette: January 22, 1937.
Place/date of birth: Maryhill, Glasgow, February 20, 1905.
Place/date of death: Not known.
Place of memorial: Not known.
Town/county connections: Glasgow, London.
Remarks: Educated Allan Glen's School, Glasgow. Entered RAF as Boy Apprentice January 18, 1921. AC2 February 20, 1923. Cpl December 6, 1932. Fitter Aero Engines. Total service was 15 years 315 days. Address on discharge: 191d Balham High Rd, London. Later moved to Gloucester Terrace. He was listed as DI/SI for over 3 months after the incident. Also awarded IGS 1908 (bars NWF 1920-21, NWF 1935). Presented with AM by His Majesty the King at Buckingham Palace February 25, 1937. He is believed to have died shortly afterwards.

Citation

His former Majesty King Edward VIII was graciously pleased to award the Albert Medal to Corporal Archibald Charles Wood, No. 60 (B) Squadron, R.A.F., Kohat, in recognition of his conspicuous gallantry when the Royal Air Force aircraft in which he was a passenger was wrecked near Nidhauli, India, on the 8th February, 1936.

Corporal Wood, who was uninjured but dazed as a result of the crash, re-entered the blazing wreckage in an endeavour to save the pilot. In doing so he received very severe burns as a result of which his left hand had to be amputated.

WOOD, Douglas.

Rank: Lt.
Unit/Force: 19 LF.
Other decorations: Nil.
Date of deed: April 17, 1916.
Date of Gazette: August 17, 1917.
Place/date of birth: Not known.
Place/date of death: Not known.
Place of memorial: Not known.
Town/county connections: Not known.
Remarks: To France October 20, 1915. Later served in RAF. Also awarded 1914-15 Star, British War and Victory Medals. Presented with the AM by His Majesty the King at Buckingham Palace February 5, 1917.

Citation

The KING has been pleased to award the Albert Medal of the First Class to Lieutenant Douglas Wood, Lancashire Fusiliers, in recognition of his gallantry in saving life when instructing a class in bomb throwing in France.

At Warloy, on the 17th April, 1916, while a class of thirty men was under instruction in bomb throwing, one of the men threw a live bomb, which failed to clear the bank behind which the throwers were sheltering, and started to roll down the bank towards the class. Lieutenant Wood sprang forward and tried to seize the bomb while it was falling. He failed to do so, but picked it up from the bottom of the trench, and was in the act of throwing it away when it exploded, blowing off his right hand and severely injuring his back.

But for the officer's prompt and gallant conduct, there is no doubt that several lives would have been lost.

T. H. WOODMAN
Source: Mrs J. Lancaster

WOODMAN, Thomas Henry.

No. 551825.
Rank: SPR.
Unit/Force: RE. 29 Lt Rly Op Coy RE.
Other decorations: Nil.
Date of deed: April 30, 1918.
Date of Gazette: August 30, 1918.
Place/date of birth: Fulham, London, January 25, 1895.
Place/date of death:
London, March 1, 1970.
Town/county connections: London.
Remarks: Educated St Lawrence's School, Brentford. Joined staff of London Underground Railway in about 1910. Married Rosa Helen (née Bennett) at St Faith's Church, Brentford in 1920. 1 daughter, born 1925. Eventually became Divisional Inspector and retired in 1960 after 50 years' railway service. Also awarded British War and Victory Medals. A member of the AM Association.

Citation
See citation for BIGLAND, J. E.

WRIGHT, Douglas William.

Rank: 2 Lt.
Unit/Force: 22 RF.
Other decorations: Nil.
Date of deed: April 8, 1917.
Date of Gazette: July 18, 1919.
Place/date of birth: Not known.
Place/date of death: Not known.
Place of memorial: Not known.
Town/county connections: Not known.
Remarks: Enlisted 10 Bn RF as Pte 878. Comsd November 22, 1916. To France July 31, 1915. Also awarded 1914-15 Star, British War and Victory Medals and Silver War Badge. He was badly wounded in this incident: left leg amputated, right arm off below elbow, right leg badly smashed and subsequently amputated. He was unable to attend Buckingham Palace for presentation of the AM and it was sent to the WO.

Citation

The KING has been pleased to award the Albert Medal in recognition of gallantry displayed in saving life:-
Mr. Douglas William Wright, formerly Second-Lieutenant, 22nd Battalion, Royal Fusiliers.
In April, 1917, Lieutenant Wright was in charge of a rifle-grenade practice at St. Pol. One of the party accidentally released the safety lever of his grenade before he was ready to fire, and thereupon threw his rifle on the ground, calling to Lieutenant Wright to escape. The officer, however, fearing that the man would be unable to get away in time, rushed past him, seized the rifle, and held it to his body in order to minimise the force of the explosion. He was so severely injured as to necessitate the amputation of both legs and one arm. The man who was firing escaped from the trench by another exit.
Lieutenant Wright undoubtedly risked his life in endeavouring to save the life of another.

D. C. YOUNG
Source: Family

YOUNG, David Coley.

Rank: Capt.
Unit/Force: 4 GR.
Other decorations: Nil.
Date of deed:
August 31, 1906.
Date of Gazette:
August 26, 1913.
Place/date of birth: December 5, 1869.
Place/date of death: Neuve Chappelle, March 12, 1915 (KIA).
Place of memorial: Rue des Berceaux Military Cemetery, Richebourg-L'Avoue, Pas de Calais.
Town/county connections: Not known.
Remarks: Son of Col David Butler Young. Educated Sedbergh School (Sep 1883-Jul 1884). Prefect. Sandhurst 1888-1889. Comsd DLI Sep 1889. To 1 Bn 4 GR Feb 1902. ADC and DAAG to Gen Sir O'Moore Creagh VC, N. China 1901-02. Lt Col comd 1/4 GR. Killed while attempting to save life of a wounded member of Leics Regt. He was posthumously MID for this action. Married Sara Jane Ragsdale (a widow) of Sands Rd, Paignton, Devon in 1902. 2 sons, 1 daughter. Also awarded IGS 1854 (bar Waziristan 1894-5), China 1900, 1914-15 Star, British War and Victory Medals (MID).

Citation
See citation for BATTYE, B. C.

The following Warrant Officer of the R.C.N.V.R. is included herein because he was discovered too late for inclusion in "'Gainst All Disaster" (see Bibliography) and he has elected not to exchange his original award for the George Cross.

E. A. WOODING
Source: E. A. Wooding

WOODING, Ernest Alfred.

Rank: Wt Elec.
Unit/Force: RCNVR.
Other decorations: Nil.
Date of deed: October 13, 1943.

Date of Gazette: April 17, 1945.
Place/date of birth: July 16, 1916, Toronto, Canada.
Town/county connections: Toronto, Canada; Ontario, Canada.
Remarks: Educated Northern Vocational School. Employed Minneapolis Honeywell Regulator Co until 1939, then joined Queen's York Rangers. Transferred in 1940 to RCNVR. Rated PO on completion of training in Halifax, N.S., then transferred to electrical inspection of ships under construction. Demobbed 1945 and returned to Honeywell. Retired as Manager of Technical Services for Commercial Construction Dept. Married 1947. 1 son, 1 daughter. Although, so far as is known, he has not claimed them, presumably he would be entitled to several other awards, including any for WWII service. One of only three people still wearing the AM at the time of writing.

Citation
The KING has been graciously pleased, on the advice of His Majesty's Canadian Ministers, to give orders for the following award:-
For bravery in saving life:

The Albert Medal

Mr. Ernest Alfred Wooding, Warrant Electrician, R.C.N.V.R.
for outstanding courage and presence of mind at the time of an explosion in a Motor Launch in harbour. Though not on board at the time, he rushed on deck when the explosion occurred and pulled two of the three men in the engine-room compartment to safety. Knowing that a large quantity of high octane gasoline was in the tanks of the boat his action showed complete disregard of himself. He did gallant rescue work of the men who were in the boat at the time of the explosion, and was certainly responsible for saving the lives of the two men from the engine-room at great personal risk.

Appendix I
Albert Medallists who served in HM Forces but won their medals as civilians

A number of Albert Medallists are known or believed to have served in HM Forces either before or after their award. Indeed, one such man, Alfred Hunt, spent the greater part of his adult life in the army and won his AM during one of the brief periods when he was not actually in uniform. There are other examples and a roll, not claimed to be exhaustive, is included below. None of those listed here survived to exchange the AM for the GC.

BROWN, Thomas William	Royal Fleet Reserve during WWI.
CHISHOLM, William	Believed to have served in the infantry in WWI.
CLARK, Alexander Doctor	Private in 7 DLI during WWI. No overseas service.
DIAMOND, Frank	Private Norfolk Regiment in WWI. KIA.
ECCLESHALL, Arthur	Private 2/6 South Staffs Regiment in WWI.
EWINGTON, Herbert Frederick	Private/Corporal in Army Ordnance Corps in WWI.
FARRER, Anthony	Lieutenant in Princess Patricia's Canadian Light Infantry. Killed on manoeuvres in Canada, 1930.
HARDWICK, Albert Victor	Believed to have been a Corporal in WWI. Unit not known.
HOPKINS, Frank	Royal Artillery in WWI. KIA in Merchant Navy during WWII.
HUNT, Alfred	Served South Africa War, WWI and WWII.
JONES, John	Believed to have served in 10 Hussars in WWI.
LEECH, Henry James	Royal Flying Corps in WWI.
LEWIS, Thomas	Private in Royal Welch Fusiliers in WWI.
MANN, Algernon Edward	Officer in Royal Engineers in WWI and WWII.
MELLY, André Mesnard	Officer in Royal Field Artillery in WWI.
MURPHY, Colin	RAF post-WWII.
SWAINSTON, Albert	Royal Field Artillery in WWI.
THOMSON, John Wardrop	WO2 in Army Service Corps in WWI.

Appendix II
Service Albert Medallists with other orders/decorations/medals

Name/Rank	*Other Awards*
ANDERSON C. A., Major General	KCB, KCIE
ATKINSON, E. L., Surgeon Lieut-Commander, RN	DSO
BARTLETT, C.E.C., Lieutenant, South Staffordshire Regt	MC
BATTYE, B.C., Captain, Royal Engineers	DSO
BEARNE, L. C., Major, Army Service Corps	DSO
BELBEN, G. D., Lieutenant, Royal Navy	DSO, DSC
BEVAN, G. P., Captain, Royal Navy	CMG, DSO
BLAND, G. H., Captain, Indian Army	MC
BURT, A., T/Brigadier-General	CMG, DSO*
CAMPBELL, J. P., Lieutenant, Royal Field Artillery	MC
CAMPBELL, M. S. C., Major, Royal Artillery	CB, CIE
CARLIN, G. W., Sister, Territorial Force Nursing Service	ARRC
CARPENTER, A., Lieutenant, Royal Navy	DSO
COTTON, A.S., Lieutenant-Colonel, Royal Artillery	CB, CMG, CBE, DSO
DARLEY, C. C., Flight-Lieutenant, Royal Air Force	CBE
DAVIS, E. P. M., Flight-Lieutenant, Royal Naval Air Service	AFC
FISKE, C. W., T/Captain, East Kent Regiment	MC
FITZPATRICK, P. J., Staff-Sergeant, Indian Army	DCM
FOLEY R., Driver, Royal Field Artillery	MM
FURLONGER, A. H., Acting Company Sergeant Major, Royal Engineers	DCM
GALBRAITH, I. W., Captain, Indian Army	MC
GEAKE, W. H. G., Lieutenant, Australian Imperial Force	MBE
GOODHART, F. H. H., Commander, Royal Navy	DSO
HALSTEAD, A., Lieutenant, West Riding Regiment	MC
HANKEY, T. B., 2 Lieutenant, King's Royal Rifle Corps	MC
HEALY, M., Sergeant, Royal Munster Fusiliers	DCM, MM*
HIGGS, H. J., Lieutenant, Royal Engineers	OBE
HINE, F. W., Chief Engine-Room Artificer, Royal Navy	DSM
HOARE, K. R., Lieutenant-Commander, Royal Naval Volunteer Reserve	DSO*, DSC

Name/Rank	Other Awards
HOSKYN, C. R., Captain, Royal Army Medical Corps	OBE
HOUGHTON, F. L., Captain, Royal Warwickshire Regiment	MC
LECKY, H. S., Lieutenant, Royal Navy	CB
McCARTHY, E., Private, Royal Leinster Regiment	MM
MacMAHON, M., Lieut-Commander, Royal Naval Reserve	DSO
MADDOX, J. E., Lieutenant, Cheshire Regiment	MM
MALCOLM, P., Lieutenant, 4 Gurkha Rifles	CB, DSO, MVO
MARSHALL-A'DEANE, W. R., Commander, Royal Navy	DSO, DSC
MONTGOMERY, R. J. A., Sub-Lieutenant, Royal Navy	CB, CMG, CVO
MORGAN, W. M., Lieutenant, Royal Welch Fusiliers	MC
NEVITT, A., Lieutenant, Royal Welch Fusiliers	MC
NEWALL, C. L. N., Major, 2 Gurkha Rifles	GCB, OM, GCMG, CBE
RATHBONE, W. L. C., 2 Lieutenant, London Regiment	MC
REEKIE, S. M., 2 Lieutenant, Royal Fusiliers	MM
RICHARDSON, E. H., Lieutenant, Royal Naval Reserve	DSC
RUTLAND, F. J., Lieutenant, Royal Navy	DSC*
SCOTT, R. J. R., Lieutenant-Commander, Royal Navy	CB
SCURFIELD, B. G., Lieutenant-Commander, Royal Navy	DSO, OBE
SMITH, W. R., Major, Royal Field Artillery	CB, CBE, DSO, MC*
STARTIN, J., Commodore, Royal Naval Reserve	KCB
STARTIN, R. A., Lieutenant, Royal Navy	OBE
TEHAN, A. G., Trooper, 12 Lancers	MM

Appendix III
Known locations of Albert Medals

AIMANSING PUN	Gurkha Museum, Winchester
ANDERSON, C. A.	Private collection
BAILEY, A. V.	Private collection
BARTLETT, C. E. C.	Staffordshire Regiment Museum, Lichfield
BEARD, E. E.	Private collection
BEARD, W. R.	Private collection
BECKER, W.	Canadian War Museum, Ottawa
BEECHING, G. W.	Stolen (from Order of St John Museum, London)
BENNETT, G.	Private collection
BODDY, J. G.	HMS *Sultan*, Portsmouth
BRIDGES, W. J.	Los Angeles County Museum, USA
BROWN, J. E.	Lost (probably at sea)
BUSH, G. R.	Private collection
CARPENTER, A.	Family
CONNOR, D. M.	Private collection
COTTON, A. S.	Family
COYNE, D. E.	Family
CREAN, T.	Family
DARLEY, C. C.	Private collection
DICKSON, T. J.	Private collection
DONOVAN, C. C.	Newcastle-under-Lyme Museum, Staffs
DUNN, J.	Guards Museum, Wellington Barracks, London
FANCONI, A.	Private collection
FARREN, J. C.	Royal Engineers Museum, Chatham
FELDWICK, A. E.	Private collection
FISKE, C. W.	Private collection
FITZPATRICK, P. J.	Private collection
FITZSIMMONS, H.	Private collection
FOLEY, R.	Royal Artillery Museum, Woolwich
FOSTER, W. H.	Private collection
FOY, C.	Private collection
FRENCH, H. C.	Family
FURLONGER, A. H.	Royal Engineers Museum, Chatham
GEAKE, W. H. G.	Australian War Memorial
GERRIGHTY, A.	Royal Marines Museum, Eastney
GILES, E.	South African National War Museum
GRIFFITHS, I. T.	Family
HEALY, M.	Family
HINE, F. W.	Lost in house move, USA
HOARE, K. R.	Family
HORN, A.	Private collection

JOYCE, E. E. M.	Scott Polar Research Institute, Cambridge
JOYCE, M.	Private collection
KELLY, F.	Duke of Wellington's Regiment museum
LASHLY, W.	Private collection
LAWRENCE, J.	Royal Logistics Corps Museum, Deepcut
LECKY, H. S.	Private collection
McCARTHY, J.	National Army Museum, London
MCCREATH, A. B.	KOSB Museum, Berwick-upon-Tweed
McDOWELL, G. P.	Private collection
McLAUGHLIN, J.	Private collection
McQUE, W.	Patiala Museum, India
MARIEN, K. F.	Naval Museum, HMAS *Cresswell*, Australia
MILLAR, C. D.	Private collection
NEALE, J.	Private collection
OATLEY, G.	Private collection
PAFFETT, F.	Royal Naval Museum, Portsmouth
PETHEBRIDGE, C. A.	Private collection
PLACE, A.	Leeds Museum, Yorkshire
PURKIS, A. E.	Private collection
PYSDEN, E. J.	Private collection
RAMSAY, J.	Private collection
RATHBONE, W. L. C.	Private collection
REEKIE, S. M.	Private collection
RICHARDSON, E. H.	Private collection
ROBINSON, H. V.	Private collection
ROSS, E. F.	Private collection
RUR SINGH	Private collection
RUSSELL, E. P. S.	Private collection
SCOTT, R. J. R.	Imperial War Museum, London
SHACKLADY, E. A.	King's Regiment Officers' Mess
SHOOTER, W.	Private collection
SMITH, H.	Private collection
STICKLEY, A.	Private collection
STOKER, A. E.	Private collection
STONES, R.	Glenbow Museum, Calgary, Canada
STREAMS, A. E.	Royal Marines Museum, Eastney
TANNER, C. C.	Family
TEHAN, A. G.	Private collection
THOMPSON, M.	Private collection
THORPE, J. W.	Family
TRIGGS, T. K.	Canadian War Museum, Ottawa
TURNER, A. T.	Royal Marines Museum, Eastney
VAISEY, G. M.	Gloucestershire Regt Museum, Gloucester
WARDEN, A. R. S.	Private collection
WARNE, A. E.	Private collection
WARWICK, P.	Private collection
WEBB, J.	Private collection
WILD, H. E.	Private collection
WILLIS, P. H.	Family
WOOD, A. C.	Private collection
WOOD, D.	Lancashire Fusiliers Museum, Bury
WOODING, E. A.	Still being worn
WOODMAN, T. H.	Family
YOUNG, D. C.	Private collection

Note: A small number of specimens were produced for exhibition purposes by museums and similar institutions. A few have got out on to the market and are to be found in private collections. There are three examples in the Royal Collection at Windsor Castle: one Gold and one Bronze for Land Service and one Bronze medal for Sea Service.

Glossary

Royal & Commonwealth Navies/Reserves

HMAS	His/Her Majesty's Australian Ship
HMCS	His/Her Majesty's Canadian Ship
HMHS	His Majesty's Hospital Ship
HMML	His Majesty's Motor Launch
HMNZS	His/Her Majesty's New Zealand Ship
HMS	His/Her Majesty's Ship
HM S/M	His/Her Majesty's Submarine
HMT	His Majesty's Transport
RAN	Royal Australian Navy
RANR	Royal Australian Navy Reserve
RCN	Royal Canadian Navy
RCNVR	Royal Canadian Navy Volunteer Reserve
RFR	Royal Fleet Reserve
RIM	Royal Indian Marine
RN	Royal Navy
RNAS	Royal Naval Air Service
RNR	Royal Naval Reserve
RNVR	Royal Naval Volunteer Reserve
RNZN	Royal New Zealand Navy

Ranks/Rates (RN/RM)

Adm	Admiral
AB	Able (Bodied) Seaman
Capt	Captain
Cdr	Commander
Cdre	Commodore
CPO	Chief Petty Officer
LS	Leading Seaman
Lt	Lieutenant
Lt-Cdr	Lieutenant-Commander
Mid	Midshipman
PO	Petty Officer
R Adm	Rear-Admiral
Sub-Lt	Sub-Lieutenant
V Adm	Vice-Admiral
Wt Offr	Warrant Officer

Specialists

Ch Sto	Chief Stoker
CERA	Chief Engine Room Artificer
EM (E)	Electrical Mechanical (Electronics) followed by class
ERA	Engine Room Artificer (followed by Class: 1, 2, 3)
MNE	Marine (RM/RMLI)
QM	Quartermaster
SBA	Sick Berth Attendant
Sto	Stoker

Army

Ranks/Appointments

Capt	Captain
Cdr	Conductor (WOI)
Col	Colonel
Brig (-Gen)	Brigadier (-General)
CPL	Corporal
CSM	Company Sergeant-Major (WOII)
DVR	Driver)
RFN	Rifleman) All these
Tpr	Trooper) rank as PTE
Pnr	Pioneer)
LCPL	Lance-Corporal
Lt	Lieutenant
2Lt	Second Lieutenant
Lt Col	Lieutenant-Colonel
Maj	Major
Maj-Gen	Major-General
PTE	Private
QMS	Quartermaster-Sergeant (WOII)
Sgt (SJT)	Sergeant (Serjeant)
SGT-MAJ	Sergeant-Major (rank unspecified)
SSGT	Staff Sergeant
Sub-Cdr	Sub-Conductor (WOI)
WOII	Warrant Officer Class Two

Indian Army

HAV	Havildar (Sergeant)
LNK	Lance-Naik (Lance-Corporal)
Sub-Maj	Subadar-Major (Senior Indian native officer, ranking above WO but below commissioned officer)
TPTR	Trumpeter

RFC/RAF

Ranks

AC	Aircraftman (followed by class: 1 or 2)
Air Cdre	Air Commodore
AM	Air Mechanic (followed by class: 1 or 2)
Cpl	Corporal
Flt Sgt	Flight Sergeant
F/O	Flying Officer
Flt Lt	Flight Lieutenant
Gp Capt	Group Captain
MRAF	Marshal of the Royal Air Force
Sgt	Sergeant
Sqn Ldr	Squadron Leader
Wg Cdr	Wing Commander

General abbreviations

A/	Acting (rank)
(A)	Air (branch of RN)
ADC	Aide-de-camp
AGS	Africa General Service Medal
Amb	Ambulance
AMD	Army Medical Department
AIF	Australian Imperial Force
AO	Army Order
AOC	Air Officer Commanding
Att	Attached
Aust	Australian
Aux	Auxiliary
Bde	Brigade
BGRA	Brigadier-General Royal Artillery
Bn	Battalion
BP	Buckingham Palace
BRA	Brigadier Royal Artillery
Brev	Brevet (rank)
Bty	Battery
Cav	Cavalry
CCS	Casualty Clearing Station
CO	Commanding Officer
Col	Column
Comd	Commander
Comsd	Commissioned
Coy	Company
CWGC	Commonweath War Graves Commission
DAAG	Deputy Assistant Adjutant-General
DDOS	Deputy Director of Ordnance Services
Dist	District
Dischgd	Discharged
Div	Division
DOW	Died of Wounds
(E)	Engineer Officer, Royal Navy
Elec	Electrical
Engr	Engineer
Fd	Field
Flt	Flight
Fus	Fusiliers
GHQ	General Headquarters
GOC	General Officer Commanding
Gp	Group

GR	Gurkha Rifles
GSM	General Service Medal, 1918
HMK	His Majesty the King
HO	Home Office
Hon	Honorary
IA	Indian Army
IGS	India General Service Medal
Inf	Infantry
IOD	Indian Ordnance Department
KIA	Killed in action
KSA	King's South Africa Medal
K St J	Knight of the Order of St John of Jerusalem
Lt	Light
LS&GC	Long Service and Good Conduct Medal
M	Married
MID	Mentioned in Despatches
Mil	Military
Mor	Mortar
MT	Motor (or Mechanical) Transport
MWS	Military Works Service (India)
NGS	Naval General Service Medal, 1915
OC	Officer Commanding
Op	Operating
PA	Personal Assistant
POW	Prisoner of War (Prince of Wales, when applied to a regimental title)
QSA	Queen's South Africa Medal
R	Royal or Reserve
RAAF	Royal Australian Air Force (in this book)
RAOC	Royal Army Ordnance Corps
Regt	Regiment
Retd	Retired
Res	Reserve
RFA	Royal Field Artillery
RFC	Royal Flying Corps
RGA	Royal Garrison Artillery
RHS	Royal Humane Society
RMA	Royal Military Academy (Woolwich)
RMP	Corps of Royal Military Police
S & M	(Bombay) Sappers and Miners
SA	South Africa
Spec	Specialist
s.s.	Steam Ship
Sup	Supply
Svc(s)	Service(s)
T/	Temporary (rank)
(T)	Territorial
TD	Territorial Decoration
TF	Territorial Force
Tps	Troops
Tpt	Transport
Trg	Training
TS	Training ship
Vol	Volunteer(s)
Wksp	Workshop(s)
WOAS	While on active service
*	Indicates a bar to an award

Appendix IV
Albert Medal awards by Regiment & Corps

Name	Abbreviation used	No awarded
CAVALRY		
12 Royal Lancers	12L	2
16 The Queen's Lancers	16L	1
1 Dragoon Guards	1DG	1
Lancashire Hussars (Yeomanry)	Lancs Hrs	1
Cheshire Yeomanry	Ches Yeo	1
FOOT GUARDS		
Grenadier Guards	GG	2
Coldstream Guards	CG	2
Scots Guards	SG	3
INFANTRY OF THE LINE		
Argyll & Sutherland Highlanders	A&SH	1
Cameron Highlanders	CAMERONIANS	1
Dorset Regiment	Dorset R	1
Duke of Cornwall's Light Infantry	DCLI	1
Duke of Wellington's Regiment	DWR	1
Durham Light Infantry	DLI	2
East Kent Regiment (The Buffs)	Buffs	2
East Yorkshire Regiment	E Yorks R	1
Gloucestershire Regiment	GLOSTERS	1
Gordon Highlanders	GORDONS	1
Highland Light Infantry	HLI	3
King's Own Scottish Borderers	KOSB	1
King's Royal Rifle Corps	KRRC	2
Lancashire Fusiliers	Lancs F	2
Leicestershire Regiment	Leics R	1
Leinster Regiment	Leinster R	1
London Regiment	Lond R	4
Manchester Regiment	Man R	3
Middlesex Regiment	Middx R	2

Name	*Abbreviation used*	*No awarded*
Northumberland Fusiliers	NF	2
Royal Fusiliers	RF	3
Royal Irish Regiment	RIR	1
Royal Lancaster Regiment	RLR	1
Royal Munster Fusiliers	R Munster F	1
Royal Warwickshire Regiment	R Warks R	1
Royal Welch Fusiliers	RWF	3
South Staffordshire Regiment	S Staffs R	1
South Wales Borderers	SWB	1
West Riding Regiment	W Riding R	1
West Yorkshire Regiment	W Yorks R	2
Army Service Corps	ASC	9
Machine Gun Corps	MGC	1
Mounted Military Police	MMP	1
Royal Artillery	RA	12
Royal Army Medical Corps	RAMC	9
Royal Engineers	RE	14
Royal Flying Corps	RFC	9
Royal Gurkha Rifles/Indian Army	—	21
Royal Marines/Royal Marine Light Infantry	RM/RMLI	6
Territorial Force Nursing Service	TFNS	2
		Total 146

Note: This total includes awards of the Albert Medal of both classes to Army personnel. A very few of the above survived to exchange their original awards for the George Cross in 1971 and the list is included here for comparative purposes. For the same reason the following table illustrates the distribution of the Albert Medal to the United Kingdom and the Commonwealth Navies and their Reserves. Again, it includes awards of both classes and those few who exchanged their awards in 1971.

NAVAL AWARDS

Royal Navy	RN	87
Royal Naval Reserve	RNR	15
Royal Naval Volunteer Reserve	RNVR	11
Royal Australian Navy	RAN	2
Royal Australian Volunteer Reserve	RANVR	1
Royal Canadian Navy	RCN	1
Royal Canadian Navy Volunteer Reserve	RCNVR	5 (including 1 to Royal Canadian Sea Cadets)
Royal New Zealand Navy	RNZN	1

There were only two awards to the Royal Air Force and one to the Royal Australian Air Force (the latter survived to become a holder of the George Cross in 1971).

Bibliography

ABBOTT, P. E. and TAMPLIN, J. M. A., *British Gallantry Awards,* Nimrod Dix, 1981.

FRAME, Tom, *Where Fate Calls,* Hodder & Stoughton, 1992.

HENDERSON, Major D. V., GM, *Heroic Endeavour,* J. B. Hayward, 1988.

KEMPTON, Chris, *Valour & Gallantry,* Military Press, 2001.

O'SHEA, Philip, LVO, *An Unknown Few,* P. D. Hasselberg, Government Printer, Wellington, New Zealand, 1981.

SMITH, Michael, *An Unsung Hero: Tom Crean—Antarctic Survivor,* Headline, 2001.

STANISTREET, Allan, *'Gainst All Disaster,* Picton, 1986.

STANISTREET, Allan, *Brave Railwaymen,* Token Publishing, 1989.

WIGMORE, L. and HARDING, B., *They Dared Mightily,* Australian War Memorial, Canberra, ACT, 1963.

WILSON, Sir Arnold, MP, and McEWEN, Captain J. H. F., MP, *Gallantry,* Oxford University Press, 1939.

YOUNG, Desmond, *Rutland of Jutland,* Cassell & Co., 1963.

British Medical Journal, various obituaries.

Journal of the Orders and Medals Research Society, various articles.

London Gazette, Various, HMSO Crown Copyright.